Expository Sermons on 2 Peter

Expository Sermons on
2 Peter

D. M. LLOYD-JONES

THE BANNER OF TRUTH TRUST

THE BANNER OF TRUTH TRUST
3 Murrayfield Road, Edinburgh EH12 6EL
PO Box 621, Carlisle, Pennsylvania 17013, U.S.A.

*

© *Mrs Bethan Lloyd-Jones 1983*
First printed in THE WESTMINSTER RECORD *1948–50*
First Banner of Truth edition 1983

ISBN 0 85151 379 4

*

Set in 10 on 12pt Linotron Sabon
and printed and bound in Great Britain at
The Camelot Press Ltd, Southampton

Preface

The twenty-five sermons which make up this volume were first preached on Sunday mornings in Westminster Chapel, London, commencing October 6, 1946, and concluding on March 30, 1947. The date is of particular interest owing to the fact that this was the first extensive series of sermons on any one book of Scripture undertaken by Dr Lloyd-Jones. They were preached during the period when the congregation at Westminster Chapel was being rebuilt following the difficult years of the Second World War and they led to other series which were to be memorable in the subsequent twenty-one years.

Dr Lloyd-Jones believed that congregations need to be raised gradually to the demands which expository preaching makes upon them and in that connection some difference may be noted between these sermons and those of later years which are already in print. The treatment here is broader, less detailed and, intentionally, it does not deal with every verse in the Epistle. For some readers that will prove a help. Just as the 2 Peter sermons when first preached led the congregation at Westminster Chapel forward in their appreciation of expository preaching, this volume will provide an excellent starting point for a type of reading with which some Christians are unfamiliar.

Many who have seen these sermons as first printed in *The Westminster Record* (March 1948–February 1950) have long asked for them in this more permanent form. It was characteristic of Dr Lloyd-Jones' reticence that this volume did not appear in his own life-time. Apart from minimal revision, chiefly from the hand of Mrs Lloyd-Jones, the text is the same as originally printed.

When Dr Lloyd-Jones' first expository volume, *Studies in the Sermon on the Mount*, was published in 1959, he felt it necessary to comment in his Preface that the contents were unmistakably sermons. Far from disguising that fact in any way he expressed the hope that the book might 'in some small way stimulate a new interest in expository preaching.' That hope has been abundantly fulfilled and one consequence has been a world-wide demand for more published sermons of a kind which only twenty-five years ago many regarded as unsaleable.

Dr Lloyd-Jones believed that when the church gives to prayer and to preaching their true biblical priority she is able, under God, to meet the challenge of any generation. May God, through these pages, confirm that same faith in many others!

July 1983   THE PUBLISHERS

Contents

I
Precious Faith

'Simon Peter, a servant and an apostle of Jesus Christ, to
them that have obtained like precious faith with us
through the righteousness of God and our Saviour Jesus
Christ: Grace and peace be multiplied unto you through
the knowledge of God, and of Jesus our Lord.'

Chapter 1:1–2

We have here a letter written in the early days of the Christian
church to a number of Christian people. They were scattered
abroad, we gather from the first Epistle, throughout a considerable
part of the then civilised and known world. It is a letter written to
people who were confronted by difficulties and by problems. The
first Epistle, in the same way exactly as this Epistle, makes it quite
clear that the object that the Apostle had in mind when he wrote both
these letters was to comfort and to encourage and to strengthen these
people. They faced difficulties, both from without and within, for
their world, as one is never tired of pointing out, was a world very
similar to ours.

If we regard history from a spiritual standpoint we must be
impressed by the fact that the essential character of life in this world
does not change. We may regard certain things today as being
terrible and serious, and we feel that by contrast with these things,
the circumstances confronting the people two thousand years ago
were almost trivial. Yet we have to realise and to remember that the
problems they experienced were as grievous and as serious to them as
our problems are to us today. The way of conducting war has
changed, the way of living in certain superficial respects has
changed, and yet the facts remain essentially the same. The world is a
place of difficulty and thus, I say, we find that these people in their
age and time, as we in ours, were conscious of terrible problems. They

had believed the Christian Gospel and, perhaps, at first had partly misunderstood it, thinking that everything was suddenly going to be all right and that they would have no further problems. But they had now reached the stage in which they had discovered that that was not the case. They had opposition from without; there were persecutions, there were trials, there were difficulties even in the matter of food and clothing and in various other things.

Then in addition to all these things there were troubles also arising from within the church, and this second Epistle of Peter is particularly concerned about these problems. For the problem that ever confronts Christian people in a world like this is, ultimately, just the one problem of unbelief. We can therefore understand why the great message of this second Epistle of Peter was written to strengthen Christian people against various forces and factors that were tending to shake and to unsettle them in their faith. Certain doubts and queries were insinuating themselves into their minds. Peter tells us at great length in the second chapter that false teachers had crept into the churches and that these, with their false teaching, were trying to undermine the faith of these early Christian people.

In particular, questions were being raised as to the value of the promises of God. An essential part of the preaching of the Gospel, from the very beginning, was the message of the second coming of our Lord and of the various things that would accompany it. All those first preachers preached a Gospel of judgment. You remember how often we are told in the Gospels and in the book of the Acts of the Apostles that their message in the first instance was that men and women should flee from the wrath to come. The Gospel was always presented in terms of judgment. It was put in that historical form, it was emphasised and stressed that this self-same Jesus who had been crucified and buried, and who had risen again, would likewise come again in judgment, and that when He came He would judge the world, and that therefore all should make certain of being found in a right relationship to Him. But these false teachers and others had crept into the churches and they were raising questions and queries. 'Where is the promise of his coming?' they said. 'Years have passed and nothing has happened, the world is still the same as it was – what, then, of this preaching, what of this Gospel?' And there was much in the hearers themselves that made them ready to listen to this. Unbelief can be very insidious and insinuating. It comes and takes advantage of various conditions through which we are passing – when we are tired or ill, when we are passing through bereavement or sorrow, or when we have just emerged from a world war; in that kind of position of lassitude and tiredness these thoughts come in. The danger was that the faith of this infant church should thus be shaken.

Now such is the background which we have to bear in mind. This is a letter written to people who are besieged by difficulties without, and at the same time attacked by difficulties within.

I need scarcely point out how apposite and appropriate this letter is to our state and condition at this present time. The Christian church avowedly and frankly is facing an extremely difficult period. We would have to go back a very long time, at least two hundred years, to find a time when she had to face such grievous difficulties. And I would say that the besetting sin at such a time as this is probably the sin of discouragement. There is a tendency because of all these things to ask certain questions, and there are always those who are ready to help us to yield to doubts and fears and to encourage us in them. I therefore believe, as I am never tired of saying these days, that the first thing that is necessary at the present time is that Christian people should be certain of their position. I borrow the words of the Apostle when he says, 'I will not be negligent to put you always in remembrance of these things, though ye know them'. That is profound psychology! It is a very great mistake to think that because we know a thing we need not be reminded of it repeatedly. I would therefore suggest that if we are concerned about the state of the church and of the world, if we really do look for revival and reawakening at the present time, we must concentrate on the church rather than on the world. The church is the bearer of the message of salvation; and if the church herself is lifeless or uncertain or unhappy, how can she do the work? It seems to be increasingly clear that the main problem at the moment is in the church herself. The world is sinful. Of course, the world is always sinful. We have no right to expect anything but sin from the world. We should never be surprised at the state of the world or the condition of the masses of the people. It is the essential teaching of the Bible that as long as men remain in the world and outside Christ they must be like that. Is it not the case, however, that perhaps the main explanation of why so many are outside the church and why the church is passing through this difficult period, is the state of the church herself? As Paul puts it in writing to the Corinthians, 'If the trumpet give an uncertain sound, who shall prepare himself for the battle?'

If we are uncertain about our position, how can we confront the world, and why should the world look at us and be convinced and convicted of its sin as it sees us? Surely the highway to revival, as the history of the great revivals of the past shows us so clearly, is that the church herself must be a living church. When that happens her impact upon the world invariably becomes something powerful and mighty. Now that is the object of this particular letter; it is to strengthen Christian people. You notice how Peter puts it in a phrase in this very first chapter. The need, he says, is to 'make your calling and election sure'. That is the thing on which we must concentrate.

Now the great message of the Gospel divides itself up in a perfectly simple and natural manner. What does it say to people in this state and condition? It is quite clear at once that there are two main things. The first is, they must be absolutely certain of that which they believe. They must make quite certain of the basis and the foundation of their faith. Then, having done that, they must add to it and grow in it. Peter states all that, really, in these first two verses, and the whole Epistle is nothing but the out-working of this statement which he makes at the very beginning. These are the two points: you must know what you have, and then you must add to it and increase it. 'Simon Peter, a servant and an apostle of Jesus Christ, to them that have obtained like precious faith with us through the righteousness of God and our Saviour Jesus Christ: Grace and peace be multiplied unto you through the knowledge of God, and of Jesus our Lord' – that's it! In a sense that is the whole of the Christian life. We first make certain of our beginning and our foundation; then we go on adding to it. We 'continue in the faith' with which we begin; we 'hold the beginning of our confidence steadfast unto the end.' This is the way other writers in the New Testament put exactly and precisely the same thing. Peter keeps playing on this theme, and he ends the letter on the very same note, 'But grow in grace, and in the knowledge of our Lord and Saviour Jesus Christ.' You have got it: very well, you must proceed to grow in it.

Now this is surely a message for us at this present time. The first thing we have to do is to make certain of the foundations. We need not stay to labour this point. We all must be ready to agree that the main effect of the various movements in the realm of thought and in the realm of religion (alas!) during the last hundred years has been to query and to question the foundation. The trouble still in the church is a matter of foundations. There are those who would have us believe that it is a good and right thing to form great unions, to have a great ecumenical church, and that then we shall be a great body of people confronting the whole world. But the question is, what is this great ecumenical church to stand for? What is she to believe? What is her foundation? We are not concerned primarily about numbers, for however great a body the ecumenical church may be, she will have no influence upon the world unless she has a truth to present, unless she has a solid and firm foundation on which to stand. Surely that is the great emphasis of the Bible. What the Bible is concerned about is truth, and in a very extraordinary manner it ridicules our pathetic faith in big battalions and in great numbers. It seems to go out of its way to teach a doctrine of the remnant and to show what one man can do when that one man is truly Christian. It shows our Lord taking a handful of men and making them apostles and the sole guardians and custodians of the faith – that is its message! The emphasis is not upon numbers of men but upon this truth of God, this foundation, upon this deposit of faith. And I suggest, therefore, that at this time this must be the first thing on which we must concentrate and of which we must make doubly certain. We must know exactly where we stand and in whom we believe.

Well now, let us briefly look at some of the things that the Apostle tells us here about this very basis and foundation of our faith. He puts it all in these very suggestive words, 'Simon Peter, a servant and an apostle of Jesus Christ, to them that have obtained like precious faith with us through the righteousness of God and our Saviour Jesus Christ'. Now what does he mean by this? Let us try to divide it up.

The first thing that he emphasises is that *there is only one faith.* The Apostle is writing to Christian people. Many of them were Gentiles, as the first Epistle shows quite clearly, and yet, says Peter, the faith you have, the faith you have obtained, is the same, it is a like precious faith with that which I and my fellow apostles, and the Jews likewise, have obtained and which we enjoy. Now this is something which we can put in a number of different ways. The faith, if you like, is the same for all classes and groups and kinds of people. That is one of the central and essential glories of the Gospel of our Lord and

Saviour Jesus Christ. 'God', Peter tells us elsewhere (Acts 10:34) 'is no respecter of persons.' The Gospel of Jesus Christ cuts out once and for all our artificial human divisions and distinctions; it announces that the whole world is made one, face to face with God. In other words, when we come into the house of God, and when we face the Gospel, our antecedents are in a sense utterly irrelevant – there is neither Jew nor Gentile, bond nor free, for we are all one in Christ Jesus. Every middle wall of partition has been broken down, and it matters not at all whether we are able or ignorant, learned or lacking in intelligence. Power, social status, wealth, position – all these things are utterly irrelevant. There is only *one* faith, the 'like precious faith'. We all have to face the same truth.

But, again, we can go on to add that there is only one faith, in the sense that the only faith is the *faith of the apostles*. You have obtained 'a like precious faith with us', says Peter; and this is as true today as it was in the days when the Epistle was written. Here, perhaps, is the very essence of the modern heresy. We are so conscious of changes on the surface that we tend to believe that changing times and changed times demand a changed or different Gospel. One of the most difficult things for the natural man to believe is that a Gospel which was preached nearly two thousand years ago can possibly be adequate today. Yet I say that that is the very foundation of our whole position. 'The faith' today is still the faith of the apostles. The Christian church is built upon 'the foundation of the apostles and prophets', and however much knowledge may have been garnered with respect to scientific matters, or indeed with respect to men's hearts, and to the mind and its working, and all such matters, still we come back and see that there is no faith today apart from the apostolic faith. 'Like precious faith with us.' This is surely something remarkable and extraordinary. The passing of nearly two thousand years has not changed the position at all; indeed history itself bears very eloquent testimony to, and proof of, the soundness of that contention.

Look back across the past two thousand years, look at all the striving and efforts and endeavours of man; consider all the organisations and movements; consider all the Acts of Parliament; consider all the various experiments and forms of government; look at man as he has tried to delve into the mysteries of life; look at the amazing record of education and culture during the past two thousand years! Yet must we not agree that when you come back to the primary problems and questions of man himself, of life and of living, the problem of how to live together in this world without killing one another, and without destroying one another and our world, there is no advance at all? Surely, then, the evidence of history supports this contribution of the Scriptures themselves. There is only one Gospel, says Peter. You may be a Gentile, you may be living far away from Jerusalem and Judea, but if you are truly Christian you have the same faith as I have, and all the other apostles and all the other Christians have. And you and I are in that same position today. You can search the world, you can search the heavens, you can go down into the depths, you can go to the remotest part of the world in an attempt to discover an answer to the problem of life, but ultimately you come back to this. There is only one faith, there is only one Gospel, and the passing of the ages and the centuries does not affect it. It is an everlasting Gospel; it is changeless.

Very well, *what is this Gospel?* Peter answers that question; and you will notice that at the very centre of it he puts Jesus Christ. 'Oh, how very elementary all this is,' says someone. My dear friend, I have emphasised the fact that it is elementary. We are living in days when it is the elements of the faith that are being forgotten. 'Jesus Christ!' 'Simon Peter, a servant and an apostle of Jesus Christ, to them that have obtained like precious faith with us through the righteousness of God and our Saviour Jesus Christ', or as some would translate it, 'through the righteousness of our God and Saviour Jesus Christ'. What is the faith? Obviously you cannot answer the question without seeing at once that Jesus is central. You notice how many times Peter mentions Him. In the very introduction in the first two verses of his letter Jesus is there in the very centre, and there is no Gospel apart from Him.

Now that, I think, needs to be put today in some such form as this. There are many who, when confronted by the state of the world as it is today, are beginning to say that we must get back to religion. There are many who, seeing the havoc of the Second World War and the utter futility and hopelessness of the inter-war period, and who remember the First World War, look at these things and say, 'Well, we seem to have tried and exhausted everything else; there is only one answer, the people must be brought back to God.' There is much talk of the need again of acknowledging God, of a need for people to subscribe again to the great general statements of religion. There is a feeling that if we are to put a check upon the moral delinquency in young people we must get back again to religion and religious education in the schools. But I say that at this point a very great and real danger arises. There are many movements in this modern world that are exhorting people to believe in God and to surrender themselves to God, but I think you will find that in many of them the name of Jesus is never mentioned. They advocate and teach a belief in God; they preach a message that urges people to submit themselves to God; but Jesus Christ is not central, Jesus Christ is not essential. There is no talk about Christ. You can go direct to God, they tell us. Now that, of course, is an utter travesty of the New Testament Gospel. It is the religion of the Jew, it is the religion of the Mohammedan, who believes in God. To believe in God alone is not enough to make us Christian, to have a general belief in God as Creator and God as Father is not in itself Christian. You need the Christ of the apostle Peter. He cannot keep away from the name of Jesus Christ. Christ is there in the very centre and forefront of the picture, in the very salutation and introduction. He shows us what is the very essence of the Christian faith: it is none other than the Person of Jesus Christ Himself.

Not only that, Peter becomes still more specific – 'You have obtained like precious faith with us through the righteousness of God and our Saviour Jesus Christ.' Now that is Peter's way of putting in a phrase the great doctrine of justification by faith which is expounded so wondrously by the apostle Paul in the Epistle to the Romans. That is the essence of the Gospel. The message is, that there is only one way whereby man can be right, or righteous, in the sight of God; and that is by the righteousness that is given to us in Christ. The problem confronting man is how to be just with God. It is certainly very right to come back to God and to believe in God, but the first question is, How can I do this? God is Holy, God is Absolute, 'God is light, and in him is no darkness at all.' I am sinful. What can I do? The Old Testament contains a law, and the law said, If you do these things you will be right with God. And the tragedy is that so many people still try to do that. Yes, they say, we must be right with God. But how do I become right with God? How can I live that new life? I read the Commandments, I do my best to keep them – I try to get right with God. But by my own efforts and exertions I will never put myself right with God. To believe that I can is in utter antithesis to and a contradiction of the Christian Gospel.

What is the Gospel? It is this – 'Like precious faith with us through the righteousness of God and our Saviour Jesus Christ.' The message which the apostles preached round their world was simply this, that Jesus Christ of Nazareth was none other than the only begotten Son of God, and that He had come on earth for one thing only, and that was that He might bear the sins of man Himself. In Christ God has dealt with the sin of mankind; He has punished sin there, He has done away with it. How can man be right with God? Believe that, submit yourself to it, and say: I have no righteousness of my own; I accept the righteousness that God gives me in Christ. I am unworthy and sinful, but I can be clothed with the righteousness of Christ; and, clothed with that, I can stand and face God and the righteousness of God. That is the essence of the Christian faith. The Christian church, therefore, has in this modern world to tell men that they cannot save themselves, that all their efforts and exertions will end in utter futility, but that God has done something in Christ; He has made a new way of righteousness – 'the righteousness of God . . . by faith'. God tells me that here is the way to get rid of sin and its guilt and power: here is a new nature and a new life and positive righteousness. God is offering a way back to Himself in and through Jesus Christ and Him crucified – that is the nature of the faith.

Now let us observe one other thing with respect to it, because Peter describes it as a 'precious faith'. 'To them, that have obtained a like *precious* faith with us.' This word 'precious' is the apostle's favourite word. You will find that he uses it in his first Epistle and here again he does so. He goes on using it again and again. What does it mean? It means something valuable, it means indeed something that is beyond price, beyond computation; there is nothing like it – 'precious' – something that is in a sense of greater value than life itself. Let me put it in the form of an illustration. You see a man who has been taken ill – he has lost his health and he consults a doctor. This is what he says to him: If you know of any remedy, or anything that can be done, I beg of you to let me know about it. I do not care what it may cost me, I must have it. What is the value of wealth or position or anything else I may have if I have lost my health? My health is more precious than anything else. I will mortgage my goods to get this treatment, because health is precious, it is beyond computation, it is more valuable than anything else. That is what Peter says about this faith, and I know of no better test of our Christian profession than that we should ask this simple question: Is this doctrine about Christ our righteousness precious unto us?

What is it that makes this doctrine precious? Let me just mention some of the things to you, that we may rejoice together with the Apostle as we think of them. Why is the faith precious? Well, it is the faith that justifies. It is the faith that enables me to know that I stand guiltless in the presence of God. Can anybody measure or compute the value of that – a conscience void of offence, a knowledge that God has forgiven me, fear of death and the grave gone, the feeling that I can face any accuser that may ever rise up against me and point to Jesus? 'Precious faith!' Money and learning and all that the world can give me can never give me peace of conscience, peace of mind, but the Gospel of Jesus Christ with its doctrine of justification in Christ gives me that at the very beginning. What else? Sanctification! What does sanctification mean? Sanctification means that not only am I guiltless in a legal sense, but that I have the precious promise of this Gospel that the Holy Spirit is working in me that which will ultimately rid me of every spot and blemish and of all pollution; not merely that I am forgiven and remain the same man, but that I receive a new nature. And, ultimately, glorification. What does that mean? It means that we shall stand in the presence of God in a perfect state. We know not yet what we shall be, says the Apostle John, but we know that when we shall see Jesus Christ we shall be like Him. The glorification of the saints means their being taken out of earth to be with God and Christ and ultimately to live with God and Christ for ever and ever. It is the faith that gives me these things; it is by faith I believe them. It is by faith I know that God has forgiven me, it is by faith I know that I shall spend eternity with God. 'Precious faith!'

And then think of these matters in terms of the way they come to us – by the calling of God. God looked upon us from heaven and singled us out. Why are you a member of the Christian church? Why are you not like millions who are unconcerned about these things and who feel that they are idle tales? It is because God called you. It was not your decision. Why are you different? Is it not that the Holy Spirit of God has done something to you? He has apprehended you, He is dealing with you. Oh! what precious faith it is, that tells me that, though I am an insignificant pygmy in this extraordinary world, the

Father of Lights, the God of all power, and dominion, is interested in me, and knows me, and is concerned about me, and has placed His almighty hand upon me – 'precious' faith that tells me that! It tells me also of sonship, of regeneration, of being made a son, adopted into God's family. Have we this precious faith? Go on then to think of it subjectively. You find, says the Apostle, that it leads to peace within and peace with God and peace with every man – this amazing 'precious' faith!

There is the foundation, says the Apostle. It does not matter who you are, or where you come from; if you are a Christian, that is your faith, that is what you believe. You will find it all in Christ. You see that without Him you are lost and nothing, but in Him you are complete, for He 'of God is made unto us wisdom, and righteousness, and sanctification, and redemption'. He is my All – Christ is all and in all. He is everything. Jesus Christ! And the faith in Him is 'precious' to my soul because of these amazing things He has done for me, and is still doing to me, and will yet do for me until I stand complete in Him in the presence of God. Is the faith precious to you? It is precious to all who are truly Christian.

2

Exceeding Great and Precious Promises

'According as his divine power hath given unto us all
things that pertain unto life and godliness, through the
knowledge of him that hath called us to glory and virtue:
Whereby are given unto us exceeding great and precious
promises: that by these ye might be partakers of the
divine nature, having escaped the corruption that is in the
world through lust.'

Chapter 1:3–4

The Apostle now goes on to show us that to be in the faith, in and of
itself, is not enough. That is the first thing – if there is something
wrong with the building, examine the foundation, if there is
something wrong with the stream look at the source. But you do not
stop at that. The next step, he says, is something like this. The result
of believing that Gospel, and having that faith, is that we have grace
and peace. But now the Apostle's desire and anxiety is that grace and
peace may be multiplied unto believers, that they may grow and
increase and develop; and this, he says, happens 'through the
knowledge of God, and of Jesus our Lord'. And in these next two
verses (3 and 4) he begins to tell us how that is going to happen. I
have my faith. Very well, I need to have that faith increased and
strengthened. But how is that to take place? Again we must give a
kind of skeleton outline of what was in the mind of the Apostle. It
happens like this.

First of all there are certain things done for us; then we proceed to
do certain things ourselves. What is done for us is described in verses
3 and 4 and what we have to do follows in verses 5 and 6. 'And beside
this, giving all diligence, add to your faith virtue; and to virtue
knowledge; and to knowledge temperance; and to temperance

patience; and to patience godliness.' But before he exhorts us to do anything ourselves, he reminds us again of what is done for us. In other words, what we have, in these two verses now under consideration, is a magnificent statement of the nature, or the character, of the Christian life, which results from believing and accepting the faith that he has already been describing. Surely we are confronted here with one of the most remarkable descriptions of the Christian life that is to be found even in the New Testament itself; and nothing is more necessary for us who are Christians at this present hour, than that we should remind ourselves again of something of the character of the Christian life in which we find ourselves. Here is the description – 'According as his divine power hath given unto us all things that pertain unto life and godliness, through the knowledge of him that hath called us to glory and virtue: whereby are given unto us exceeding great and precious promises: that by these ye might be partakers of the divine nature, having escaped the corruption that is in the world through lust.'

That, I say, is the description of the quality or the type, the character or the kind of life that is to be possessed and lived by the Christian. I ask again, Is not this the first thing of which we need to remind ourselves? I make no apology for saying once more, in passing, that it does seem to me increasingly that this is the first message on which the Christian church needs to concentrate at the present time. I, personally, am much more concerned about the state of the church than I am about the state of the world. We are all clear about the world. The world is in its muddle, its wretchedness, and unhappiness, because it is heedless of the Christian message. It does not pay any attention to the Gospel of Christ and I suggest that one chief cause of that is the fact that it does not see this quality of life in us. When it does see it, then it will begin to pay attention. I would urge once more therefore that it is the business of the church to concentrate on herself and not on the world that is outside. Revival starts in the church, and revival comes when Christian people begin to realise how far short they fall of the standard that is depicted in the New Testament.

Now here, I say, we are told the nature and the character of the Christian life. Well, what is it? What is the object of this life, what is the essential life of the Christian, what is it we should be striving after? According to Peter it can be put in two statements. The first thing is *to know God*, and the second thing is to *become like Him*. That is the basic definition always in the New Testament of the character and quality and nature of the Christian life. What is it that as a Christian I should desire above everything else? It is not to have certain experiences; it is not that I may be better than I used to be; it is not that I am to hold certain views of life and the world and society and various other matters. The supreme objective of the Christian man is to know God. You remember how our Lord put it – 'This is life eternal, that they might know thee the only true God, and Jesus Christ, whom thou has sent.' What is the *summum bonum* of the Christian life? Our Lord put it in one of the Beatitudes, 'Blessed are the pure in heart: for they shall see God.' To know God! And you notice how Peter keeps repeating that here: 'Simon Peter, a servant and an apostle of Jesus Christ, to them that have obtained like precious faith with us through the righteousness of God and our Saviour Jesus Christ: Grace and peace be multiplied unto you through the knowledge of God, and of Jesus our Lord, according as his divine power hath given unto us all things that pertain unto life and godliness, through the knowledge of him that hath called us to glory and virtue.' There is always this emphasis on knowledge. In the first chapter of Paul's letter to the church at Colosse we find exactly and precisely the same emphasis. It is the knowledge of God – that is the great thing! Therefore the question which we ask ourselves before we proceed any further is, Do we know God? Is God real to us? When we get on our knees and claim that we pray, are we speaking to God? Do we know that God is there? Are we aware of a sense of contact and communion and fellowship with God? For prayer is not uttering certain pious hopes and fears and aspirations; it is talking to God – to know God, to be certain of God. You need to grow in grace, says Peter, because the knowledge of God is the ultimate objective of the Christian; that is the peculiar thing that makes the Christian life exactly and precisely what it is.

But you notice that Peter does not stop at our knowledge of God – he adds that *we are to become like God*. 'Whereby are given unto us exceeding great and precious promises: that by these ye might be partakers of the divine nature, having escaped the corruption that is in the world through lust.' Now this is one of those statements in the New Testament which are utterly staggering and amazing. Peter's conception of the Christian is that he is one who is a partaker of the divine nature. By this he means that he is one who becomes like God; He is one who develops the divine character and manifests the divine characteristics. He has already described and referred to the Christian life as a life of godliness, or, if you prefer it, a godly life, a god-like life. That is the Christian, according to Peter. Or let me put it in a different form. What is a Christian? Is he just a man who is born in a certain country? Is he just someone who was christened when he was an infant? Is he someone who was confirmed at a certain age, or immersed in water at a particular point? Is he merely a man who tries to live a good life, one who is philanthropic in his ideas and who is out to uplift the status and improve the lot of mankind? According to the New Testament, while many of these things may be true of the Christian, they do not make a man a Christian. A Christian is one who is a partaker of the divine nature. He is one in whom are, essentially, the traits and characteristics of God Himself, the divine life. He is like Christ. The life of godliness, the divine quality of life, the divine characteristics are in him, are being formed in him, and he is manifesting these divine characteristics. That, according to Peter, is the thing to which we are called; that is what is demanded and expected of you and me as Christians. We not merely believe that our sins are forgiven in Christ – thank God that we do believe that – but we must not stop at that. I am not merely one who is forgiven, I am to be a partaker of the divine nature; I am to be a new man, a new creation, a new being; and I am to reveal and manifest these characteristics. That is the calling.

Now, the Apostle, having spoken in this way, seems to imagine someone coming and saying, That is very wonderful, but how is it to be done? Isn't it an utterly impossible task to set us? We are living in a world that is against us, a world that is contradictory, and you tell us we have to be like God, you are asking us to be like Christ, you are asking us here on earth, just as we are, to be living and showing forth certain of the virtues and the excellences of God Himself. It is impossible, it cannot be done. The world is against us, and we are weak. You are setting the standard too high. No, says Peter, that is the thing that makes a man Christian; that is to be Christian, nothing less.

How can we do it? The Apostle here answers our question. He first of all answers it by saying that all things that appertain unto life and godliness have already been given unto us. 'According as his divine power hath given unto us all things that pertain unto life and godliness.' How can we do it? The answer is that everything we require is there for us. There is no excuse, there is no need, for failure. All things – and that is all-inclusive, you cannot add to it – all things that pertain unto life and godliness have already been given us. Well, how have they been given us? In a sense the Apostle gives the answer like this: they have been given 'through the knowledge of him that hath called us to glory and virtue: whereby are given unto us exceeding great and precious promises'. That is how it happens. In other words, all these things that are necessary for life and godliness are given unto us in and by and through the knowledge of God that we have in Jesus Christ and his Gospel. Very well, how does that work out? This is Peter's exposition of it. What is this knowledge that I have in the Gospel, which supplies me with all things that are necessary to life and to godliness? What is it that I have in this knowledge given me by the Gospel, that enables me here on earth to live this life which is similar in character to the life of God and of Christ?

First and foremost the Gospel *gives me knowledge with respect to my state and condition by nature*. The Apostle puts that last here, but in experience it is the first. 'Having escaped the corruption that is in the world through lust.' Let us look at it like this. The first thing a man needs to be enlightened upon is himself and the nature of his life in this world. What is man? What is the meaning of life in this world? What is the purpose of being here? What are we going on to? We must realise the nature of life as it is in this world. As to this, the teaching of the New Testament, indeed the teaching of the Bible from beginning to end, is summarised perfectly by the Apostle in these words, 'having escaped the corruption that is in the world through lust.' The world, according to the Bible, has fallen from God; the world is therefore corrupt, and in a state of corruption. God made man perfect, He made him body, soul and spirit. He put His own image upon him. In other words, His own divine characteristics were given to man at the beginning. But, alas, a foreign element called sin came in, and the effect of sin upon man was that his whole life was corrupted. Sin is that which comes between man and God, and, when he sinned, man lost that peculiar quality of life which God had given him at the beginning when He placed His image and stamp upon him. As a result of sin and the fall, man no longer lives the life that he had been living before; he has become alienated from God and the godly way of life, and the world in which he lives is likewise in a state of corruption. In other words, the world in which we live is a world that is inimical to our best and truest and highest interests; the world is for ever trying to come between us and God. If we listen to the world, as we all do by nature, it makes us not only think less and less of God, but even makes us feel that God is against us. It may even create an enmity against God, and a hatred of God within us. It gives us a positive liking and longing for the things that are hurtful to us, the things that debase us, the things that lower us, the things that drag us further and further away from God. Such is the corruption that is in the world through lust. The characteristic of man's natural life is that it is a life lived according to desire. Man by nature does not ask, 'Is this good, is this god-like, is this pure, is this clean, is this elevating, is this spiritual?' He asks, 'Do I like it?' He is governed by his desires, by that which pleases him, and by that which panders to his lower nature. That is what Peter means by corruption – it is the corruption that results from lust or inordinate desire.

But there is no need to elaborate. You have but to keep your eyes open, and look around and about you at the present time, to see exactly what I mean. Look at your newspapers. Why do they give lengthy reports of police court cases? They know that that is what people like – the lust, the gloating, the peculiar interest in that which is unclean, the morbid curiosity about trials and even executions. All that kind of thing is a perfect illustration. Look at the faces of men. Look at the kind of life men live. Listen to their conversation. Is it not something that appeals to the lower and animal nature? That is the corruption that is in the world through lust. Now the first thing the Gospel does is to awaken us to the fact that by nature we are subject to this corruption, that we do not desire to know God as we ought, that to know God and to be like God is not the big thing in our life. We forget Him; days may pass and we may never speak to Him; we do not read His word, we do not meditate upon Him. We give ourselves to these other things that are in us and in the world that is round about us. But the Gospel makes me see that I am in a dangerous condition, that I am corrupt within, and that there is a corruption without, that I am far away from God and separated from God. It makes me see that I am in that corrupt state and condition and that I must get out, and escape from it, if ever I am to know God and to be god-like, and if I am to spend eternity in His Holy Presence. It is the knowledge of God and the Lord Jesus Christ in his Gospel that alone reveals that fact to me. That is the first thing. I can never know God, and I can never be like God in my life, until I have seen myself as I am, and until I realise that the world is all against me and is dragging me down. But the moment I see it I have taken the first step, and that only comes through the Gospel.

What else? Well, the next thing is what Peter calls the 'exceeding great and precious promises'. You see the steps. I see my nature, I see that I have been living a careless life, living the way of the world, saying that everything is all right, feeling rather sorry for the people who are still religious, feeling that they are rather antiquated; and then I suddenly awake to the fact that the Gospel is right, and that I am in a state of corruption. I begin to see through the kind of life I have been living, and now I ask myself how God can forgive me for it, also how I can ever get out of it, and how I can live a conquering overcoming life in spite of it. That is the logical sequence. Very well, says Peter, when you are awakened and see the corruption in your own heart, and the corruption that is around and about you in the world because of lust, and when you begin to ask your questions, thank God all things that are necessary for life and godliness are provided for in the exceeding great and precious promises.

What are they? Well, let me just note some of them. These are the elemental things of the Gospel. First of all, 'Forgiveness'. 'He that believeth on him is not condemned.' 'God so loved the world, that he gave his only begotten Son, that whosoever believeth in him should not perish, but have everlasting life.' 'There is therefore now no condemnation to them which are in Christ Jesus.' 'Being justified by faith, we have peace with God.' I could go on almost endlessly repeating these exceeding great and precious promises that come when a man sees himself as being corrupt, and fallen away from God, and therefore guilty in the presence of God. What gracious promises of God, everything pardoned and forgiven! Oh yes, but as I have already reminded you, that is not enough. It is a grand thing to be forgiven; but I now realise that I am corrupt in my nature. What can I do about that? Well, here again is another gracious promise, 'But as many as received him, to them gave he power (or authority), to become the sons of God.' 'Being born again, not of corruptible seed, but of incorruptible, by the word of God which liveth and abideth for ever.' Thank God, when I am aware of the corruptness of my nature the Gospel tells me that I can be born again, receive a new nature and a new character, be made a new man. 'If any man be in Christ, he is a new creature.' What a wonderful, gracious, exceeding great and precious promise that is!

What else? Well, realising all this, and having arrived at this point, naturally I need more light. I realise I have spent my lifetime in reading things that do not help me in this respect; I have been relying on the wisdom of man. But I begin to see that it is all earthbound, it does not rise to this spiritual life, it does not tell me about God, it does not really tell me how I can live the life I want to live. Well, where can I get light except in the promises of this Book, the Gospel of Jesus Christ and its instructions? 'But,' says someone, 'I try to read the Bible and I find it uninteresting. My mind has been so accustomed to the corrupt literature I have read – exciting novels and biographies which I have enjoyed – that when I come to this Book I find it dry. I do not seem to have the faculty for it. How can I get to like it?' Here, then, comes the gracious promise and comfort of the Holy Spirit, 'Ye have an unction from the Holy One,' says John, 'and ye know all things.' By the illumination of the Holy Spirit I am enabled to see and appropriate and to comprehend something of this precious truth.

Then as I look at the world in which I live and see its state and all its temptations, and all the insinuations of Satan round about, I ask how I shall know which way to go. Here comes the great and exceeding precious promise of the leading and the guidance of the Holy Spirit, who will lead me, not only into all truth, but also in my personal life and decisions and conduct and behaviour.

And then there is that other great need, the need of power as I confront the principalities and powers, and the rulers of the darkness of this world, and the spiritual wickedness in high places. I say I am weak, and then comes the answer 'but Thou art mighty' – the indwelling of the Holy Spirit, through whom I can become more than conqueror over every enemy that meets me and is set against me. And then, as I go on in this life with these exceeding great promises, there are times when I feel tired, and I wonder whether I am ever going to arrive. I feel the contradiction of it all, the enemy is so powerful and so strong, and tends at times to besiege and assail me. What else is there for me? What is the ultimate exceeding great and precious promise? The *blessed hope*, the knowledge that I shall not only be held thus, and instructed and led and guided through this world, but that when I die and go out of it, 'this corruptible shall have put on incorruption,' that even my body shall be changed – this my 'vile body', as the Authorised Version puts it, or if you prefer the Revised, that 'the body of our humiliation may be conformed to the body of his glory'. I shall be completely emancipated and set free, without fault or spot or blemish; I shall be perfect in the presence of God.

One other thing! In addition to all this, there is this mighty power that is working for us – 'grace and peace be multiplied unto you through the knowledge of God, and of Jesus our Lord, according as his divine power hath given unto us all things that pertain unto life and godliness through the knowledge of him that hath called us to glory and virtue.' My dear friends, we are called unto a supernatural life. This whole doctrine of the rebirth needs the action of God. Man does not make himself a Christian by deciding to become Christian. It is the action of God, by the mighty power of the Holy Spirit, placing this new disposition within him, which gives him this new life and quality. It is His divine power; and that divine power not only starts us off in the Christian life, it accompanies us, it works in us, it will mould us, it will fashion us until we arrive in that ultimate state of glorification. You remember Paul's prayer for the church at Ephesus; he prays that the eyes of their understanding may be enlightened that they may know certain things. What are they? '... the hope of his calling, and what the riches of the glory of his inheritance in the saints, and what is the exceeding greatness of his power to us-ward who believe.' This, he says, is so great that he can compare it with nothing but the power that raised the Lord Jesus Christ from the dead. That is the last and ultimate precious promise on which we need to concentrate, and on which we must ever meditate. We are not just left to ourselves; this important task is not just left to us. 'We are God's workmanship', created, fashioned by Him. It is a process initiated by God and worked out by the Holy Spirit, so that as I confront that goal of the knowledge of God and of likeness to God, and as I see the corruption that is in me and in the world round about me, I have the comfort not only of these exceeding great and precious promises, but I know further that in me, and about me, and through me, is working this mighty power of God Himself. Therefore I say confidently and with assurance with the apostle Paul, 'He which hath begun a good work in you will perform it until the day of Jesus Christ'.

Do we know God? Are we like God? Can we say that we are partakers of the divine nature? That is what makes one a Christian. That is the witness and the testimony we should be bearing at this present time. To the extent that you and I, and every professing Christian, manifest this divine nature, to that extent shall we by our lives convict the world of its sin and its corruption, and draw and attract men and women to Jesus Christ our Lord.

3
The Balanced Life

'And beside this, giving all diligence, add to your faith
virtue; and to virtue knowledge; And to knowledge
temperance; and to temperance patience; and to patience
godliness; And to godliness brotherly kindness; and to
brotherly kindness charity.'

Chapter 1:5–7

As we come to the statement recorded in these three verses it is very
important that we should observe their exact connection with what
the Apostle has already been saying. In other words, nothing is more
important at this point than that we should observe carefully the
logical sequence which is followed by the Apostle in writing this
letter. This deserves a comment in passing. There is nothing, finally,
that is such a proof of the divine inspiration of Scripture as the way in
which a man like Peter – a man who was a fisherman by calling and
by trade, a man certainly who had not had the special advantages in
an educational sense that a man like Paul had, a man whom we think
of as being governed by impulses and who was rather impetuous –
having become an Apostle of Jesus Christ by the grace of God, and
under the influence of the Holy Spirit, not only writes a letter which is
full of transcendent thought, but at the same time shows and displays
a logical order, an extraordinary sequence, in the way in which he
presents us with the various aspects of the truth that he is concerned
to convey.

In the first four verses, as we have seen, he reminds his readers of
the glorious character of their 'precious faith' – its origin in the mind
and heart of the Triune God, what it has done to us and the glorious
prospect it holds out before us of being 'partakers of the divine
nature' and of knowing God.

Now then, says Peter in effect, having said all that, let us go forward. 'Beside this,' says the Authorised Version, but it is generally agreed that at this point the Authorised Version really does mislead us a little. It does not bring out the exact emphasis which the Apostle had in mind. 'For this very cause,' he said, or, 'because of this,' because of what has already been said, 'giving all diligence, add to your faith virtue,' etc. Here is something which is truly important, and something which is again basic and fundamental to the whole Christian position. The order in which these things are put is something which is absolutely vital. The Apostle does not ask us to do anything until he has first of all emphasised and repeated what God has done for us in Christ. I say that this is basic and for this good reason. How many times, especially during the last hundred years, have men taken it for granted that the real essence of the Christian Gospel is in this text we are considering! How often during the past hundred years have men given the impression that to be Christian means that you display in your life a kind of general belief of faith, and then you add to it virtue and knowledge and temperance and patience and godliness and brotherly kindness and charity! To them the Christian message is an exhortation to us to live a certain type of life, and an exhortation to put these things into practice. But that is an utter travesty of the Gospel. The Christian Gospel in the first instance does not ask us to do anything; it first of all proclaims and announces to us what God has done for us.

That is so for quite a number of reasons. It is one of the very essentials of the Christian Gospel to show that man as he is by nature cannot do anything. He is 'dead in trespasses and sins', he is without life, and all his righteousness is but 'as filthy rags' – that is the scriptural teaching. In effect the Gospel is not interested in any of our actions or our conduct and our behaviour until we become Christian. The first statements, surely, of the Gospel are these, 'There is none righteous, no, not one'; 'We have all come short of the glory of God.' Man at his best and highest is a lost creature; he is a sinner doomed in the sight of God. Any man, every man! Though a man may strain and strive and pray, and go from one end of the earth to the other, in an attempt to seek for righteousness, he will be no nearer to God, and to a true knowledge of God, at the end than he was at the beginning.

The first statement of the Gospel is not an exhortation to action or to conduct and behaviour. Before man is called upon to do anything, he must have received something. Before God calls upon a man to put anything into practice, He has made it possible for man to put it into practice. Many New Testament analogies put this point quite clearly. We can look at it like this. There is no point in addressing an appeal to a dead person. The only person to whom you can with any logic address an appeal is one who is alive; and that is precisely the teaching of the Gospel. When a man becomes a Christian he is born again; whereas he was dead, he now lives. The Bible compares it to a birth. Before there can be activity there must be life, there must be muscles, there must be the faculties and the propensities. And that is the position of the Christian; he has been given all this. He has these muscles, these spiritual muscles – all things pertaining to life and godliness are given. Therefore, because of this, 'add to your faith', etc. Or take the analogy of a farm, which is a very good one. The whole statement of the Gospel is that the farm as such is given to us by God's gift: 'by grace are ye saved through faith; and that not of yourselves: it is the gift of God'. We are given the farm, we are given the implements and all that is necessary, we are given the seed. What we are called upon to do, is to farm. It is no use telling a man to farm if he has not a farm; if he is without land and without seed and without the implements, nothing can be done. But all these are given us, and therefore, having received them, we are asked to farm. But even then we are reminded that that does not guarantee the increase. 'It is God who gives the increase.' The farmer may plough and harrow, he may roll the land and sow the seed, but in the absence of the rain and the sunshine, and many other factors, there will be no increase. Now there, it seems to me, is the perfect balance which is ever preserved in the New Testament. That is the order in which it invariably puts these things. It is because you have obtained a like precious faith with us, says Peter, it is because you have all things that pertain to life and godliness, it is because of these exceeding great and precious promises, it is because of the power of God that is in you, that I now beseech you to add to your faith virtue, and to virtue knowledge, and so on.

Here, then, we stand face to face with something that is very necessary as an emphasis at this present time. There are two errors into which we always tend to fall. We go on repeating in every age the experiences of the first Christians that are depicted in the New Testament – the errors of extremes. There are those of whom I have been speaking who think that by their own efforts they can make themselves Christian, that by adding these virtues to their natural life they can fit themselves to stand in the presence of God. And on the other side there is the error of passivity. This is the error of saying, 'Of course one can do nothing; salvation is of Christ; and therefore any effort or any attempt at spiritual culture, or any effort to discipline the Christian life, is wrong, and means falling back on works, and trying to justify oneself by works.' To go to one extreme or the other has always been the tendency, and you have these two errors described in the New Testament itself. On the one side there are those who preach justification by works, and on the other those who can be described as antinomians, and who say, If you are saved, you are saved, and your actions do not matter at all. These are in both instances contradictory to the teaching of Scripture, and upset the balance of its teaching. Let us, then, follow the logical order and sequence that are indicated by the Apostle. God gives the inward capacity which makes everything possible; without that we can do nothing and we are not asked to do anything. But, having been given, and having received that gift, then nothing is more important than that we should give ourselves with all our energy to spiritual culture and to the development of the Christian life. In other words, we can translate this fifth verse like this: 'For this very cause, therefore, do you on your part supply in your faith, virtue' and so on. That puts it perfectly, as if Peter were saying, I have already told you what God has done on His part; now, because of that, do you, on your part, supply in your faith virtue and so on.

Having thus pointed out the all-importance of this logical order and sequence, let us now turn to the details of the text. The first thing we must notice is this word 'add'. Here, again, it is agreed that this translation is perhaps not as good as it might be, and that a better word would be 'supply', or 'furnish'. This word is interesting; it was used for fitting out the chorus in connection with the Greek plays. It was a word that was used to describe the action of one who paid the cost of supplying, or fully furnishing with everything that was necessary, the chorus, which was always such a vital part of a Greek play. So it is rightly translated by the words 'furnish' or 'supply abundantly'. That is what the Apostle Peter meant when he said, In your faith, or to your faith, supply abundantly, virtue, then to the virtue supply abundantly knowledge, and so on with all these things.

He does not just mean that we mechanically add each one of these to the one that has gone before; what he is concerned about is that there shall be a perfect whole, a perfect balance, that the chorus of the play shall be fitted out not only abundantly and completely, but with that perfect balance that will produce a perfect performance and a perfect result. That is the meaning of this word 'add'.

Very well, let us consider exactly what the Apostle asks us to do when he names these various things. I believe that they can be grouped together into three main headings. He first of all reminds us of the character of our faith; then in the second place he emphasises our inward dispositions; and thirdly, he deals with our relationship to others. It is a perfect list; you cannot add to it. It deals with the whole of the Christian life, and all is dependent upon faith. The most important thing is that we should be right about the character of the faith. Then the next thing is to remember that we are in a world which is antagonistic and hostile, and therefore we must be quite certain about our own inward dispositions. Thirdly, we must be careful about our relationship to others.

First of all, take this definition of the character of the faith. Supply in your faith, 'virtue'. What does this word mean? Well, here again is a word about which we have to be careful. Nowadays this word 'virtue' is given a very different meaning. We talk about a man's virtues, and we mean certain excellences in his character. The temptation, therefore, is to think that Peter is here saying, Supply in your faith 'virtue' in that sense. But clearly it cannot be that, for this good reason, that all the other things that follow are in that sense virtues; so that if Peter were just saying that, he would be saying, Supply in your faith virtues, and then he would go on repeating the virtues. No, this is a word which has undergone a change in meaning since the days of the Authorised Version, and it is all-important that we should take it in the meaning which the Apostle Peter obviously attached to it. 'Virtue' here means 'moral power', or, if you like, moral energy – it means activity or vigour of the soul. See to it, says Peter, that your faith is a living faith, see that it is an active faith, see that it is a vigorous faith, see that it is a manly faith, see that it is an energetic faith.

Now this is an exhortation, surely, that we all need. I wonder sometimes whether we are not dealing here with something which keeps large numbers of people from the Christian life and faith. Is

there not something languid, so often, in our Christian life and
Christian activity, as you contrast it with the life of the world
outside? Is there not this curious tendency for the element of
passivity in our conception of the Christian faith to predominate, as
if we regard faith as nothing but an attitude of waiting? A kind of
lethargy and languor spreads over us, a curious kind of lassitude. No,
no, says Peter, let your faith be energetic, let it be vigorous, let it be
alive; stir yourself up, see that you are active and alert. That is
something that you and I are called upon to do. In other words, we
must not just recline on beds of ease and wait for something to move
and disturb us. Our faith is to be a living, energetic, active faith, and
we are to see that, on our part, we give all diligence to making it so:
'add to your faith virtue'.

Then you notice he goes on to say that that virtue or energy or
vigour should be furnished with 'knowledge'. What does he mean by
'knowledge' at this point? Obviously he does not mean the kind of
knowledge that leads to faith; he has been emphasising that already
at great length. He has used the introduction of this letter to remind
them of that. That is taken for granted. What, then, does it mean? It
must mean 'insight', 'understanding', 'enlightenment'. Here again
we see the wonderful order which is preserved by the Apostle. He is
exhorting these people to a vigorous, energetic, alert life – 'Don't just
settle down in spiritual lethargy and lassitude,' says Peter, 'waiting
for amazing things to happen; be up and doing, be vigorous, seize the
opportunity, put "virtue" into practice.' But, he continues, do not
stop at that. If he left it at that there would be a terrible temptation to
rush into false activity and false zeal. So it is needed that this vigour,
this energy, this activity be governed and controlled and qualified by
intelligence, by understanding and by enlightenment. In other
words, it does not just mean the display of energy without control; it
must be controlled energy, it must be enlightened virtue. Surely we
cannot look at these words without feeling, in a sense, that Peter was
writing from his own experience. Peter by nature was a very
impulsive man, and you cannot read the pages of the four Gospels
without seeing a perfect portrayal, as you study Peter, of uncontrolled energy. Poor Peter, because he was not controlled and intelligent
and enlightened, did things at times which he bitterly regretted
afterwards. No doubt he remembered all that, and, realising that
these people were like himself, he says, Furnish that vigour of yours

with intelligent understanding.

Without going into these points in detail, I would say in passing, that as one looks at the present religious situation in Britain, and in other countries, one does see the importance of adding knowledge to vigour. There is the danger of our being overwhelmed by a state of mere activity, of having an excess of organisations. Let our spiritual energy and activity be intelligent, let it be enlightened, let it be controlled. Let us make certain that the knowledge of God and of Christ and of the Christian faith is ever in the saddle, controlling this amazing, wonderful steed that is ever ready to take the bit between his teeth and bolt. We are not called upon to indulge in any unenlightened activity in the kingdom of God; it must always be controlled by understanding.

Let me now say a word about the important group that comprises the inward dispositions. In this group we have two terms, temperance and patience. These two words include everything at this point. What are the two things which I as a Christian have to watch, and to watch unceasingly? I have to watch myself. Though we are born again, though we have the divine nature, there is another man here. There are impulses and desires, there are lusts and passions; and though a man may have believed the Christian Gospel, and though he may have known the power of God, there is still a fight to wage within – 'the flesh lusteth against the spirit and the spirit against the flesh'. Also there is always the enemy and the adversary of our souls to drive us into sin. It may even be in connection with our work. In a moment of success he may come and fawn upon us and flatter us, and in that elation we may fall to these lusts and passions that are within. Therefore, says Peter, always remember self-discipline, always watch these things that are within, and be temperate. As the Apostle Paul puts it, 'Mortify, therefore, your members that are on the earth.'* You remember the list which he gives in the third chapter of Colossians.

This is something we can never afford to neglect. You and I who have this faith are told that this is something we do on our part. We must not expect that while we are sitting down in a chair all these things that are within will suddenly be taken out of us. No, we are all to practise temperance, discipline, self-control. We are all to mortify

* Put to death therefore whatever belongs to your earthly nature. (*N.I.V.*)

these members. It is a positive exhortation to us – 'temperance'. Need I remind you at this point that I am still only saying these things in the light of what we have already been told. It is because of God's power, it is because He has given us all things that pertain to life and godliness, that we can do this. I am not asking an unenlightened man to discipline and control himself; I am calling upon the man who has this new life to do something which he is capable of doing.

And then comes 'patience', which means, of course, 'patient endurance'. In this life, and in this Christian warfare, the problems are not only within; there are problems without also. There is, for instance, the danger that arises from other people and other things. Oh, the need of patience – patient endurance! Peter again was probably falling back on his own experiences. He it was who had said to our Lord, 'Though all men forsake thee, I will follow thee'; and then, poor Peter had denied Him three times. There is not much point in making great professions and great promises if we do not carry them out. What we need to cultivate is patient endurance, not a sudden stepping out and then becoming discouraged and falling back and bringing the Christian faith into disgrace in the sight of the world. No, we must be careful to add this sense of patient endurance. Remembering the things that are ahead, remembering what has been given, we just go on, and in spite of everything we must be manly, vigorous, self-controlled. We must go on with patient endurance. At a time like this, when so many are scoffing at these things and so many have turned their back upon the Christian church, the temptation is to say, 'Why should I go on, why should I be different and just go on and be patient?' The answer is that we should remember that we are God's children, marching on to a glorious eternal inheritance which we shall enter 'after we have suffered awhile'. 'Let us not be weary in well doing: for in due season we shall reap, if we faint not.'

Next we come to our relationship to others. Here again there is a complete list, godliness, brotherly kindness, love. What does Peter mean? The first thing, of course, always, is that our relationship to God should be right. All Bible students, I think, will find it very interesting to work out these problems and find out why the Apostle puts godliness at this particular point. To me there is only one explanation. He puts it here because he is dealing here with the realm of relationships. And we must always put our relationship to God first. In other words, while you are controlling these things within, and while you are going on in the spirit of patient endurance, remember why you are doing it all; remember that it is all for the glory of God. Self-culture must not be practised for its own sake, and the danger is to be falling back on our disciplined nature in and of itself. But if we worship discipline we are not being godly. There is no point in any of these things unless they are centrally related to God. Godliness, therefore, first. Before I think of my relationship to anybody else, I must always be certain that my main motive and ambition in life is to honour God, is to glorify God, and to tell forth His praise. Then, having put that first, we are to consider the brethren – 'brotherly kindness'. There, of course, Peter is referring to other Christian people. He was exhorting these first Christians to love one another, and to be patient towards one another. How difficult it is at times! How easy it is to become impatient, and perhaps more impatient with those who are Christian than with those who are not, because we expect more of them. How much harm is being done in the church because of the lack of brotherly kindness! Let us together read the thirteenth chapter of the first Epistle to the Corinthians. Let us take it to heart, let us have that brotherly attitude towards one another that 'hopeth all things'. Then, finally, the Apostle says, over and above the brethren, love all men – have a great charity in your heart towards all. Try to see the souls in the sinners, try to see their need; have within you a great love such as the love of God Himself who 'maketh his sun to rise on the evil and on the good, and sendeth rain on the just and on the unjust'. Let that love reign in you, says Peter.

We see that each one of these qualities adds and contributes to the others; every one has its own importance and yet each one influences the others. We see the importance of vigour, and yet we see the importance of controlling vigour by knowledge. Every one has its own function, and yet each one affects the others and therefore contributes to the whole. In other words, what impresses me most of all about this list is its perfect balance; and there is nothing about the Christian life that is so glorious as its perfect balance. There is no other life that has this balance. There are people who are highly intellectual and very cultured, but perhaps not moral; there are others who are morally blameless but not very intelligent; and there are those who have great will power, but somehow there is something lacking. There is no life that shows this perfect balance but the Christian life that is depicted here. To show that, let me put it in the form of two pictures. That word 'add' has already given us one. Isn't it the perfection and the balance of a great chorus, as we now know it – the soprano, the alto, the tenor and the bass? They are all necessary to the chorus, and you must not have too much of one or too little of the other or you will upset the balance. You must estimate and assess the volume and the strength of the voices in order to render a great chorus or oratorio perfectly; you must get your balance, you must get your proportion. That is one way of looking at it. Or perhaps you prefer to look at it in another way. You can look at the various items in this list as the ingredients in a bottle of medicine – perhaps this puts it in a still better way. It is like a mixture, in which the efficacy of the whole depends upon each ingredient being duly proportioned and yet intimately bound with all the others. Every ingredient is important and has its own particular action and yet each ingredient helps the others. There is a kind of synergistic action. And here, if you like, you have the perfect mixture for the Christian life. Oh, the importance of putting in just the right amount of each ingredient into the bottle in order that you may have the perfect whole! Or, lastly, perhaps you can look at it like this. In the Christian life you start with faith and you always end with love. Without faith you can do nothing, but given faith, and the practising of the faith, you must inevitably end with love, for God Himself is Love. May God in His infinite grace thus enable and stimulate us to manifest this perfect poise and balance in our Christian lives, and in our Christian witness, in this our day and generation!

4
Assurance of Salvation

'Wherefore the rather, brethren, give diligence to make
your calling and election sure: for if ye do these things, ye
shall never fall.'

Chapter 1:10

We have seen that the Apostle in his endeavour to help and
encourage these early Christians has been emphasising the importance of the two sides to the Christian life. In verses 1–4 he deals with
the given side – what God does to us. In verses 5–7 he exhorts them in
the light of that and because of that, to play their part and to work
that out in practice.

Coming now to verse 8, we find that from the beginning of verse 8
to the end of verse 11 he, in a sense, simply repeats that exhortation.
But it is such an interesting repetition that we cannot really deal with
it in one discourse. We shall have to divide it up into two main
sections. I begin with the tenth verse because, here, he again makes
the same appeal that he has already made in verses 5–7; but in
addition shows us why we should respond to it. I have been insisting
and urging you, says Peter, to add to your faith knowledge and
temperance and patient endurance, etc., because I want you to make
your calling and election sure. That is the object. These troubles from
the outside are tending to make you uncertain. These heresies within
and the teaching of the false teachers are having the same effect. They
are shaking your faith and you are becoming uncertain. I exhort you,
says the Apostle, to furnish out your faith in order that you may
make your calling and election sure. That is the basis of the
argument, and what we desire to do is to consider the exhortation in
this form. It is true to say that this tenth verse is really the key verse of
the whole Epistle, that the object of the entire letter is to enable us to
make our calling and election sure.

What does Peter mean by this exhortation? On the surface it sounds rather self-contradictory – we are to make our calling and election sure! Now there are those who would interpret it by saying that this is just an exhortation for people to make themselves Christian and to make certain of the fact that they are Christian. According to that argument, if you do the things enumerated by the Apostle, the result will be that you will become Christian in a true sense. Yet, surely, that is an interpretation which we cannot accept for a moment, and for this good reason, that it would be a complete and entire contradiction of the whole doctrine of the Bible and very especially of the doctrine of the New Testament. The Apostle is not here exhorting these people to make certain of their calling and election in an ultimate and eternal sense, for that is something of which they are incapable. The election and calling are on God's side and are God's action. The Apostle has already been making that clear. Did you notice in the first verse that very significant statement, 'Simon Peter, a servant and an apostle of Jesus Christ, to them that have obtained like precious faith'? They have not created it, they have not generated it; they have obtained it, they have received it as a gift. The faith is something that we 'obtain', we 'receive'.

This is the great doctrine we find everywhere in the New Testament, is it not? 'By grace are ye saved through faith; and that not of yourselves: it is the gift of God.' 'For whom he did foreknow he also did predestinate to be conformed to the image of his Son . . .' Let us be quite clear about this – the calling and election are on God's side. Peter gives the word in the third verse – 'According as his divine power hath given us all things that pertain unto life and godliness.' It is His glorious power, it is He alone who can give us the gift of life. Paul tells us that 'we were dead in trespasses and sins'. But while we were dead in trespasses and sins God 'quickened us'. A dead person cannot regenerate himself; a man cannot give life to himself; he cannot quicken himself. He is incapable of any action. A man cannot give birth to himself. That has always been a stumbling block to many, but it is one of the central doctrines of the New Testament. It tells us that salvation is entirely the gift of God by grace. No, Peter is not telling us here to elect ourselves or to choose ourselves or to call ourselves. It is God who calls, it is God who chooses. It is a great mystery – let us acknowledge and confess it. The mind of man cannot grasp and understand it. Let me go further and say that the mind of man would never have thought of it; no man would have thought of this. These terms 'election' and 'calling' are only to be found in the Bible.

'Well, if this is so,' says someone, 'I feel God is not fair.' But so long as you are anxious to understand you will not accept this doctrine. To me the essence of faith is to believe where I cannot understand, because I find it in the Word of God. It is not for the Christian preacher to understand the mind of God but to accept His gracious revelation and submit to it. If I could understand the mind of God, my mind would be equal to the mind of God. I cannot understand the mind of God. But it is an essential part of the Christian preacher's work to say this, that any man who examines himself and his life and experience, and who at this moment, finds himself in the Christian position and the possessor of the Christian life, as he looks back across his experience must acknowledge and admit and confess that he is what he is by the grace of God. Look at the world and you will see with your own eyes a confirmation of the New Testament teaching. There are those who are concerned about and interested in the things we are discussing; and there are the large masses of people who are not only unconcerned, but who dismiss them with scorn, and to whom all this is insulting. What is the cause of the difference and the cleavage? Why have we this understanding and concern? Why are we not like many thousands of heedless people in this modern world? Is there any answer but this, that God has called us, that the grace of God has dealt with us? No, the calling and election are from God. It is God's action; God initiated the movement. There would be no salvation if God had not acted.

Well, what is this exhortation? It is that you and I may be certain of our salvation. The exhortation is that you and I shall do these things in order that we may know and be aware of the fact that, in the words of Philip Doddridge, ''Tis done, the great transaction's done'. The election and the calling are of God; but the question is, Do I know that I am called and elected? And Peter here exhorts these Christians to be certain about that. John, in the fifth chapter of his first Epistle says the same thing. 'These things I have written unto you that ye may know that ye have eternal life' – that you may be sure! So what the Apostle is pleading for is what, traditionally, has been called the assurance of salvation.

Now having defined the meaning of the text in that way, let me go on to ask another question. Who should have this assurance, or for whom is the assurance meant? Here again there has been a great deal of confusion. Is this meant for all, or only for certain special people? Is every Christian meant to have an assurance of salvation, or is it only for a certain special few – certain outstanding people? Oh yes, says someone, the Apostle Paul had an assurance of salvation, but surely it is not meant for all of us; it is not meant for people like ourselves. Yet, surely, that is again an utter travesty of the New Testament teaching. Peter is writing here to ordinary Christians. There is no differentiation amongst them into small and great; and he says, 'make your calling and election sure'. John, in the same way, wrote to those first Christians, most of them slaves, all of them very ordinary common people, nothing exceptional in ability and culture. They were not men living segregated lives; they were not men who had made a vocation of the spiritual life; they were ordinary people doing the most menial tasks in the world. And yet they were expected to make their calling and election sure, and to know that they had eternal life.

If you consult the subsequent history of the church, you will find that at all times of revival and reformation, when the church has really been alive, nothing is more characteristic of her life than this fact, that her people have this assurance of salvation, and 'know in whom they have believed'. A well-known incident in the Evangelical Revival of the 18th century, illustrates this very well. The first time that great 18th-century preacher, and man of God, George Whitefield, met one of the Welsh Methodist leaders, Howell Harris, in Cardiff, the first question he put to Howell Harris was this, 'Mr Harris, do you *know* that your sins are forgiven?' That is it! Have you assurance, are you certain, can you say, that your sins are forgiven? And Howell Harris was able to reply that he had rejoiced in that knowledge for a number of years. That is the thing of which my text speaks – the knowledge of sins forgiven, the knowledge of possessing divine life and being partakers of the divine nature – 'that ye may know that ye have eternal life'. Nothing is more important for each one of us than to face the question put by George Whitefield to Howell Harris – Do you know that your sins are forgiven? Do you know that you are a child of God? Can you say you have eternal life? You remember how John puts it in his first Epistle and the fifth chapter, '. . . this is the record, that God hath given to us eternal life . . .' That is the question for us, as it was the question for those early Christians. You must be certain of this, says Peter, because if you are not certain, you will not be able to function as you ought. Make certain, therefore. Are we modern Christians certain of our salvation?

There is confusion about this because people have certain preliminary objections. I want to try to deal with them in order that we may be able to implement this exhortation.

People say you must not talk in this way about knowing that your sins are forgiven, or that you have eternal life. Why do they feel like that? There are some who are utterly antagonised by the doctrine of assurance because of the glib way certain people use these expressions. I think we have to face this quite definitely and frankly. There are people who talk about an assurance of salvation with such glibness, and with such superficiality, and in a spirit that seems to be so utterly contrary to the spirit of the New Testament, that they very definitely antagonise others against this doctrine. There are people who use this expression with a self-satisfied smile and smugness and say that they are 'gloriously saved'. There is almost a levity in their speech which is offensive; and I say that it is offensive to the New Testament doctrine itself. There is no glibness about the language of the New Testament; there is no levity, there is no superficiality in it. There is no laughter or joking here. There is none of that cultivated joviality which is often manifested when certain types of people testify to their salvation – there is none of that in the New Testament! The New Testament joy is the joy of a man who has seen himself as a hell-deserving sinner. The New Testament joy is the joy of one who realises there is still corruption within him and who attributes all he now is to the grace and the mercy of God. The New Testament man is a man who realises that he has been forgiven that he may be called unto holiness, that he may be like God and like Christ. The more a man seeks to be like Christ, the less glib, the less superficial he is. Let us be quite clear about that.

Then there are others who feel it is presumption to speak of having assurance. They say, 'How can I in a life and world like this, say that I know my sins are forgiven? Isn't it presumption? Am I not, as it were, derogating from the sovereignty of God, if I say that I know my sins are forgiven and that I have eternal life?' The answer to that is what I am going to show in a moment, that, were we not taught this doctrine in the New Testament, it would be the height of presumption. But we are reminded in the New Testament that not only is it not presumption to claim this, but that not to do so is to detract from the glory and the wonder of the Gospel and its great salvation.

Another difficulty is that of the people who feel they cannot make this statement until they are perfect. To them it is ridiculous to say that 'I know whom I have believed', and that I am the possessor of eternal life, while I still sin and while I am still conscious of corruption within. In other words, they feel that only those who can claim sinless perfection have a right to claim the assurance of salvation. But there, again, is a confusion of doctrine. We are not told to make our calling and election sure by being sinless and perfect; the idea of sinless perfection is not in the New Testament. We are told to claim assurance and to make certain of it on other grounds. There is no need to wait until we are perfect to claim this. The New Testament doctrine emphasises that there are still two natures resident within us, the new and the old, and the old is continually warring against the new; but the fact that the flesh is there does not mean that the spirit is not there.

Those are some of the objections. Let us now go on to another practical question. Why should we have this assurance? Surely there is nothing more important at this present time than that the church of God should consider why we should have this certainty and assurance. Let me suggest some answers. First and foremost is the reason *that God offers it*. It is taught in His Word. It is not something that man would have thought of. My first reason, therefore, for making my calling and election sure, is because God asks me to do so. It is a part of God's method of salvation that men and women should have this certainty and assurance. It is a doctrine that is inculcated everywhere in these New Testament Epistles. We can argue very easily that the object of every single New Testament Epistle is to give people certainty, to give them the knowledge of this assurance. God offers it; and it is for us. So that though a man may give the appearance of being very modest and very spiritual when he asks, 'Who am I to make such a claim, and what right have I, such a miserable sinner, to make such an exalted claim?' the truth is that it is false modesty, it is a spurious form of humility.

The apostle Paul does not hesitate to say he knows – 'I know whom I have believed and am persuaded he is able to keep that which I have committed unto him against that day.' 'I am persuaded,' says Paul, 'that neither death, nor life, nor angels, nor principalities, nor powers, nor things present, nor things to come, nor height, nor depth, nor any other creature, shall be able to separate us from the love of God, which is in Christ Jesus our Lord.' Also, 'Henceforth there is laid up for me a crown' – I am going to have it. Would you charge such a man with lack of humility? Is that possible? Not at all, for he also says, 'I am the least of all the apostles and am not worthy to be called an apostle', and 'This is a faithful saying, and worthy of all acceptation, that Christ Jesus came into the world to save sinners, of whom I am chief.' Says Paul, I am the chief of sinners, and yet I am certain of my salvation. It is something that is offered us, and we must beware of that subtle false humility. There is nothing incompatible with the greatest humility in claiming the assurance of salvation. Let me go further and say that the most humble men that the church and the world have ever known have been those who have been certain of their salvation. They realised that it was entirely due to God, and the more a man realises that, the more certain and the more humble he is on that account.

Again, we should make certain of our calling and election because otherwise we are incomplete Christians, and under-developed and not fully grown Christians. The Christian is one who rejoices in his salvation. If we are not certain, we cannot rejoice; so that the work of God in us by grace is incomplete unless we have assurance. In a sense we are spiritual monstrosities. If we lack assurance we are rather like the blind man described in the eighth chapter of the Gospel according to Mark, who came to our Lord. Our Lord began to heal him, and at first he said he saw 'men as trees walking'. In a sense he had sight, but it was an imperfect sight, it was incomplete; and our Lord proceeded to deal with him until he saw all things clearly. If the Christian lacks assurance he is like a man who sees imperfectly. He does not really manifest salvation as he ought.

Another reason, and this is very much more important in a practical sense, is that to have this assurance makes us better witnesses for Christ. 'The joy of the Lord is your strength', says the Old Testament – how true it is! The best worker for God and for Christ is the man who is most certain and sure of his position before God. If a man is uncertain of his salvation and position, how can he preach and recommend the Gospel? How can he speak to others about it truly? While there are doubts and fears and uncertainties, one, in a sense, has not the right to speak. There is nothing so crippling to our witness and testimony as uncertainty about this matter. That is why, as you look back across the history of the church you will find that men like George Whitefield, and many others whom I could mention, who have been most used, had certainty and authority in their proclamation. Or, to put it in another form, it is this quality that makes the Gospel attractive to others. Men and women of the world are looking at us and watching us. They seem so certain of everything, and then, one day, death comes along, or misunderstandings, or wars, or troubles and tribulations. These things shake them and they do not know where to turn. But if they see someone else in the same position, who nevertheless remains calm and collected, with a peace undisturbed, and a joy beneath all the surface anxieties and troubles and tribulations, they begin to ask, 'How can we obtain it, what is the secret?' In other words, the man who is certain is the man who attracts. It is the man who seems to know his case and understands his business; it is the man who radiates a certainty and an authority who attracts you; and that is the kind of man that the Christian church needs to-day. The world is looking for that man; the more certain and sure you and I are of our calling and election, the more shall we attract others to Christ, and the more shall we be able to help them.

How then, is this certainty to be obtained? How can I make my calling and election sure? There are two main dangers at this point. The first is that of over self-examination. Briefly, there are some people who never examine themselves at all – that is one danger. But there are others who overdo it and become morbid –they spend their lives in feeling their spiritual pulse. The result is they are so concerned with examining themselves that they never do anything else. Then there is also the danger of waiting for some big experience, or some kind of vision or extraordinary manifestation. The New Testament does not mention such things.

What is the New Testament way of obtaining certainty? First of all, the objective belief of the facts concerning the Lord Jesus Christ. If you are uncertain, if you are unhappy, the first thing is to look at the Lord Jesus Christ. If you look at yourselves and nothing else you will see nothing but sin and blackness. No man can be sure by looking at his own heart. Look unto the Lord, look at the Son of God dying for your sins. Be objective – look out to Him, look away to Him from despair or sin. He came, not for the righteous, but for the sinners, not for the guiltless, but for the guilty. He has died for sinners; therefore, if you see your sins, look unto Him, start with Him, be objective.

What next? The next thing, according to Peter, is to fill out your faith, furnish it out. You start by basing your hope entirely on Him and His finished work for you. Then, having done that, you add to your faith, etc. That is the New Testament method. Do not just sit in contemplation of Christ, but go out and practise the Christian life. It is a remarkable thing, but the more we do for Him the more certain we are of Him. We are not justified by works – He is our only hope. But having seen that, the more you do, the more certain you will become. So add to your faith virtue, and to virtue knowledge, and to knowledge temperance, and to temperance patience, etc. That is how you do it. These things interact one upon the other. The more we do the work of the Lord and practise the Christian life, the more certain we are of the Lord.

If we see clearly, and remind ourselves constantly, that our only hope is in Christ and His work for us; and if because of that, because we believe that, we do everything we can to please Him and to fill out our faith, as we do so the Holy Spirit will 'testify with our spirit that we are the children of God'. So we do not sit passively waiting; we do all we can; we add to our faith, we manifest the life, and the more we manifest it, the more certain we shall be of it. In other words, if you do not exercise your muscles, the less you will be able to use them. The more you exercise them the more certain you are of them, and the more powerful they become. That is the rule for the Christian life – believe and do. Act and practise; and as we do these things we shall make our calling and election sure.

God grant that as we come, by His grace, to implement these things, we all may be able to face that question of George Whitefield without fear and with assurance.

Do you know that your sins are forgiven? Can you say, 'I am a partaker of the divine nature,' 'I am a child of God', 'I am born again'? That is the question, and that is the way to be able to answer the question in a satisfactory manner.

5
Life and Death

'For if these things be in you, and abound, they make you that ye shall neither be barren nor unfruitful in the knowledge of our Lord Jesus Christ. But he that lacketh these things is blind, and cannot see afar off, and hath forgotten that he was purged from his old sins. For so an entrance shall be ministered unto you abundantly into the everlasting kingdom of our Lord and Saviour Jesus Christ.'

Chapter 1:8, 9, 11

In these verses we have a continuation of the exhortation in verses 5, 6 and 7 which the Apostle had addressed to the Christians to whom he was writing.

The central exhortation is this – 'Beside this,' he says, 'giving all diligence, add to your faith virtue, and to virtue knowledge, and to knowledge temperance, and to temperance patience, and to patience godliness, and to godliness brotherly kindness, and to brotherly kindness charity.' That is the exhortation and then he adds the verses which we are now considering. In other words, what the Apostle does here is to supply reasons and inducements to help these Christian people to put into practice his exhortation with respect to furnishing their faith with those other graces; for he has shown that one effect and result of doing that would be that they would make their calling and election sure. Not only would they be saved, they would know that they were saved; and they would have a joy and assurance in the happiness and the certainty of that knowledge of God as Father, and of their relationship to Him in our Lord and Saviour Jesus Christ.

But now I am anxious to consider with you these further reasons, the further inducements, which are put forward by the Apostle in his attempt to persuade the Christians to furnish out their faith with these other graces. The appeal made here by the Apostle is something which is very typical and characteristic of the New Testament teaching everywhere with respect to holiness and sanctification. There are two general comments which one can make immediately with respect to it, because it is so characteristic of the New Testament method. The first is that the New Testament appeal for holiness is never in terms of a law. The New Testament never comes to us presenting us with a law; it never comes to us merely dictating to us that we ought to do this and we ought not to do that. It does not deal with us as children in that sense. It does not, as it were, insult us by putting us under a rigid law; and anyone who has a view of holiness which is in that sense legalistic has departed from the essential teaching of the New Testament. That is not the way in which the New Testament teaches holiness. It puts it rather as an appeal to our reason, as an appeal to our understanding. The New Testament presents it in this kind of way, as if to say, If you claim you have believed certain things, if you really mean what you say, don't you see it follows inevitably and of necessity that you ought to do certain things? In other words, the New Testament, in its appeal for holiness, is always reasonable and rational. You claim, it says, that you believe certain things; you claim that you have become a certain type of person; very well, follow out your own logic, put into practice and apply what you yourselves really claim to believe. Of course, if you do not claim to believe, there is no appeal; but if you do claim to believe, well then, says the New Testament, be reasonable. You believe that you are the sons of God, 'partakers of the divine nature', therefore, because of it, don't you see that it is inevitable you should of necessity furnish your faith with virtue, and virtue with knowledge, etc.? The New Testament makes holiness the most reasonable and commonsense thing imaginable, and its whole case with respect to those who are not concerned about holiness is that they are utterly unreasonable and self-contradictory.

That brings me to my second comment, which is that according to the New Testament itself there is nothing which is so utterly unreasonable and illogical as a professing Christian who objects to the New Testament call to holiness. It savours of something that is completely illogical. Now the New Testament is not at all surprised that people who do not claim to be Christian object to this standard.

The New Testament is not at all surprised that men and women outside the church are not interested in these things, or that they should regard the Christian life as something which spoils and ruins life, and makes life really something utterly hateful. The New Testament is not surprised that the people outside speak like that. It expects them to take that view of itself and its teaching. It does not expect the non-Christian to like it, indeed it expects to arouse antagonism. Some of you may recall the advice that Martin Luther gave to his friend Philip Melanchthon when he was setting out on his career. 'Always preach,' said Luther, 'in such a way that if the people listening do not come to hate their sin, they will instead hate you.' The non-Christian of necessity regards the Christian way of life, and the holiness that is taught in the New Testament, as something utterly distasteful, something narrow. He regards it as an impossible standard. But, says the New Testament, if a Christian feels like that about it, well then he is just contradicting himself. He calls himself a Christian and claims to believe certain things; and yet he feels that its demands are too great and too stringent, and says that they make life impossible. Now that, according to Peter in these verses, and according to the New Testament everywhere, is to be utterly illogical and unreasonable, and to put ourselves in a hopeless and self-contradictory position. There is no better test of whether we are truly Christian or not, than our reaction to this exhortation of the Apostle. How do I feel when I face this exhortation, to add to my faith virtue, etc.? How do I feel when I face the call to deny myself and take up the cross and follow Christ? Is it against the grain? Do I feel opposed to it, do I dislike it, is it objectionable to me? I say my reaction to these questions proclaims exactly where I stand; and ultimately one of the tests as to whether my profession is of any real value or not, is my response to this New Testament appeal. That is the argument which Peter works out here in detail, and he puts it in this way.

There are three main reasons why we should all want to give this diligence to making our calling and election sure, why we all should be straining every nerve to furnish our faith with these other qualities. Two of the reasons are positive and the other is negative. Peter puts a positive argument first, then the negative one in the middle, and then ends with a positive argument. But perhaps it will be more convenient for us, and for our memories, if we start with the negative and then go on to the two positives.

The negative reason for furnishing our faith with virtue and knowledge, and so on, is given in verse 9. Put in the form of a principle, it states that not to add to our faith virtue, and so on, is to display an ignorance of the fundamental purpose of the Christian life. This is how Peter puts it – 'He that lacketh these things is blind, and cannot see afar off, and hath forgotten that he was purged from his old sins.' So that a man who is not concerned about making his calling and election sure, who is not concerned about pressing on to holiness, and fitting out his faith in all these ways, is a man who, according to the Bible, is ignorant of the fundamental purpose of the Christian life. Peter says in the first instance that he is short-sighted – 'he that lacketh these things is blind, and cannot see afar off'. He is a man who cannot see distant things; he is a short-sighted man; he is a man who only sees that which is immediately in front of him. He does not see the distant scene; he is a man who is only concerned about the temporal and the present. He is a man who wants to enjoy life here and now, and forgets the other life that is to come. He is a man who sees so much of the world round about him, and its glittering prizes, and its so-called happiness and joy and everything for which the world lives, that he sees nothing else. He sees that which is right in front of him, but cannot see the things that are further away. What the Apostle obviously means therefore is that this type of person does not see the ultimate end of the Christian life: he does not see the final goal. He is a man who claims to have set out on a journey, but he has forgotten where he is going; he has forgotten why he started out, and the purpose he had in starting out. What is the goal of the Christian life? what is it that we are ultimately attaining unto? what is our final goal and destiny? There is no question about that in the New Testament. The object of it all is that we may see God and enjoy Him for ever. Very well, says Peter, if that is the ultimate goal, if you see that, as a Christian, the end you are ultimately out to attain is to see God, and to spend eternity in His holy presence and enjoy Him for ever, if you believe that, then this is the argument.

There are certain statements made about that ultimate goal and objective, and here are some of them. 'Blessed are the pure in heart, for they shall see God.' I want to see God. Very well, what have I to do? Purify my heart – it is inevitable. Or listen to the Epistle to the Hebrews saying the same thing: 'Follow peace with all men, and holiness, without which no man shall see the Lord.' I want to see the Lord. Very well, says the writer, follow after holiness, for without it no man shall see the Lord. Or listen to John in his First Epistle saying the same thing again. 'Every man that hath this hope in him' (that is, of seeing Christ) 'purifieth himself, even as he is pure.' That is the way the New Testament puts it. Do you say you want to see God? Well, remember that God is holy and perfect and pure; and if you really want to see Him you haven't a moment to spare, or a second to waste. Begin to purify your heart. Be pure as He is pure. If you do not do these things, you are short-sighted, you cannot see afar off, you are blind, you have forgotten what you really set out to do.

But not only that, says Peter; such a man has 'forgotten that he was purged from his old sins'. In other words, he is a man who not only cannot see forwards, he cannot see backwards either. I have no doubt that when Peter wrote these words he was an old man. Perhaps he was getting near the end of the journey in a physical sense, and it struck him as being a very good analogy and illustration. A short-sighted man, he couldn't see forward, and he couldn't see backward. 'He has forgotten that he has been purged from his old sins.' What does he mean by that? That he has forgotten the initial purpose of the Gospel, he has forgotten the whole point of salvation! Why did the Lord Jesus Christ ever come into this world? What is the purpose of the Incarnation? Come back to the first chapter of Matthew and there you will find the answer is given. 'His Name shall be called Jesus.' Why? 'Because he shall deliver his people from their sins.' That is why He came. He would never have left the courts of heaven but for that. Do I believe that Jesus of Nazareth is the Son of God? Do I believe in the Incarnation? Do I see why the Substance of the Eternal Substance vacated the courts of heaven and came on earth? There is only one answer; He came to deliver His people from their sins. Why did He die on that Cross on Calvary's Hill? What is the meaning of it? What do the communion bread and wine represent? Why was His body broken and His blood shed? Is it just a picture, is it just a dramatic incident? No, the purpose and the object which He had in doing it has been stated once and for ever by the Apostle Paul in the second chapter of the Epistle to Titus, and the fourteenth verse, when he says that 'He gave himself for us, that he might redeem us from all iniquity, and purify unto himself a peculiar people, zealous of good works.' You believe that Jesus of Nazareth is the Son of God; you believe that He went deliberately to that death on the Cross on Calvary's Hill? If you believe these things, says Peter, the logic of it is this – if you believe that He humbled Himself and divested Himself of the insignia of His Godhead, that He came and shared the life of men and women, that He suffered the contradiction of sinners for so long, that He was there in the garden sweating drops of blood, that He endured the shame and the agony of the Cross that you might be delivered from the power and pollution of sin, that you might be made perfect, spotless and holy – if you believe that that is the background to and the beginning of your whole position, there is only one thing to do, you must get as far away from sin as you can, you must hate it. If you believe He delivered you from it, how can you continue in it? You cannot! You must give all diligence to making your calling and election sure. You must be anxious to furnish your faith with virtue and knowledge, with temperance and patience, and all these other things. The man who does not do that has forgotten that he has been purged from his old sins; he has forgotten the whole purpose of the Incarnation and the humiliation of Christ and the agony and the death on the Cross and the glorious resurrection. He is utterly inconsistent with himself. He says he believes on the Lord Jesus Christ in order that he may be delivered from his sin, and yet he continues in sin. He is guilty even of making merchandise of the Cross of Christ. Such a man has forgotten the very initial and fundamental purpose of the Christian life.

But to proceed to the second argument. Peter exhorts men and women thus diligently to make their calling and election sure in that way, because to do these things produces an active and a fruitful life. That is the message of verse 8. 'For if these things be in you, and abound, they make you that ye shall be neither barren nor unfruitful in the knowledge of our Lord Jesus Christ.' Now it is generally agreed that the word 'barren' is a mistranslation. The margin in the Authorised Version puts the right word – it is the word 'idle'. If these things be in you, they make you that ye shall neither be 'idle nor unfruitful', etc. Now that is the second reason for doing these things; and you see it is a positive one. The trouble with so many of us Christians is that our Christian life is a very idle one. We say we believe these things, but what do we do about them? We are very active in connection with other things in which we believe; if it is a club we take our part; if it is a game we enter into it wholeheartedly;

if it is business we put our energy into it. Yet, here, we claim that God is interested in us, and that Christ has died for us – here we make the biggest claim a man can ever make – but what are we doing about it? Is it leading to any sort of activity?

I wonder how we fare when we compare ourselves with our own forefathers? Sometimes I wonder whether the main difference between the modern Christian and the Christians in the last century is not just at this very point – that they were so active and we are so idle. Those men believed in prayer meetings. They went to prayer meetings, and they prayed; they had their fellowship meetings, their class meetings, their society meetings. They wanted to talk about these things, about the spiritual life and the problems of the spiritual life. They lived their Christian life; they organised missionary societies. There was a great activity in their life. But somehow the idea has crept in that to be a Christian means a general subscription to certain views, and an occasional attendance at the House of God and the means of grace. We sit and listen, we receive, but we do nothing – there is no Christian activity in our lives. Let every man examine himself in the light of this word.

'Very well,' says someone, 'I do see that and recognise it; I have to admit and confess that I am idle in my Christian life. What have I got to do, what is your exhortation to me, that I may get rid of this spirit of idleness that seems to have descended upon me?' Now here the Apostle has something very important and vital to say. Peter at this point states that activity must always be the result of character; and that is a very fundamental distinction. We must be something and become something before we do anything. Let us not misunderstand the Apostle's exhortation here. He is not just exhorting us to be rushing ourselves into activity. Neither Peter nor anybody else in the New Testament ever believed in mere bustling and busy-ness, and rushing hither and thither in order that we may be very active. That is not the New Testament's appeal at all. The New Testament is not interested in activity for its own sake. The New Testament is not interested in mechanical efforts and activities. In the church today we have multiplied our institutions and our conferences, and there are people who are tremendously active; but it is not the activity that is spoken of in the New Testament. The Apostle puts it like this. He does not exhort these people to be busy in doing things; he exhorts them and urges them to strive to become like Christ. That is how he puts it. Beside this, giving all diligence, add to your faith virtue and to virtue knowledge, etc. Then, he says, 'If these things be in you, and abound, they make you that ye shall not be idle.' You see how it works. Peter urges you to concentrate on becoming a holy man, because if you become a holy man you will of necessity become an active Christian. That is the difference between the true Christian method and carnal busy-ness. We are to be diligent in the cultivation of the virtues and graces of Christ, for if we do that, 'if these things be in you and abound, they make you that ye shall not be idle'. Your activity then will be determined by the Holy Spirit and not by your own fleshly excitement, not by your own nervous pressure, not by your own delight in being busy and active. It will be the outcome of a nature like that of the Son of God Himself. He went about doing good, He was what He was, and did what He did, because of His holy nature; and you must be like Him, says Peter.

Then he goes on to show that this kind of activity will be a fruitful one. That other type of activity, that mere mechanical activism, is not very fruitful. Just look at it as regards the church today. Look at the busy-ness and the organised activity of the church. But what is it producing, to what is it leading? Though we have multiplied our organisations and institutions, the number of church members is dwindling, the number of people attending places of worship becomes less and less, and the world is not better. The busy-ness is unfruitful; but if we indulge in true Christian activity it will become fruitful as well. And it will be fruitful in this way. If we concentrate on developing the Christian character we become attractive to others. Men and women, when they look at us, will see good people and holy people, and they will ask, 'What is it that these people have got, why are they so charming and attractive, what is this peace and composure they possess, what is this atmosphere of holiness and goodness that we sense in them, what is it that they have which we lack?' If we develop character, it will draw. Not only that, it will make us sympathetic and understanding; we shall be able to understand and consider their problems. In addition, it will give us knowledge and understanding, and we shall be able to teach. When therefore they come to us in distress and anguish of soul, we shall be able to give a reason for the hope that is in us, we shall be able to guide them to Christ, we shall be able to comfort their hearts with the promises of the Gospel. The man who is busy in a carnal sense cannot do that; but the man who is truly Christian is a man who has something to pass on. A Christian is one who is like Christ Himself; and if we endeavour to develop the character of Christ, our lives must become fruitful. We read of Him, 'Then drew near unto him all the publicans and sinners for to hear him.' The little children went to Him; the outcasts, the distressed, went to Him, though He was sinless and spotless. What was it? Ah, it was just His grace. And we are to be like that; and so we are to put our energy into cultivating these graces. Then we shall not be idle, and our lives will be fruitful even as His life was fruitful.

But that brings us to the last reason for cultivating these graces, and this again, I would remind you, is positive. We are to add to virtue knowledge, etc., for this reason, that it leads to a happy and a glorious end to life. You see the Apostle's logic. It means that you start in the right way, you are continuing in the right way, and it will mean that you will end in the right way. If you only do these things, says Peter, you will cover the whole of your life. As we contemplate this last argument we see once more the utter folly of neglecting these things. We see once more how blind and short-sighted the man is who does not give diligence to add to his faith virtue and knowledge and other graces. What a short-sighted man he is! He has forgotten the thing that is coming to meet him.

Once more I would say that there is nothing perhaps which so tests and reveals exactly where we are and where we stand as the way in which we face the end. The thing that ultimately is going to test the value of our professed Christian faith is the way in which we face old age, is the way in which we face death. Haven't you sometimes been rather sadly disappointed when you have watched certain people in old age? It can be rather tragic sometimes. Old age tests us, for when we enter that stage our natural powers are failing. So many of us in this life and world live on our own activity. That is why many a man dies suddenly after he has retired from business; and often a wise doctor will advise such a man not to give up altogether, but to go two or three times a week to his business. The man has been living on his business, and after he has retired there is nothing to keep him going. That also applies in connection with Christian work. A man may live on his own preaching instead of on Christ, just as a man can live on his business. But when old age has come he cannot do these things; his powers are failing him, and he cannot appreciate the things of the world. And there he is, left to himself! That is the test. How does one face old age, how are we going to die? Well, says the Apostle, the man who adds to his faith is the man who dies gloriously and triumphantly – 'so an entrance shall be ministered unto you abundantly into the everlasting kingdom of our Lord and Saviour Jesus Christ'. You notice how Peter plays upon words. Take that word 'ministered'; do you know that that is exactly the same word as the word 'add' in verse 5? 'Ministered' unto you – if you do certain things an entrance shall be ministered unto you – you minister these things, and this entrance will be ministered unto you. You will die gloriously and triumphantly. How does it work? This is what Peter says. When I come to be an old man, and when I come to die, if I am truly Christian, death to me will be but an entrance, an entrance into a glorious life. I can put that best by contrasting it with what Tennyson said. Do you remember how Tennyson describes death? He puts it like this:

> *Sunset and evening star,*
> *And one clear call for me!*
> *And may there be no moaning of the bar,*
> *When I put out to sea.*

No! – with the greatest possible respect to the great poet – that is not Christian. The Christian when he dies, does not cross the bar and set out to sea. No; it is rather, as Charles Wesley put it:

> *Safe into the haven guide,*
> *O receive my soul at last*

– that is the Christian view of death. It is going home, it is entering into harbour, 'An entrance will be ministered unto you'. Not a setting out on to an uncharted ocean, not going vaguely into some dim, uncharted world. Not at all, but an entrance into the haven, going home. What does it all mean? It means that the Christian dies like that because he knows God. He has striven diligently to know Him better and better. He knows Christ. He knows where he is going. He does not feel lonely as he is dying, because Christ is with him. He has promised, 'I will never leave thee, nor forsake thee', and

'When thou passest through the waters, I will be with thee'; and He is there. He does not feel a stranger, and he knows something about the land to which he is going. He has been meditating upon it, he has been looking at it by faith. He has been looking at 'the things which are unseen and eternal'; he has 'set his affection on things above'. Therefore he faces death and says, I am going home, I am going to be 'with Christ which is far better'. So the fear of death is gone – he does not object to going because he knows exactly where he is going, and to whom he is going. He thinks also of the 'abundant' entrance. What does that mean? It means something like this. The Christian who has responded to Peter's appeal and who has been giving all diligence to living a full Christian life, does not die full of regrets at his failures and shortcomings; he is rather one who can say with Paul, as he views the end, 'I have fought a good fight, I have kept the faith; henceforth there is laid up for me a crown'. That is the way the true Christian dies. He has been giving this diligence, he has been living the life, so he does not feel guilty; he does not feel that he has been wasting his time. He does not say, 'If only I could go back, I would be better'. There are no bitter regrets, he is sure of 'the abundant entrance'. He is not just saved 'as by fire'.

And over and above that, he gets an abundant welcome. He is met by the angelic hosts of heaven. He is like the man Lazarus that our Lord spoke of. You remember the angels came and took him into Abraham's bosom. That is how the Christian dies. You remember how John Bunyan puts it. He describes Christian and Hopeful's going and he says that a multitude of the heavenly hosts with harps in their hands met them, and sang songs which no man could understand but those, and such as are thought worthy to be admitted into that blessed place. The welcome of the angels and the glorified spirits!

But above all, as the Christian is entering the harbour a voice says, 'Come, ye blessed of my Father, inherit the kingdom prepared for you from the foundation of the world – enter the joy of your Lord.' That is how the Christian dies. Don't you feel, as you hear that, that you want to say with one of old, 'Let me die the death of the righteous and let my last end be like his'? Well, there is but one way which guarantees the abundant entrance in the everlasting Kingdom. It is this: 'Blessed are they that do his commandments, that they may have right to the tree of life, and may enter in through the gates into the city.' If you want to have the abundant entrance furnished, ministered, unto you when you come to die, give all diligence to furnish your faith with – or minister unto your faith – virtue, knowledge, temperance, patience, godliness, brotherly kindness, love. You minister these, and the other will be ministered unto you.

6
Things We Must Never Forget

'Wherefore I will not be negligent to put you always in remembrance of these things, though ye knew *them*, and be established in the present truth. Yea, I think it meet, as long as I am in this tabernacle, to stir you up by putting *you* in remembrance; knowing that shortly I must put off *this* my tabernacle, even as our Lord Jesus Christ hath shewed me. Moreover I will endeavour that ye may be able after my decease to have these things always in remembrance.'

Chapter 1:12–15

In the first eleven verses, the Apostle has stated his main case. His readers are in trouble and dejected because they have tended to forget the things which they believed when they first became Christian. This is most important, so in these four verses he deals with the whole question of bearing them in mind and keeping them in remembrance. That is his whole object in writing, that is why he has been saying the things he has already said.

As we look at this statement of his, we shall discover a number of general principles as well as a specific and peculiar emphasis and message. There are certain general points which are of great value to us, and which we share with those who are non-Christian. Take, for instance, certain facts and points with respect to memory itself. Is there anything more characteristic of life than our tendency to forget? Now it is good that we should stop for a moment to consider that. How easily we forget people; how easily we forget friends! We have all had the experience of thinking, when certain people have died, that we could never forget them, that their memory would be ever present with us, that there would never be a moment when they would be out of mind. But that has not proved to be the case. We forget. We say sometimes that time is a wonderful healer, but that is just a way of saying in another way that we have this constant tendency to forget. In the same way we tend to forget certain great and exalted moments. This is true in the life of the individual, as it is true in the life of nations. We all know what it is, in some sense or another, to be on the mountain top – it may be a spiritual experience, or it may be a great moment of insight with respect to one's work or profession.

This is something, too, that is true in the life of nations. Reference is constantly being made to the spirit of Dunkirk, and how this nation rose to a great height and suddenly became one, how lesser differences were forgotten and the whole spirit of the nation was suddenly unified. At that time men and women felt in a new sense the real nature of the war, and the value of the country and the greatness of the country. They said that nothing must be spared in order that the country might be free and triumphant. But how easily we fell from the exalted moment, how easily did we drift away from such a time of exaltation and vision! Or take it in the matter of vows and pledges. As the result of some experience, we have made a vow and pledge. We said, 'Henceforward I am determined that I am going to live in such a way and manner." But how easily we forget the vow and pledge and the solemn oath! How easy it is for days to come when we entirely forget, and drop to a lower level and go on living as we had been living before. Alas! we are all well aware of this. We all remember the experiences after the first World War, the great idealisms, the great speeches, the high resolves and determinations on the part of this nation and the nations of the world, to live in a different way: but how soon it all was forgotten! There was a genuine determination to keep the memory of those things green, but it was soon forgotten. There is in us this constant tendency to forget.

Now I am drawing attention to this for a good reason. I sometimes think, as I read the Bible, and meditate upon it, that the fact of sin, and the biblical doctrine of sin, is more clearly demonstrated and manifested in this matter of memory than perhaps in any other respect. For is not this the simple truth, that we always tend to forget the very things we want to remember, and conversely we find it almost impossible to forget the things we would like to forget? I have instanced certain things which we would like to remember. These, alas, are the things that somehow seem to slip out of our memory and that we tend to forget. But there are other things of which we say we would give the whole world at times if we could but forget them;

certain base actions, certain unworthy motives, certain things that one has said in the heat of the moment; things we have done, or something that someone else has done to us. We know perfectly well we should forget it, but we see the person and back it flashes upon us. We may not have thought about it for years, and then something happens and back it comes. Now all that, I say, is a manifestation of sin. That is what sin has done to the human race; that is how it perverts. That is the accursed element in sin, and that is where sin is so hateful and so annoying. It stands between us and that which is best and highest; and nowhere does it show itself more than in this particular matter of memory.

Let us consider another principle. The Apostle is careful to emphasise the difference between being aware of a thing and really living by it. You notice how he puts his doctrine, 'I will not be negligent to put you always in remembrance of these things, though ye know them, and be established in the present truth.' Now I suppose that psychologically this is one of the most important points of all. The danger always is that we imagine that, because we are aware of a thing, that thing is in our memory. But it may not be. There are many ways in which this can be illustrated. Anyone who has ever been a student knows exactly what I mean by this principle. You are sitting one day in the lecture theatre and you are told a number of facts by the lecturer. As you sit and listen, you say, 'Yes, I know that, I remember reading that, I am aware of that.' So you do not trouble to make notes. But a few months later you are sitting in the examination hall, and you have a question on that very matter. You remember the lecture, you remember reading about this subject, but somehow or another you cannot recall it exactly. You are aware of it, but you do not really possess it. Now that is the kind of principle the Apostle has in his mind. Here again is a principle that is of general and universal application as well as in this particular Christian sense.

I sometimes think that this is the real explanation of the pathetic period between the two wars. Men and women were aware that certain principles govern life, but they were not equally careful to observe that they were put into actual practice and operation. The danger is that sin will persuade us that, as long as we are aware of certain moral standards, all is well; that awareness does duty for practising. There is all the difference in the world between knowing what is good and doing it. 'To him that knoweth to do good, and doeth it not, to him it is sin.' You remember the words of our Lord Himself, 'If ye know these things, happy are ye if ye do them.' If I am not careful to differentiate between awareness and the actual practice of a truth it will avail me nothing. I know perfectly well that you know these things, said the Apostle, you are established in the truth that you have at the moment, and you are well aware of the things I have been saying to you; but I know myself well enough to know that I must have them right in the centre of my mind and life if they are to be of any value to me.

But perhaps we can put that still more clearly by going on to another principle. Memory, according to the Apostle's teaching, is something that needs to be roused and stimulated. 'Yea, I think it meet,' he says, 'as long as I am in this tabernacle, to stir you up by putting you in remembrance.' Now here again is a vital principle. He does not mean that he wants these people to live on memories – that is a very subtle danger. What he means is that certain principles must be actively present in the centre of our minds. Now, there, perhaps, is a point at which we see so clearly the difference between the Christian view of a day, such as Armistice Sunday or Remembrance Day, and the non-Christian view. Those who take the psychological view would argue like this, that we recall a memory and then go on to live by and on these memories. But that is something you cannot do. You cannot live on the past, you cannot live on memories. That is not living, that is existing. This is sometimes very sad and pathetic; it is the essential difference between a sentimental view of life and the truly Christian view of life. You do not really respect the dead by trying to live back in the past; that is not living in the present; that is existing. It is no use trying to go on living by memories, living on memories; that is an attempt to walk forwards looking backwards at the same time, and it is something that is wrong in and of itself. That is not what the Apostle means. He does not say he is going to stir them up in order that they may live on memories. He says, I am going to stir you up in order that these principles may be actively in your minds in the present, and that you may live on them and by them. So it is not living on the past or drawing on the past; it is keeping certain perennial principles permanently present.

Thus, we come across another great central principle in the biblical teaching. We may say to ourselves, 'Yes, I know exactly what you mean, I believe it and accept it and therefore I am all right.'

Not at all, says the Apostle, you must keep it ever before you. In other words, the discipline of the Christian life demands that never a day should pass but that we should remind ourselves of certain things. It is not enough to say we have Christ as our salvation; the moment we realise that, we must have Him every day, we must stimulate the memory. That is the value of reading the Bible, that is the value of prayer and meditation; and I say that we are but tyros in the Christian life if we have not discovered that we are opposed by an evil system. We must forcibly remind ourselves daily of certain principles, otherwise they will merely remain vaguely in the realm of memory, and they will not be actively operating in our daily life.

That leads to the next principle, which is my last general principle with regard to memory. It is this, that the business of the church and of preaching is not to present us with new and interesting ideas, it is rather to go on reminding us of certain fundamental and eternal truths. Now, there, we come to the point at which the Gospel of Jesus Christ is relevant today, and is relevant to this country and the countries of the world in the present hour and situation. Large numbers of statements are made today with respect to the world situation, and to the whole condition of this country, and other countries; but I say, the primary business of the Christian church and of her message and her preaching is not to indulge in vague general statements. It is to repeat the centralities of the Christian Gospel, to remind men and women of the truth of God as it is in Christ Jesus. The world is more liable to forget this than anything else. The world is interested in the general situation, politics, economics, social conditions, the possibilities of another war, and other similar things. The world, therefore, rather delights in these vague general state-ments that never lead to anything. But the business of the Christian church is constantly to remind men and women of certain things which they constantly tend to forget. What are they? Let me remind you of some of them. These are the great things of which the Apostle was reminding these Christians and which the Christian church is here to proclaim to the world at this moment. Here are some of the things that we should constantly be holding in the centre of our life today.

First of all, *life itself*. The Gospel has a very special pronouncement to make with respect to life itself. It tells us about the greatness and the glory of life. The world today, outside the church and outside the

Gospel, has a very poor and low view of life. New kinds of cynicism and despair are spreading through the minds of the people. We do not hear very much today about those grand idealisms and optimisms which were so popular in the last century and before the 1914–1918 war. Man does not appear to be nearly so wonderful now as he was before the 1939–1945 war. Men have passed through concentration camps and through bombing and horrors of that kind since then; and the tendency today is to think of men in rather a debased manner. We hold biological views of man which are not very complimentary to him. They emphasise the bestial that is in him, and that which is degrading; and the tendency today is for men to think of life in that low and debased manner. 'Let us eat, drink and be merry, for tomorrow we die.' What is life? they ask; what is the point of it? We have had troubles, more seem to be coming; surely, they say, the essence of wisdom is that man shall make the best he can of it and get through it somehow.

Now the Bible is here to proclaim and pronounce that life is a great and grand and big thing. 'Dust thou art, to dust returnest, was not spoken of the soul.' Man, according to the Bible, is not a mere thinking animal who has evolved out of lower types; man is not just a creature that has come up through the jungle and the backwoods and evolved a cerebral cortex. Man is the special creation of God. God made him and fashioned him; God said, 'Let us make man in our image.' Man is great and has this stamped upon him – he was made for tremendous and mighty things. Now that is the Gospel teaching; that is what it really teaches and emphasises. The pagan religions are full of pessimism and despair, but the Christian Gospel reminds us of the true dignity and greatness of man as the individual and special creation of God. Let us remind ourselves of that in times like these when men are thinking only about comforts and wealth and houses, and when man is thinking about himself in materialistic terms. Let us call to remembrance God's idea of man and God's pattern and plan for man.

And then let us consider the *nature of life*. Here you notice the Apostle puts this in a very interesting manner. 'Yea, I think it meet, as long as I am in this tabernacle, to stir you up by putting you in remembrance; knowing that shortly I must put off this my tabernacle, even as our Lord Jesus Christ hath shewed me.' That is the nature of life according to the Bible. I am here in this world; my body is nothing but the tabernacle or tent in which I dwell for the time being. You remember how John puts it. He says of the Lord Jesus Christ that He came and 'tabernacled' amongst us. What is the body? It is nothing but a kind of tent. In other words, I am reminded that this is not my permanent place of abode. I am told to differentiate between myself (my personality) and my body. The tragedy is that men identify themselves with their bodies, and the life in the body, and the life in the flesh. Thus life in this world seems to be the only life. No, says Peter, I myself have been put and sent into this world, and I am in this tent for the time being. I am only a sojourner, I am only staying here for a while. Life is a pilgrimage, man is a traveller, the world is a kind of inn in which we spend a night as we are moving on. We have come, God has put us here, and we are going on to God, and the life that we live here in the flesh is lived in a tent and in a tabernacle. Now there again, I say, is a great emphasis upon the dignity of our life in this world. We are reminded that we are going on to a great destiny.

That, in turn, reminds us of the *whole purpose of life*. Here again is something of which we constantly need to be reminded. If I have that view of the nature of my life in this world, then, at once I will see the purpose of my life in this world. What is the answer, I wonder, when we stop to ask ourselves certain questions? What are we doing here? Why have we ever been placed here? What about those who were here with us and who have now gone? What is it all about? Is there any sense or rhyme or reason in it all? Is life just an accident, a chance? Does man just find himself here, is he but a part of this biological process of reproduction? We come and go – is that the whole story? Am I just to live for the sake of eating and drinking and being merry; to enjoy the pleasure-loving, animal kind of existence that the vast majority of people are living today? Well, of course, there is an eternal 'No' to all that, if you take this Christian view.

Man is here to glorify God. God made man to that intent and purpose; that is the object of our lives. We did not come into this world just to stay in it or shuffle through it; we are to realise that we are meant to be the sons of God, the children of God. God made man that His own glory might be manifested. God has a great purpose for man; and the world is a part of God's great plan to bring to pass His eternal, ultimate purpose. Thus we remember that what we do in this world and life is of great importance; every action counts, every moment is of significance. We are told that we shall have to give an account of every idle word we have spoken. Even our time is precious in the sight of God; and it is as we remind ourselves of the dignity and greatness of it all that we shall be animated by a new purpose and object.

That in its turn leads us to another inevitable question. 'If that is the right view of life,' says someone, 'why is life as it is? If you say that God made man and God made the world; if you say that God is the Author of life and that man is the unique creation of God, how do you explain the state of the world today? We remember two world wars and the sacrifices that have been made. Men have died for a certain purpose, but why war at all? Why fight, why should there be fightings and wars; what is the matter?' 'Surely,' says this person, 'the very state of the world belies what you have told us is the biblical teaching with respect to man and life.' But there is no contradiction, for the Bible teaching alone supplies us with the true and only real and adequate explanation. The Gospel never fails to remind us that all the troubles and trials and tragedies can be explained by one thing only, and that is, sin. Oh, yes, I am referring to that once more! I am doing what the apostle Peter says, 'I will not be negligent to put you always in remembrance of these things, though ye know them, and be established in the present truth.' The one thing the world hates is to be reminded of its sin. We like to think of ourselves in optimistic terms; we try to minimise troubles. All along we are trying to paint our bright pictures, but the facts remain. If we want to put things realistically we must recognise and admit that the cause of all the trouble is nothing but this wrong relationship to God, and that although the world today tries to buoy up its hope and persuade itself that the future is going to be bright, it has no real confidence in its own words, but knows that all is wrong. The Gospel is here to remind us constantly that a wrong attitude to God, individually or nationally, or as a world, leads inevitably to sorrow and trouble and final destruction. That, and that alone, surely, is the message of these past years. It is the Lord God Almighty saying to mankind, 'I have been allowing you to see what you make of yourselves and of your world when you try to live without Me.' There is no hope for men, or the world, until they acknowledge God and come back to His way of living. The Gospel is here to remind us perpetually of the fact of sin.

Very well, we ask the next question. What is the objective in man's life? Here again we get this great word of the Apostle, 'Moreover I will endeavour that ye may be able after my decease to have these things always in remembrance.' What is death; what happens when we pass on? This word 'decease' is a great word. It tells us that death is really an exodus. I am going to remind you of these things, says Peter, until my 'exodus' comes. You see the suggestion. Death to the true Christian is just a passing from the bondage and captivity of Egypt into Canaan, the new land. It is like the Exodus of the children of Israel, there under the heel of the Pharaoh, the cruel oppressor, there in bondage and serfdom; then, the Exodus, the going out, the crossing of the Red Sea and the Jordan, and the entry ultimately into the land of Canaan and all its amazing possessions. That is the way in which, according to the New Testament, the Christian should face the end. Not a terror, but just the folding up of the tent and moving out – an exodus, a crossing of the river and an entrance into the everlasting and eternal kingdom.

But we must not only consider it like that. The Bible has its view of the whole of life and the ultimate destiny of man. It tells us that God has a great plan and purpose for this world, and God is carrying out that plan and purpose. There is the great teaching in biblical prophecy. The teaching is this, that as long as sin remains, there will be trouble, and that eventually there will be a final cataclysmic event. There is no superficial optimism in the Bible. It talks about wars and rumours of wars, but it tells us that the Son of God who has already conquered death and sin and the grave, will return again finally to cleanse the world, and that all the forces that are inimical to God will be finally routed. There is a glorious crowning day coming, there is a final exodus to look forward to, there is an ultimate apocalypse. As it asks us to look back to what He has done, it asks us to look forward to what He is yet going to do.

In other words, the ultimate thing of which the Bible always reminds us, and which it always urges us to keep in remembrance, is that the greatest and the most vital thing in this world is to know the Lord Jesus Christ. You cannot live on memories, you cannot live on hopes; but on the Lord Jesus Christ you can live always. What we must never forget is His sacrifice and His rising again. There, I say, is the fact that transforms every other fact, the fact of life – yea, and, thank God, the fact of death itself. In Him, and in Him alone, we have a true conception of man and a true conception of life. In Him we triumph over death and the grave and have eternal and everlasting life. Beloved friends, these are the things to keep in remembrance. Let every other memory be sanctified by the memory of Him 'who gave himself for us and rose again'.

7
The Doctrine of the Second Advent

'For we have not followed cunningly devised fables, when we made known unto you the power and coming of our Lord Jesus Christ, but were eyewitnesses of his majesty.'

Chapter 1:16

As we continue our consideration of this chapter it is again of vital importance that we should bear the background in mind, and that we should keep a firm hold and grasp on the whole object and purpose which animated the Apostle when he wrote these words. He is writing, let me remind you, to Christian people who are in difficulties. This is not a theological disquisition, it is not a mere philosophical essay; it is a pastoral letter written by a pastor to actual Christian people, members of churches. His object is to help and encourage them, to establish them, to strengthen them. As he himself puts it, his object is to enable them 'to make their calling and election sure'. He wants these Christians to have certainty, and to be in such a position that, whatever may happen outside, whatever may happen inside, they shall remain unaffected and strong.

Now as the Apostle goes on to this particular matter dealt with in the 16th verse, he connects it with everything that has gone before, 'For,' he says, 'we have not followed cunningly devised fables, when we made known unto you the power and coming of our Lord Jesus Christ, but were eye-witnesses of his majesty.' Here is something additional, and in a sense we are entitled to say that at this point, we are introduced, for the first time in this explicit manner, to what is in reality the central theme of this whole Epistle. In other words, the Apostle here refers to what is commonly known among us as the

Second Advent, or if you prefer it, the Second Coming of our Lord Jesus Christ.

Now it is a matter of interest for those who are concerned about, and interested in, the mechanical part of exposition, to consider whether this is really a reference to the Second Coming or to the First Coming. The two views have had their advocates among expositors. There are those who feel that Peter refers to the First Coming of our Lord, to the Incarnation, to what Peter himself and others had witnessed when our Lord was here in the days of His flesh. But it does seem to me, as it does to the majority of commentators, that this is clearly a reference, not to the First Coming, but rather to the Second Coming. I think if you read the Epistle right through again you will see that this is the great burden of the Apostle. The thing that Peter is ultimately out to deal with is the activity of the scoffers to whom he refers in the third chapter, the scoffers who were asking, 'Where is the promise of his coming?' That is the great matter. He takes this up at the beginning of the second chapter, and then he goes on dealing with it. As this is his central theme, it seems more likely that even at this point, the Second Coming is in his mind and not the First. At the same time we can agree that some of the things here in this immediate context do have a bearing upon the First as well as upon the Second Coming; but the central doctrine here is the doctrine of the Second Advent of Christ, the return of our Lord.

Now this was one of the great central doctrines of the early church. No one can read the New Testament, even in a cursory manner, without at once seeing that this was a subject which not only meant a great deal to the first Christians, it was even something by which in a sense they lived. You cannot read the New Testament without being given the impression that those first Christians were men and women who lived in the light of this great event, the return, the coming back of Christ. You see that in every part of the New Testament. You find it in the teaching and doctrine of our Lord Himself. In the thirteenth chapter of Mark we have a reminder of it. You find it in the corresponding chapters of the other Gospels; it is there the whole time. Many of His parables have reference to it. It is seen explicitly in the three sections of the twenty-fifth chapter of Matthew, in the parable of the ten virgins, the parable of the talents, and finally the picture of the judgment of the nations. It is there implicitly in many another parable and statement in the same way. So it is in the teaching of our Lord Himself!

We need not, perhaps, tarry with this, for this good reason. You remember how until the early years of this century there was the so-called 'liberal' view of our Lord and Saviour Jesus Christ. In the last hundred years or so there have been those who felt that they could reconstruct what they called 'the Jesus of History' – that movement which took out the supernatural and the miraculous and tried to turn our Lord into nothing but a Jewish teacher. They said He was an exceptional teacher. They pictured Him as a kind of agitator and social reformer, one whose interest was largely political and social; and they tried thus to rid Him of everything else, and to produce this picture. But it is now generally agreed by scholars, by practically all scholars who are interested in these matters, that that attempt to paint and picture 'the Jesus of History' was finally demolished completely by the work of one man, Dr Albert Schweitzer, in his book, *The Quest of the Historical Jesus*. I mention these things just as a matter of interest, but he established even in terms of criticism and history that, if there is one thing that is essential to the New Testament and Gospel picture of our Lord, it is His own belief in the apocalyptic and transcendent element in His life and work. Schweitzer proved this satisfactorily to the minds of scholars who, like himself, are far removed from our evangelical position.

In other words, I would remind you that at the very heart of the Gospel teaching is this doctrine of the final consummation, the return of Christ, the apocalyptic element. Then when you go through the other books you find it in exactly the same way. You find it in the first chapter of the Acts of the Apostles. You remember how, when our Lord was taken up into the heavens, an angel came and told the wondering and amazed disciples that He would again return in like manner. There it is at the very beginning. You get it in the preaching of Peter to the authorities in Jerusalem. He talks about 'the restitution of all things' – the same doctrine. And as you go on through the various Epistles, you find it everywhere. An attempt was once made to try to prove that the Apostle Paul only believed this doctrine at the beginning, and that you do not find it in his later Epistles; but it is now agreed that you find it in his Epistles everywhere. It is in his very last Epistle. Lastly you come to the Book of the Revelation, which is a book that cannot be understood at all except in these terms. Here was a message, here was a truth which was vital to the first Christians. These men lived in the light of this particular doctrine, and their whole outlook was governed by it. They were prepared to sacrifice because of it, they were prepared to suffer because of it; and when they endured grievous persecution this was the thing that sustained them.

Now as we put it like that, the question obviously arises as to whether that is equally true of modern Christians? Does this particular matter, this particular doctrine, stand out as prominently in our minds, and our lives, and in our witness, as it did in the case of the early church? Can we say, as we review ourselves as Christian people, that this idea, this truth, this doctrine of the return and the Second Coming of our Lord, is there in the prominent, primary and central place that it occupied in the lives and minds of these people? Well, I think we will all have to agree that that is not the case, and perhaps we will have to admit, further, that that is one of the main differences between the New Testament Christians and ourselves.

There is in the New Testament a note of urgency. You are given the impression here of people who regard this life as but a sojourning. They looked at themselves as travellers; there was ever in their minds the idea of the end of time, and of judgment, and of the return of Christ, and the end of all things. There is the impression in the New Testament that believers are men living between two worlds – that is the atmosphere. But that is clearly not the atmosphere in which Christian people in general live at this present time, and the obvious question is – why is there this difference? What is it that accounts for the fact that we do not attach the same significance to this particular truth as they did? Why do we not believe it? Why are we not dominated by it as they were? Now that, it seems to me, is the most important question for us to consider at this point. I suggest that there are two main answers to this question. The first is what I would call a general answer, and then there is what I would call a special and particular answer.

Let us look first at *the general answer*. Why is this doctrine somehow or another being relegated to the mere background of our faith and belief? I think the first answer is that there has been a general neglect of doctrine as a whole. And to some of us this is a most vital matter. During the last hundred years or so, and especially during this century, doctrine has become unpopular. Our grandfathers were very interested in the doctrines of the Christian faith, in biblical doctrine; they read it, they studied it, they discussed it; it was one of their favourite themes. But this is no longer the case. Men and women are not interested in doctrine today; indeed, we can go further and say there has been a reaction against doctrine, that doctrine has become offensive and is being derided. The tendency has crept in to regard the gospel as a general morality with respect to life. People say, 'We do not want doctrine; life is too busy, too overwhelming. We need a little comfort, we want something to help us along.' The result is that the tendency of preaching has been to indulge in a vague, general, moralising philosophy with respect to life. We have been exhorted to courage and endurance, and we have regarded the Gospel as a general stimulus, something that helps us to get along. That, I say, has been the tendency, and doctrine, as doctrine, has been at a discount and has been seriously and sadly neglected as a whole.

The result is that there are Christian people who are indeed woefully ignorant about the great doctrines regarding the Trinity, the Atonement, and the Holy Spirit, this particular doctrine of the Second Advent, and the doctrine of the church. There is a general ignorance about these matters even in the Christian church. Thus, but little attention is paid to the doctrine of the Second Coming because all doctrine has been at a discount. While we have been indulging in moral uplift we have forgotten doctrine altogether, and we have been concerned merely about these temporary aids, using Christian terminology in a general sense only. Or perhaps we have at times been so concerned about a personal Saviour that we have forgotten the more general aspects of the Christian doctrine. Certainly we start with the doctrine of personal salvation. That is our first, our primary need; and there is nothing wrong in being first concerned about that. It is the New Testament emphasis; but if we confine the New Testament to that, and to a personal experience of salvation alone, we are not being true to the New Testament teaching. For the New Testament has a world view; it has an outlook upon the whole of life and upon the ultimate course of history. But there has been, I think we will all agree, for fifty years and more this tendency to be interested personally only. Psychology has perhaps given a stimulus in that direction; and the difficult times through which we have been passing have encouraged it. People say we must be right personally, and they have neglected the more general aspects of the faith. All this has been a contributory factor to the neglect of these great doctrines.

Another explanation is that there have been those who say that this New Testament teaching with regard to the Second Coming of our Lord is to be explained in a different manner from that which has been traditional. They would say that the Second Coming of our Lord refers to what happened in A.D. 70, when the Roman army conquered Jerusalem and destroyed the city, and to that event alone. Others would say it refers to what happened on the Day of Pentecost. They agree that the doctrine of the Second Coming is there in the New Testament, but believe that it was surely fulfilled on the Day of Pentecost when Christ came in the Person of the Holy Spirit. That, they think, is the Second Coming. Some have thus believed that it has already happened in the past and that there is nothing yet to come.

But perhaps the commonest of all the general reasons is the truth taught by our Lord in the parable of the Ten Virgins, I mean the tendency to a general indolence and a general slackness. Do you remember how our Lord pointed out that even the five wise virgins, as well as the five foolish virgins, slept instead of watching? Certainly they woke when the Bridegroom came and they had oil in their lamps; but they were sleeping during the waiting time. In the same way it was true before our Lord first came in the flesh. This same heaviness and lethargy had descended upon Israel. And there is a tendency for us at this time to be lethargic. This general indolence tends to overcome us, and we fail to fight the fight of faith and to face the facts as they are presented in the New Testament.

Now let me mention another group of reasons, which I would describe as *special or particular reasons*. I have suggested hitherto that the main reason for the neglect of this doctrine is that people have forgotten it. I want now to suggest that the other main reason is that some people have remembered it too much. There is no doctrine, perhaps, that has suffered so much at the hands of its friends as the doctrine of the Second Advent, or the Second Coming of our Lord. There is no doctrine, I imagine, that has suffered so much at the hands of those who have been animated by a misguided and uncontrolled zeal as this particular doctrine. Let me illustrate what I mean, by a personal anecdote. I remember, when I first came to this church, speaking to Dr Campbell Morgan in the Minister's vestry one Friday evening. He looked at me and said, 'We are going to have a crowd tonight.' 'What makes you say that?' I asked him, and he said, 'I am going to lecture on the Book of Revelation, and, you know, I never announce that I am giving a lecture on any aspect of prophetic doctrine but that there is invariably an unusual crowd.' And it happened that night. I say that in order to remind you of this particular aspect of the matter. There is in the case of some people a morbid, unhealthy interest in this matter. There are people who are interested in 'the times and seasons', there are people who constantly spend their time in trying to study prophecy and to identify particular persons depicted in the Bible, and who literalise the various pictures and images that are used in the Bible. They spend the whole of their time, I say, in trying to understand these things.

I need not take your time in reminding you of the various movements that have arisen, and the various schools of teaching with respect to these matters, and all the refinements and all the ramifications of doctrine, and the dogmatism that characterises the various schools, and how some of them would even make agreement or disagreement with their particular interpretation the very test and hall mark of orthodoxy itself. I mean the kind of people who in the Second World War were perfectly certain that Mussolini or Hitler was the Beast, and those who in a previous century were perfectly certain it was Napoleon. You are doubtless, familiar with the various ideas. There has been this morbid interest in 'times and seasons' and in dates, and in an attempt to identify the various pictures of the Scriptures. This great doctrine of the Second Advent has in a sense fallen into disrepute because of this false interest, and because of this tendency on the part of some to be more interested in the how and the when of the Second Coming rather than in the fact of the Second Coming. The effect of all this has been that there are teachers and preachers and expositors who have always believed and accepted this doctrine, but who rarely refer to it because they are anxious to avoid stimulating this morbid, unhealthy curiosity. In their concern to preserve the balance of truth and of doctrine, they have been anxious to avoid pandering to what is a misuse of Scripture and a false understanding of the New Testament. Others have not mentioned it because they are anxious to avoid being embroiled in what is often bitter as well as useless controversy.

I have taken time to elaborate on the comparative neglect of this doctrine because it is a vital starting point for us as we now come to look at it briefly. I have now explained why the doctrine has not been preached and emphasised; it has been forgotten in the general tendency to ignore doctrine as a whole and it has not been stressed by others because they have been afraid of stimulating that which is false.

What then does the New Testament really teach about this matter? In other words, what is clearly and unmistakably taught here? I am not concerned about refinements and the various schools of interpretation. I am simply concerned about reminding you, as Peter reminded his first readers, of what is beyond doubt and peradventure the teaching of the New Testament.

First of all is the great fact of our Lord's return to earth. That is the big thing and the clear thing – that the Lord Jesus Christ who first came as a babe in Bethlehem is going to return to this earth and to this world. What does the New Testament teach with regard to the manner of His return? First of all, that it is going to be a personal return. The New Testament does not only say that our Lord's teaching is going to influence the world greatly and to permeate life and outlook. There are those who interpret His return in that way. They say, 'Yes, we do agree with you about the doctrine of the return of Christ after His ascension into Heaven, but,' they say, 'that has already happened, Christian teaching has already influenced the world. There has been a gradual permeation of the life of mankind by the teaching of Christ as reported in the Gospel.' Is that the return? My reply is, 'No!' The Return of our Lord as taught everywhere in the New Testament is a *personal return*. The idea of the permeation of the world by Christian teaching does not do justice to the language used in the Gospels and epistles – it is to be a personal return.

Secondly it is a *bodily return*, or if you like, a physical return. Now I put it like that in order to correct another error. There are those who will try to argue that our Lord's Return is that which happened on the Day of Pentecost. They say His return is a spiritual return – 'Look at the disciples,' they say, 'and the Apostles before the Day of Pentecost, and look at them afterwards. Isn't it perfectly clear that our Lord's return in the Spirit made all that difference?' Well, I agree entirely that that, in a sense, is a return of our Lord, and there is noble and exalted language in the Bible about our Lord coming to dwell in the believer in the Holy Spirit. That is all perfectly true, but I say that the Bible, over and above that, talks about a bodily return and says that as He ascended bodily, He will again return bodily. 'The glorious appearing,' that is the language – He is going to appear, He is going to be manifested!

That leads me to put it in another way. There are clear and unequivocal and unmistakable statements to the effect that the return of our Lord will not only be personal and bodily, it will be visible. He will come 'on the clouds of heaven', 'every eye shall see him'. It is not going to be an influence, it is not going to be a spiritual effect. In exactly the same way as His going was visible, so His return will be visible. There are many statements to that effect running right through the New Testament, and to the effect that when He does appear, men will cry out to the mountains and the rocks to hide them. 'Every eye shall see him.' He will come upon the clouds, and He will be visible.

The next point is that it is taught very clearly that this coming will be *sudden*. Now we have to be careful as we say that, because we read that there are certain things that are to happen before He comes. There will be certain signs, and He spoke the parable of the fig tree in order to remind us of that. But in spite of that, He constantly emphasises the suddenness. He points out that when He is not expected He will come. He points out the danger of being asleep instead of watching. Think of all those exhortations before His death – how He keeps on saying, Watch and pray, be on the alert, be ever ready, watch! It is a sudden coming. Then the other point that is always made is that it is going to be a *glorious event*. The first time He came, He came as a Babe and was born in a stable in Bethlehem. That was the coming in humiliation. He came as a servant and in the likeness of sinful flesh. But when He comes again, He will come in glory and in power, attended by the angels and with the sound of the trumpet, in all the glory and the majesty and the fulness of His divine Person. It will be beyond the brightness of the sun, it will be something unbelievable, a glorious, radiant coming. All that is clearly taught right through the New Testament about the manner of our Lord's Second Coming.

But, what is *the purpose of His coming*? The purpose of our Lord's Second Coming will be to wind up the affairs of this world and to put an end to time. God made the world, He started it upon its course, but at the very beginning God appointed an end. The world has not existed from eternity, the world will not exist to all eternity. There is a beginning and an end, and the ultimate purpose of our Lord's Second Coming is to wind up the affairs of earth and to wind up the affairs of time. Likewise He will come in order to produce a final resurrection. Those who are already dead, those of us who will be dead before this event, all that are dead will be raised, bad and good; those who remain on earth at the time of our Lord's coming will be changed. There will thus be a final resurrection – all, good and bad, Christians and non-Christians – and it will be a resurrection to judgment. All the dead, good and bad, great and small, will stand before God and the Books will be opened. The record of men's lives will be examined, and the Book of Life containing the names of the elect will be opened – there will be this final judgment.

That will be followed by the destruction of all the enemies of God. Jesus of Nazareth, the Son of God, the King of kings, the Lord of lords, will destroy every enemy, the devil and all his legions, and all the hosts of men and women who have not believed on Him. They will finally be destroyed for ever from the sight of God – that is clearly taught. Then there will be the destruction of the world itself. It will be consumed by a fervent heat. Creation, as we now know it, will be destroyed and there will be a new heaven and a new earth. And that ushers in the final and everlasting and eternal state of glory in the presence of God, when, the wicked and evil having been destroyed, the Christians, those who are Christ's, shall be with God the Father, Son and Holy Spirit, and all the holy angels, and shall share in that everlasting and eternal bliss and glory.

A last question. *When* is this going to happen? The answer can be put almost in a word – no one knows. That is why our friends who have tried to fix the date of the end have always been wrong. I do beseech you to read literature on this subject on both sides. You will find that some of the greatest commentators of history have gone wrong on this question of fixing dates and times. The Bible tells us we must not be concerned about times and seasons. Have you noticed what our Lord said, as recorded in Mark 13:32? Even He did not know the time of the end, but the Father alone. You and I must not be concerned about the precise moment and time. Recent years have again shown us people trying to identify certain events. I say, do not waste your time, do not become side-tracked, do not allow yourself to be distracted from the plain central teaching. The teaching of the New Testament on the time element is this – *Be ready*. 'What I say unto you I say unto all, *Watch*.'

It may seem incredible to us that these things are really going to happen. It sounded incredible to the people before the First Advent that He would come as He did. It was miraculous, it was supernatural; but it happened. And as it happened then, this will also happen; and your business and mine, my dear friends, is to be always ready, to be ever prepared. It is to watch, it is to pray, it is to believe, and realise this. As Peter says, he has not been following cunningly devised fables when he has been teaching this matter. This is the essence of the New Testament. It was and is as sure as the Incarnation and the Atonement and the Holy Spirit and the church, and all the other doctrines which are there. God grant, therefore, that we may avoid the errors at both extremes – the error of ignoring the doctrine, and the error of a morbid, unhealthy interest in it – and that we may face these central statements and prepare for them, and await the blessed appearing and coming of the Lord Jesus Christ.

8

The Message of the Second Advent

'For we have not followed cunningly devised fables, when we made known unto you the power and coming of our Lord Jesus Christ, but were eyewitnesses of his majesty.'

Chapter 1:16

As we turn once more to this verse, I would remind you that it refers essentially to the Second Coming of our Lord and not to the First Advent, and that that is, in a sense, the central theme of this particular letter. In the last sermon we dealt with this doctrine in general, without any frills or fancies, without any speculation or imagination and without any of the refinements that so often have brought this doctrine into disrepute.

But what I am anxious to do now is to show the relevance of all this. Peter called attention to it because, as he suggests in the remainder of the Epistle, in a sense, that is, perhaps, the one thing above all others that is going to strengthen and comfort and help the people to whom he wrote. It is vitally important, therefore, that we should be equally clear as to the bearing of this doctrine upon our life and outlook at this present time.

There are large numbers of people today outside the church, and there are many, one sometimes thinks, within the church, who are greatly troubled as they look upon this modern world in which we live. They are troubled in the sense that in the former case they are prevented from believing the Gospel, and in the latter that their faith is being shaken. That is why we must be interested in this matter. It is not a theoretical matter. We are not turning to it because we are anxious again to indulge in the pastime of trying to determine the times and seasons – no, we are concerned with this doctrine because it will help us, and enable us at this present time to be 'strong in the Lord and in the power of his might', and also because it will help us to speak to many who are not attracted by the Christian Gospel today and who feel, because of certain things that are happening, that they cannot accept it. I am thinking of those people who come to us and ask, 'How do you explain the state of the world today and especially after nearly two thousand years of Christian work and of preaching the Christian Gospel?' That, with many today, is the problem. Some of them are outside the church. They say, 'We would like to believe your Gospel, but we really cannot, because it does seem to us that the Gospel has failed – you claim it is the Gospel of God, you say that the Son of God came into the world, you talk about the power of the Holy Spirit, you claim that the Gospel is miraculous and supernatural, you say that all this has been working for nearly two thousand years and that it has been preached without intermission for all that time, and yet look at the world, look at the two world wars within a quarter of a century, look at the state of society, look at the godlessness and irreligion, look at the clouds on the horizon and the uncertain future. How can you,' they ask, 'stand and proclaim that that Gospel is what you say it is, and yet face the facts as they confront you in this world today?' That is the stumbling block to them, and they say that because of it, they are unable to subscribe to 'the faith' and to join the Christian church.

In the same way there are many inside the church who are discouraged by the same facts. They are frankly troubled. These first Christians were also troubled at this point because they thought that the Gospel was going to conquer the world in a very few years, that the Lord would return immediately and all would be well. And when these things did not happen they began to say, Is this faith after all what we thought it was; is it miraculous and supernatural, is it, after all, the power of God? Or, to put it in modern language, the question confronting many is, Has the Gospel failed? Has the Christian church failed? Is there anything in the Gospel after all? The state of the world as it is, and the things that appear on the horizon, are thus tending at the present time to shake the faith of many and to keep many entirely outside the Christian faith. Now what is the answer of the New Testament to that kind of attitude? What has the New Testament to say to that position? The answer, in a sense, can be put in one phrase. It is the doctrine of the Second Coming of Christ. That is the New Testament answer to that difficulty, and to all the trouble and the confusion that arises at that particular point; and it is in order to show how this doctrine does deal with that situation that I refer once more to the truth contained in this particular verse.

I have already given an outline of what the doctrine itself states. How do we apply that to the present problem? There are a number of principles that are of necessity involved, and are implicit in the doctrine of the Second Coming. What I propose to do is to take a kind of bird's-eye view of what the New Testament has to say concerning this doctrine in its various parts. I cannot pretend that in one discourse I can give an exhaustive account; I am concerned solely to emphasise principles, the great central principles. Some may ask such questions as 'Well, what do you make of such-and-such a statement in the Book of Revelation?' I am not directly concerned about that at the moment, and in any case I think my exposition of the doctrine has shown that that is the kind of false approach which tends to lead us astray. We must be concerned about principles, and must always be careful about the detailed working out of principles, for it is at the point of detail that most errors have arisen in the past.

Here then are some of the principles of the doctrine of the Second Coming. The truth concerning the Second Coming is, first and foremost, *a pronouncement to the effect that there is a plan of salvation.* Our fathers were very fond of that term – the plan of salvation. I am afraid we do not use this term as we should; we are interested in being saved and in being forgiven. They were always emphasising the plan of salvation. We, for one reason or another, have become too subjective. I suppose it is partly due to the world we are living in, and the times through which we have had to pass during this century. I suppose it is partly produced also by psychology. Everybody is interested in feelings and personal safety. That is quite legitimate, but we must never allow it so to monopolise our attention as to make us forget the plan of salvation, and the objective reality in the mind of God as it is outlined in the Bible.

The New Testament, indeed the whole Bible, makes it very plain and clear that away back in eternity, if one may use such language, God, in the eternal council, mapped out a plan for the salvation of this world. The New Testament tells us that before man was ever made, before man ever fell, God had planned the salvation of the world. God sees the end from the beginning. All things are open before the sight of God, and the Bible, I say, constantly repeats and reiterates this grand fact, that God, having seen the end from the beginning, and all things being entire and plain and open to His sight, planned before time began that at a given point and place He would create the world. He would create man. He foresaw that the Fall would take place, man would listen to the suggestion of Satan, and that then He, God, would begin the process of salvation.

This plan is outlined in the Old Testament. We read of the calling of Abraham at a given point, of the creating of the nation, and of how the nation was led down to Egypt. That seemed to be the end of everything, but God called them out and took them into the Promised Land. You remember the strange vicissitudes through which they passed in that land. As you read the Old Testament, if you did not know about the New Testament, you would be cast into the depths of despair. The children of Israel were carried away captive, but God intervened and they were brought back again – there was just a remnant left, but God was with them. Then the remnant seemed to go astray, and for four hundred years there was no prophet nor 'Word of the Lord' recorded. Then in the fulness of the times the Son of God came. But He was crucified and the end seems to have come again. But on the morning of the third day, as it had been predicted and prophesied, He rose from the grave, He manifested Himself, He ascended to heaven. Then, exactly as it was foretold, the day of Pentecost came and the Holy Spirit was given.

Now the doctrine of the Second Coming is part of that plan. The first thing it tells us is that the plan of salvation is not yet finished. We can look back upon the various steps that have taken place in the great and glorious plan of God, and then this doctrine tells us that there is still something more to happen. Everything has been foreseen; the times are fixed; God knows His own mind and purpose. Everything that God has ever planned has come to pass, and what God has still planned will yet come to pass. The doctrine of the Second Coming announces all that; so that we must not think of salvation as something contingent or fortuitous; we must not think of it all as something that is dependent upon what is happening in this world of time; we must rather come back to the plan. It is as though we are looking at a time-table, and we argue that the time-table has always been kept in the past, so it must be kept in the future. God grant we may take a firm hold of 'the plan of salvation'. The end is as certain as the beginning; and all God's purposes with respect to mankind are definitely portions of a great, whole, grand plan which is invincible.

The second thing of which it reminds us is the *reality and the terrible power of evil*. Now I do not hesitate to say that there is a sense in which no doctrine of the New Testament so emphasises the fact and the power of evil and of sin as does this doctrine of the Second Coming of our Lord. There are other doctrines that emphasise evil, such as those of the Fall of man, the doctrine of sin itself, and the doctrine of salvation; but I think that, if you examine it carefully, you will see there is nothing that so emphasises the terrible malignant power of evil as this doctrine of the Second Coming. It does it in this way. It tells us that the power of evil is so great that even the saved men and women would be defeated by it were it not that the Lord Jesus Christ is to come. No man is good enough to deal with evil, the Lord must come again before this can be dealt with finally.

Now this is where we see the relevance of this doctrine to the present hour. As we look upon the world and see its trouble, its discord, its unhappiness, there is nothing that gives so true an insight into, and understanding of, the present, save a clear grasping of this biblical doctrine of evil and the power of evil. It teaches us that there are in this world two mighty forces, two mighty kingdoms, the kingdom of God and the kingdom of Satan. Satan is the god of this world. You remember those words of Paul, 'We wrestle not against flesh and blood, but against principalities, against powers, against the rulers of the darkness of this world, against spiritual wickedness in high places [or in the heavenlies].' Do we realise that as clearly as we ought? Could we ever be surprised at the state of the world if we only realised that as the New Testament does? Do we realise that evil is a kingdom headed by a great king, the god of this world, the prince of the power of the air? That is something that is suggested by the doctrine of the Second Advent. There is a massing and gathering together of two great armies, two great kingdoms, God and Satan, Christ and Evil. These are the forces. Evil is a terrible reality, an awful power. 'Ah,' says someone, 'that is very depressing.' Yet surely we must be realistic and face facts. The world is depressed; and the greatest enemy of mankind, as well as of the Gospel, today, is the superficial person who tries to make out that things are not so bad. It is the business of every thoughtful person to face facts, and not to try to lull himself into some position of ease and security. The doctrine of the Second Coming proclaims the terrible reality and power of sin.

Our next deduction emphasises *the inevitable conflict between these two kingdoms*. It says it is inevitable. The power of evil has come into this world, and its one object and motive is to destroy the work of God. That is why sin came in, that is why Satan intervened. He hates God – that is the consuming passion of his being and of his existence – and as a hater of God, he pitted himself against God. He objected to the lordship and sovereignty of God, and the one object and mission of Satan is to destroy, not merely to mar, but to ruin and destroy God's work. He is bent upon it, he works for it, he schemes for it, he organises for it. Evil's purpose is nothing less than that. God's purpose on the other hand is good; God's purpose is loving, God's purpose is kind and beneficent. The clash between these forces is inevitable, and the whole doctrine of the Second Coming is one which, in a sense, outlines that conflict and that warfare, that mighty struggle that is going on.

Now in many of its symbols and in many of its pictures and imagery the Bible gives us an insight into the nature of this struggle. It tells us that sometimes Satan seems to take the form of world-government and power. Here you can apply the picture to different and particular world powers – if you like, the Roman Empire, and the various other empires. There are appearances that suggest it is in that form today; but the principle is the thing of importance. Sometimes Satan has used worldly dynasties and governments to try to destroy the work of God. But it has not always been in that form. Sometimes you find, according to the biblical symbols and imagery, that the enemy takes the form of false religion. The Bible does not teach religion, it teaches the Christian faith; and religion sometimes can be the greatest enemy of God and His truth. So Satan transforms himself into an angel of light and is ever ready to proclaim a false religion. Under this heading of religion we see at once that we must include quite a number of ideas, not only religion specifically as such, but philosophies – materialism, or perhaps an idealism which excludes God; theories whether political or social or economic; or more general theories about man and his nature and his existence, and perhaps ideas with respect to life in general. Satan uses and employs all these methods, anything that he can make use of that will mar and destroy the work of God or stand between man and God. Those are his methods, and as we consider these things we can see very clearly that the state of the world today is not as surprising as it appears to be at first sight. Look back across the last two thousand years and you will see the different forms which this great struggle has taken – sometimes political, sometimes philosophical, sometimes religious. Now the doctrine of the New Testament with regard to the Second Coming gives us an indication of all these things and prepares us for an understanding of this terrible conflict that goes on between the two kingdoms.

But it tells us also about *the course of the conflict*. There are two points here. First and foremost it tells us that there is a periodicity about the course of the conflict. There are times when the Gospel flourishes, when the Gospel is popular, and men and women crowd to religious meetings and rejoice in it. Then there are terrible periods when men fall away from it, when they become indifferent to it. But, thank God, God intervenes again with a glorious revival and reawakening, a new stimulus. Do you not see this as you look back across the past. Look at the curves, if you like, in the story of the church. You will find it started with a great revival. Then there was a gradual falling off. Then another period of great revival, then that gradually wanes. There you are down in the depths of the Middle Ages, the dark ages. Then comes the glorious Protestant Reformation. But that gradually seemed to pass. Then again, the great eighteenth-century revival. That is the story – there is a periodicity. The enemy seems to be all-powerful and God's people seem to be conquered, then God intervenes and He 'raises up the standard when the enemy comes in like a flood'. That is the first thing.

The second thing, and this is the one which is more important for us today, is that the end of it all will be a crisis. There is clear and unmistakable teaching to that effect, that this conquest will be consummated in a mighty clash – an Armageddon, an ultimate coming together of the two forces, and a final battle. There is no suggestion whatsoever in the New Testament of a gradual improvement of the world and of a gradual introduction of the kingdom of God; the doctrine is apocalyptic, eschatological, critical. That is the picture which is given everywhere throughout the New Testament of the final outcome of this terrifying conflict. It will end in crisis – in an ultimate clash.

The next deduction, which is the one that applies to us above everything else, is *the certainty of the final triumph of Christ and of His cause*. Thank God for that. Whatever may happen, whatever may take place, the plan of salvation guarantees that the kingdom of God is coming and the Lord of lords is going to triumph and prevail. Let me emphasise this. There will be times when it will be almost impossible to believe it. There will be times when almost the very elect themselves will be deceived and lose heart and hope. But the New Testament prepares us for all that. It tells us that at certain periods it will look as if God is defeated, but that we may know for certain that God will triumph and prevail. The end is sure, 'Jesus shall reign', beyond a doubt or a peradventure.

Very well, what is the business and the function of the Gospel and its preaching in the meantime? This is where we ultimately deal with the original question. The business of the Gospel in the meantime is not to try to improve the world gradually. This world is never going to be gradually and increasingly improved – that is the error and the foolishness of those who wonder why the world is as it is after two thousand years of Gospel preaching. The New Testament tells us that it will be like that. The business of the Gospel is not to improve the world generally; it is to take hold of men and women individually out of that world and put them into the kingdom of God; it is to take hold of you and me in this world which is under the wrath and the damnation and condemnation of God, and to save us out of it before it is finally destroyed. It is to gather out God's people, it is to take out the fulness of the Gentiles and the fulness of the Jews; it is to separate God's peculiar people, it is to take us one by one out of this present evil world and put us there in the everlasting and eternal kingdom. So we see clearly that the Gospel has not failed. The Gospel has never promised that the world is going to be better and better; it has simply stated that the world will remain evil until it is ultimately destroyed, and that we are to be saved out of it.

What then is the conclusion that we can draw from all this? What of the present world, what of the present position? We need not be surprised at it in view of what we have seen. Does not the world today conform to the biblical teaching? Is there anything that can explain the world today but the biblical teaching? The Christian should not be surprised at the state of the world and at the clouds on the horizon; he should expect it, he should be prepared for it.

The doctrine also gives us this glorious comfort – whatever may lie ahead of us, if we are in Christ we know that the ultimate end is safe and sure. But that does not lead to complacency; that above everything should stimulate us to activity. If we believe these things we can only draw one deduction – that there is not a moment to spare. As I see what God in His love has done and is saving me from, I must prepare myself for Him, I must pray to be made worthy of the kingdom of His dear Son; I must tell others and warn them, I must open their eyes to the facts that are clear to me, I must be diligent in season and out of season, I must warn men to flee from the wrath to come. God grant that in His infinite grace and pity He may give us such an insight into and understanding of this blessed glorious doctrine, that we shall not only be encouraged and strengthened and established, but that we shall, with the first Christians and all true Christians throughout the ages, look for and long for 'the blessed appearing' which will ultimately rout Satan and his cohorts and introduce that kingdom of righteousness and peace and glory which shall never cease.

9
The Apostolic Testimony

'For we have not followed cunningly devised fables, when we made known unto you the power and coming of our Lord Jesus Christ, but were eyewitnesses of his majesty. For he received from God the Father honour and glory, when there came such a voice to him from the excellent glory, This is my beloved Son, in whom I am well pleased. And this voice which came from heaven we heard, when we were with him in the holy mount.'

Chapter 1:16–18

The statement in this first chapter from verse 16 to the end of the chapter is of very great importance. Indeed, it can be said of it that it is of central importance from this standpoint of the certainty of our faith and, if you like, therefore, from the standpoint of what is generally described as apologetics. The apostle, as we recall, is concerned to help these struggling Christians who were facing difficulties – and we have followed him step by step as he reasons with them, until he brings them to what is perhaps the strongest of all comforts and consolations, namely, the doctrine of the Second Coming and the return of our Lord in glory, and holds that before them.

At that point, however, the apostle seems to imagine someone asking a question like this: 'Yes,' says someone, 'that is all right, you have been reminding us at very great length of what you and the other apostles have preached, the message which we heard at the beginning and which we accepted and which we believe. But, you know, the circumstances and conditions are such that we have to confess that there are times when we are a little bit uncertain about much of it, and there are other people, other teachers, claiming as much authority as yourself, who are suggesting to us that these things are not exactly and precisely as you tell us. Now, here, you have again reminded us of this great and tremendous event which you say is going to take place – that this self-same person, Jesus of Nazareth, whom you have preached unto us as both Christ and Lord, is going to come back to earth in honour and glory, that He will introduce a new heaven and new earth and lead us to an everlasting state of bliss and happiness and perfection. But what guarantee have we that all this is right and that all this is true? We have believed it, we have accepted it, and have had to suffer for that belief and acceptance, but how can we know that these things are really true, that they are what you have claimed for them? What are the grounds of certainty on which we can be absolutely confident and assured?'

It is to deal with that precise problem and difficulty that Peter writes these words which we are now considering, together with the words that follow until the end of the chapter. He anticipates this question, this argument, and he deals with it here in his own characteristic way and manner. At the particular time when Peter wrote, this problem had arisen in an acute form, not only because of the difficulties with which people were confronted as the result of circumstances, but also because there were current round and about them many strange and wonderful fables. It is to these he makes reference here. Anyone who is at all familiar with the history of the Jews, not only at the time of the coming of our Lord into the world, but also previous to that, will know that there was nothing that was perhaps more characteristic of their mental outlook and atmosphere at that time than the multiplicity of fables and stories that had gained currency amongst them. The Jews had developed a kind of imaginative exposition of the Old Testament and in addition had been inventing stories and fables. Not only that; anyone who has even the most cursory acquaintance with mythology will know that there was nothing more characteristic of Greek literature, common throughout the civilised world of those times, than the great variety of myths and stories and fables about various gods that had assumed human form and had dwelt on earth, and to whom and through whom certain strange and wonderful things had happened. Indeed, we can go further and say that, even in the church herself, a number of fables and stories with regard to our Lord Himself had gained a great deal of currency. There are such things as apocryphal gospels which purport to be stories and records of the life and doings of Jesus of Nazareth, the Son of God. In these fables and stories all kinds of strange and wonderful and weird things were claimed for our Lord and Saviour Jesus Christ. We can not now enter into all this; but it is important that we should bear it in mind, for the effect of all these pagan, Jewish and even Christian fables was to raise a doubt in the minds of some of believers, and they were tempted as a result to ask this particular question: 'How can we know that what you have been saying to us is not also a cunningly devised fable?'

That is the question with which we are now concerned, and, of course, there is no need to point out that it is one which is as urgent today as when Peter wrote his letter to those early Christians. In other words, it is the question of authority, and in a sense, during the last hundred years, there is no question which has been so hotly and constantly debated as this. On what grounds do we preach this Gospel? On what grounds do we believe it? On what grounds do we call upon those who are outside the church to accept it? Here we stand as Christian people confronting the world as it is today, and we claim that this is a unique message. We say that this is the only solution to all problems, and that the key to everything is that God has done something once and for ever in the Person of His only begotten Son, our Lord and Saviour Jesus Christ. But the question is asked, 'On what authority do you say this? What is your sanction?' And, not only without, but also within the Christian church there are those who, sometimes as the result of their reading, or their conversations with others who do not believe and who claim to have a scientific outlook on life, find their faith is somewhat shaken when they are confronted by certain arguments. Now this is obviously something of absolutely central importance. The whole question is, what guarantee have we for the truth of the Christian faith? What is our authority for making this unique claim for the Gospel of our Lord and Saviour Jesus Christ?

Here the apostle has two main things to say. First and foremost is the matter of the apostolic witness. Then comes the testimony of prophecy. We deal now with the first of these.

If a man comes to me and says: 'That is all very well, you claim that these things are true, and you are very happy as the result of your belief, but, you know, I want something solid to stand on before I can believe them. What are your reasons?' Let us observe how the apostle deals with the question.

Let me put it first negatively: our first argument must not be to point to the exalted nature of the teaching. So often one finds that when Christian people are pressed at this point this is the reason they give. 'My reason,' they say, 'for believing the Gospel is that it is such a wonderful and noble and exalted teaching. I have read other ideas, and I have come across nothing which is so wonderful and exalted. Look at its view of life, look at the kind of ethic to which it calls us; look at its effect when men really try to carry it out and put it into practice.' But I say that you will never find this line of argument used in the New Testament itself. There is a very good reason for that fact. If we base our confidence in the Gospel solely on the nature of its teaching, then we are finally left in a position when we really cannot argue convincingly against those who believe in various other forms of teaching. You will find that there are other religions in the world which have very noble and exalted teaching. It is no part of the preaching of the Gospel to detract from other views of life. We claim for this Gospel that it can transcend every other teaching. We do not try to detract or derogate from the others. We say that this is quite unique. In other words, let us grant quite freely that Buddhism is a very high and noble and exalted teaching. Likewise we can say the same thing about Mohammedanism, with its stern, strict morality, with its high ethic, with its inculcation of a highly disciplined type of life. Not only that, let us turn to the Greek pagan philosophers – Aristotle, Plato, Socrates – and many other teachers, some of whom, Seneca and others, were actually contemporaries of our Lord.

Read these men's writings and their teaching concerning life. If we are honest, we have to admit that, if you tabulate their teaching and then look at the Christian ethic as found in the Sermon on the Mount, you find that there is often little difference between them. We have no right to claim for the Gospel of Christ a uniqueness merely from the standpoint of ethical and moral, or of noble and elevated, teaching. And the fact is that there are large numbers outside Christ this morning for that very reason. They claim that they find the same teaching elsewhere. 'Why should I, therefore,' they ask, 'believe all this miraculous part of your Gospel? Why should I suddenly be asked to swallow what seems to belong to the realm of fable rather than fact? It seems to me more honest and intelligent to accept teaching which I find coming from those who have claimed to be nothing but human, rather than to add all this which claims to be divine and supernatural.' I say, therefore, that we must observe that the apostle's argument does not base itself on the exalted nature of the teaching alone, or in the first instance.

Let me likewise point out, in the second place, that Peter does not base it on experience, or on results which follow from belief in the Gospel. This again, is equally important, and has been particularly important during the last hundred years. You recall how, as the result of scientific research and advances and development during the Victorian period, there were those in the church who began to think and say, 'Now, unless we are very careful, we are going to lose our faith. They will try to prove with their science that miracles could not happen. But there is no need to lose our faith. We must differentiate between the reported facts of the Christian religion and the experience of the Christian religion.' They said that the ultimate proof of the Christian religion is in the experiences and results to which it leads. So many, when pressed in argument, have turned to the modern pseudo-scientific person, saying: 'You can prove anything you like, but it can never make any difference to what I have experienced.' And they feel they are defending the Christian faith.

Now I am anxious to point out that such an argument is, in a sense, to 'sell the pass' and to deny the very centre of the Christian faith. Peter does not say that the real grounds for believing this Gospel are something like this: 'I was once a fisherman, a man who lived a sinful life. But since I have become a Christian and a preacher and an apostle I have had amazing experiences.' Peter does not base his argument upon his own experience in an inward sense, or upon the results of the Gospel in his particular case. And there is a very good reason for that. If we base our certainty upon something as subjective as that, then what are we to say to the various cults that are so popular at the present time? There are many agencies which can give people very definite and remarkable experiences. It is no part of the Gospel to deny any value in any other teaching. One of the most remarkable changes I have ever seen in a life was in the case of someone who believed in what is known as 'Christian Science'. These cults and false beliefs can give people very definite experiences – turn drunkards into sober people, dishonest people into honest people, etc. Psychology can do it also; a mere treatment of the mind and brain along those lines is fully capable of producing profound changes in the realm of experience and inward sensation. So, if we base the case for the Christian Gospel on such grounds as that, what is to be our reply to these various other teachings and cults and agencies which can produce exactly the same results and same effects?

In other words, it is vitally important that we should realise the positive character and nature of the Christian apologetic. What is it? It is nothing less than the apostolic witness and testimony to certain facts, and that is the very thing which Peter tells us at this point. 'We have not followed cunningly devised fables . . . we were eyewitnesses of his majesty . . . He received . . . honour and glory, when there came such a voice to him from the excellent glory: This is my beloved Son, in whom I am well pleased. And this voice . . . we heard, when we were with him in the holy mount.' That is the nature of the Christian apologetic. The basis of our faith rests solidly upon certain facts to which witness is borne by the apostles. Read the Book of the Acts of the Apostles and observe there the nature of the preaching of the Apostles, the first preachers of the Christian Gospel. What did they say as they went around the then known world? Did they talk about themselves? Did they tell people what had happened to them? Were they there just as exponents of some mystic experience they had had? The answer is a very definite 'No'. They stated certain facts of which they themselves were witnesses and to which they bore testimony. They went from place to place and they 'preached Jesus', they preached 'Jesus as the Christ', they preached 'Jesus as Lord'. There is a perfect illustration of that in the tenth chapter of Acts, where we find Peter preaching to Cornelius, a Gentile, and you observe what he said. He talked about Jesus of Nazareth. He said, I was with Him, I saw Him do these works, I say that this is the One whom I saw after He was raised from the dead, who ate and drank with us. He preached Jesus. And if you look at the preaching of Peter and Paul everywhere you will find that it was always the same thing. Paul in the synagogues reasoned from the Scriptures to prove that Jesus was the Christ and that the Christ must needs suffer. The argument is always precisely the same. In other words, the whole basis of our position rests upon the Person of our Lord and Saviour Jesus Christ and on the facts concerning Him.

Now what are those facts? Here we are driven back to certain statements which we find in the Gospels and the Acts of the Apostles.

There certain claims are made for Him. The claim is that He is the only begotten Son of God. What evidence have we? Well, we are told He worked miracles – he could heal the sick, give sight to the blind, and raise the dead. He could command the elements, calm the sea, and bid the wind to cease. He had the lordship over the whole of creation, disease, pestilence and things of that kind. These men claim that they saw Him working these miracles. Likewise, they bear testimony to the fact of His resurrection. They say they saw Him nailed to a cross, and that He died and was buried in a grave, but afterwards they saw that same grave empty. They say that they saw Him risen from the dead, that He spoke to them and was with them forty days and manifested Himself, and that at the end of that time they saw Him ascending into heaven.

But here, Peter singles out for very special mention the fact of the transfiguration. 'We have not followed cunningly devised fables, when we made known unto you the power and coming of our Lord Jesus Christ, but were eyewitnesses of his majesty.' We were with Him, James and John and myself, says Peter in effect, there on that mount, and we suddenly saw Him transfigured, and over and above that we heard the voice from heaven which spoke and said, 'This is my beloved Son, in whom I am well pleased.' Now why does he single out this in particular? It seems to me that the reason must be that it was there on the mount of transfiguration that these men saw more clearly than anywhere else the peculiar and amazing glory of our Lord. You remember the description. Suddenly they saw Him transfigured, there was a blazing, dazzling light in His face, and His very clothing had such a whiteness that no fuller could ever produce. That amazing glory – they were almost blinded by it. Peter never forgot it. But over and above that, he says, while they were there in that amazing scene they saw Moses and Elias, they heard them speaking to him. These men, who had come from the life beyond death and the grave, appeared and spoke. Over and above all they had heard a voice from heaven, a voice such as they had never heard before, saying: 'This is my beloved Son, in whom I am well pleased.'

Our whole position at this moment depends upon this fact. I either accept that statement of the apostle Peter or I do not accept it. I am a Christian not because I see certain effects produced in certain people who believe the Gospel. Why am I a Christian? Well, my final reason is that I believe what I am told in this book; I believe the fact that is solemnly asseverated by the Apostle, that when he and James and John went up that mountain with Jesus they suddenly saw Him transfigured, saw Moses and Elias, and heard the voice from heaven. I believe them when they say He quieted the waves and silenced the wind and healed the sick and raised the dead – I have no other reason for believing, it is my only ground and basis and assurance of hope.

In the last analysis we are driven back to one of these two positions. If you like to believe the modern philosophies and the modern pseudo-scientific attitude towards life, you start by saying a miracle is impossible, and because of that you must then say a miracle has never happened; therefore, you say, 'I do not believe your Gospel, with its miraculous claims.' You are perfectly logical but that is not the argument between us. We are not here to argue whether a miracle can happen. The ultimate question is this: are these men credible witnesses or not? Am I prepared to believe what they affirm? Do I believe that science can really explain the whole of life? Am I safe in saying that in the light of modern theories a miracle is inherently impossible? I may have a psychological experience, I may become a different man – that does not make me a Christian. What makes me a Christian is to believe and accept the testimony that Jesus is the only begotten Son of God, that He was born of the Virgin Mary, that He was born in a miraculous manner, that He worked miracles, that He was transfigured on the holy mount, that He did things that man has never done, that He died for men's sins on the cross, that He rose from the grave, that He ascended into heaven. I either accept these things as facts, or else I say that they are nothing but fables and inventions. Have I anything to strengthen me and buttress me in that faith? I have one great proof, and that is the Christian church herself. How do you explain the Christian church apart from these facts? How do you explain the apostles themselves? Is it likely that the men who wrote these Gospels were liars and fabricators and frauds, that they deliberately invented these scenes? Is it likely that Peter, who denied his Lord just before the crucifixion because he was afraid of death, should afterwards make claims and statements that constantly exposed him to death and to martyrdom and indeed, subsequently, led to his martyrdom? We base our whole case upon this apostolic witness and testimony. That is how the Christian church came into being, that is how she conquered the ancient world. These men simply preached the facts concerning Him, and we are driven ultimately to one of these two positions – we either believe the apostles, or else we do not believe them. I either accept the exalted, miraculous, definite claim, or else I reject it. Either I believe that these things are facts, or else I dismiss them as fables.

Christian people, let us not be afraid of this supposed scientific attack upon the Gospel. Science can never remove facts; it can never alter events which have taken place in history. Let us not apologise for the faith. Let us not reduce the faith. Let us make the full miraculous claim. Let us not offer a restricted Jesus with noble ideas and exalted teaching. Let us make the full New Testament claim for Him and fasten our everything upon the apostolic witness and testimony, upon the evidence of the men who were with Him on the mount and who heard the voice from heaven say, 'This is my beloved Son, in whom I am well pleased.'

10

The Authority of Scripture

'We have also a more sure word of prophecy; whereunto
ye do well that ye take heed, as unto a light that shineth in
a dark place, until the day dawn, and the day star arise in
your hearts: Knowing this first, that no prophecy of the
scripture is of any private interpretation. For the
prophecy came not in old time by the will of man: but
holy men of God spake as they were moved by the Holy
Ghost.'

Chapter 1:19–21

We now proceed with the second part of what we may describe as the
'Apologetics of the Apostle Peter'. And this second great section of
his apologetics is, of course, the Scriptures. Those are the two things
on which we ultimately stand. The Apostolic witness and testimony,
and the Holy Scriptures.

In verses 19, 20 and 21 he deals with this second aspect. But here
again there is a double argument. Let me, for the sake of clarity of
thought and exposition, indicate these two arguments. First, he says,
there are the events which have verified prophecy. That he deals with
in verse 19. The other is the nature of the Scripture itself; and that is
the subject with which he deals in verses 20 and 21 and which we are
now going to study. Facts verifying prophecy, yes; but in addition to
that, the nature of prophecy itself. And not only the nature of
prophecy, but the nature of Scripture as a whole. You notice how
Peter puts it – 'Knowing this first, that no prophecy of the
Scripture . . .' Prophecy is a part of Scripture, so what is true of
prophecy is true of the whole Scripture. In the Second Epistle of Paul
to Timothy, and the third chapter, exactly the same claim is made. In
view of this we must discover what exactly Peter is saying here.
'Knowing this first, that no prophecy of the Scripture is of any private

interpretation. For the prophecy came not in old time by the will of man: but holy men of God spake as they were moved by the Holy Ghost.' It is important to know precisely what the Apostle means in verse 20, and I imagine I am right when I say that there has been no single phrase of Scripture that has produced such a variety of different interpretations as this particular verse. For those who are interested in exposition, and in the elucidation of the meaning of Scripture, I do not think there can be anything that is more fascinating than to study the history of its interpretation. It has figured very prominently in the great religious controversies of the centuries. It is a verse on which the great division between Roman Catholicism and Protestantism is partly based. It is therefore an extremely significant and important statement.

Let me give you a hurried account of some of the main lines of interpretation which have been suggested and put forward in an attempt to explain this verse. 'Knowing this first, that no prophecy of the Scripture is of any private interpretation.' That is how it reads in the Authorised Version, and here are some of the explanations put forward. Dealing with them historically, we start with the Roman Catholic exposition, and this exposition is precisely what you would expect it to be. They say that here, of course, is the statement of Scripture itself that private judgment is something which must be rigidly excluded – it is only the church that can interpret the Scriptures. No prophecy of the Scripture is of any private interpretation! Protestantism, they say, with its claim for private judgment and for the universal priesthood of all believers is, therefore, once and for ever condemned completely. Nothing, they continue, is more dangerous than that this Book should get into the hands of the common people and that they should try to interpret and understand it for themselves. There is only one safe thing to do, they say, and that is to go to the church. The church alone can interpret this great tradition that has come down, and she does so through the Councils and the Cardinals and the Pope. 'No prophecy of the Scripture is of any private interpretation'; nothing can be so dangerous as that individuals should face that Word and by themselves should try to understand it. So we see why this verse has played so prominent a part in the whole argument betwen Roman Catholicism and the Protestant position with respect to apologetics and the whole basis of our faith. Do you believe in the necessity of the church in addition to the Word, or do you say that the Word itself is the final authority and that the church is not absolutely necessary to the interpretation of the Word, but rather must herself be judged by the Word?

Another view which has been put forward is that we have a caution here against the interpretation of any particular prophecy on its own – the view which says that the only way to interpret prophecy is to interpret it in the light of the whole of prophecy. No prophecy is itself of any private interpretation. In other words, Be very careful, they say, that you do not take hold of just one prophecy and on one prophecy elaborate a great doctrine or a body of doctrines. To understand prophecy aright, they say, you must take an individual prophecy and put it in the light of the whole body of prophecy; that is the only safe thing to do.

Again, it has been put forward that what it means is that the prophets themselves were not capable of understanding all that they said in their own prophecies. You will find that Peter makes that actual statement in the first chapter of his first Epistle in verses 10 and 11 and there are those who would interpret this statement in that manner. They say, even the prophet himself did not always understand what he was saying. 'No prophecy . . . is of any private interpretation.'

Then there are those who have suggested that what it means is that prophecy is not its own interpretation, and does not carry its own interpretation in itself, but that it can only be understood when the events come to pass which it has prophesied and predicted. They say, therefore, that you cannot pretend to interpret prophecy until it has been fulfilled – that is what is meant by 'no private interpretation' – you must wait for the event before you seek for the meaning of the prophecy.

Then the last common explanation that has been put forward is that no man reading prophecy, or even the prophet himself who expresses it, is able to interpret the prophecy by his own understanding; he can only do so as he is illumined and guided by the Holy Spirit. What they say, therefore, is that no man, as he is, can understand prophecy – 'prophecy is of no private interpretation', you must have the illumination of the Holy Spirit upon your mind before you can see or understand or interpret it aright. Those are the common ideas that have been put forward in the past in an attempt to interpret this particular statement.

Now as we examine these expositions what we must surely feel is that while there are elements of truth in all of them apart from the Roman Catholic one, they all seem to fail in this sense, that they take the twentieth verse by itself and fail to consider it in the light of the twenty-first verse. But verses 20 and 21 must surely be taken together. The very word 'for' at the beginning of verse 21 makes that imperative. 'Knowing this first, that no prophecy of the Scripture is of any private interpretation. For the prophecy came not in old time by the will of man: but holy men of God spake as they were moved by the Holy Ghost.' Verse 21 surely throws a great light upon verse 20. Not only should we bear that in mind, but we must bear something else in mind.Take that word 'is' in verse 20. It is generally agreed that the translation 'is' is rather unfortunate at that point. It really means 'arises' or 'originates' or, if you prefer it, 'comes into existence'. Then let us look at the word 'interpretation'. If you trace this word you will find that it is sometimes translated by the word 'expounding' or 'expound' or by the word 'determination', so that the idea we have is something like this: 'Knowing this first, that no prophecy of the Scripture, originates or arises, as the result of any private determination.'

We now begin to see exactly what Peter is saying. If I may translate it a little more freely, we can put it like this, 'Knowing this first, that no prophecy of the Scripture originates in the prophet's own understanding of things', and put like that, you will see how naturally it leads on to verse 21. 'No prophecy of the Scripture arises or originates in the prophet's own understanding of things, for the prophecy came not in old time by the will of man: but holy men of God spake as they were moved by the Holy Ghost.' There, I think, we have the only reasonable, rational and satisfactory explanation of this particular verse. And of course it links up perfectly with what Peter has already been saying in verse 19: 'We have also a more sure word of prophecy; whereunto ye do well that ye take heed, as unto a light that shineth in a dark place, until the day dawn, and the day star arise in your hearts.' Why should I take heed unto this Scripture and prophecy? Why should I meditate upon it? Why should I base my life upon it? The answer is that this prophecy has already been verified by the Incarnation, and, in any case, prophecy is not a mere recording of the meditation and cogitation and thought and understanding and insight of man; it has not originated in any determination on man's part, it is not the expounding of man's views – 'prophecy came not in old time by the will of man: but holy men of God spake as they were moved by the Holy Ghost'. In other words these two verses go together, and the statement of verse 21 is very strong and powerful. Look at it as it is translated in the Authorised Version. 'The prophecy came not in old time by the will of man.' Now that is not as strong as it ought to be; it should read, 'prophecy never came' – not at any time – 'no prophecy ever came (or was brought) by the will of man, but holy men of God spake as they were moved by the Holy Ghost'.

There is one other word which we have to deal with, before our exposition is complete. Holy men of God spake as they were 'moved' by the Holy Ghost. Now a better way, perhaps, of putting it would be, 'Men spake from God as they were moved by the Holy Ghost'; and you are familiar with the fact that the word translated 'moved' could perhaps be still better translated 'carried along', or the one which commends itself to me above all other translations is 'driven', 'driven along'. In connection with this word 'moved', the expositors are all very fond of referring us to the twenty-seventh chapter of the Book of the Acts of the Apostles. You remember the story that is given there of the shipwreck of Paul and his companions as they were on their way to Rome. You remember the graphic way in which the story is told, how that mighty wind, Euroclydon, arose, and how that little ship was buffeted and tossed about, with the sailors and the captain of the ship at their wits' end. First of all they lightened the ship by getting rid of all unnecessary tackling, then they threw the cargo overboard. They did everything man could do at that time in order to save the ship, and in a very graphic way we are told that, having done all things, 'we let her drive'. We are told she was driven along – that is the very same word that is used here – 'holy men spake from God as they were driven along by the Holy Ghost'.

Here, then, is the statement which the Apostle makes. Scripture, he tells us, and prophecy in particular, must never be thought of as just a collection of the thoughts and ideas of men. This, of course, is absolutely vital and fundamental. The prophecy and prediction of Scripture are not the results of human insight and human under-standing. This can never be emphasised too much, especially during these present years. I need not weary you by reminding you that a vital part of the so-called higher criticism of the Bible is to hold a particular view about prophecy. 'Our fathers,' say the critics, 'were all wrong, they thought prophecy meant foresight and foretelling; what it really means is insight.' What they really believe is that what you have in the Old Testament is nothing but the writings of men who had a profound insight into life, wise men, understanding men, men who pondered the times in which they lived, men who thought and wrote and argued and reasoned, and as a result of that great process expressed their insight. Here in these writings, they say, we have insight, not foresight. Now the Apostle Peter is at great pains to point out that what we have in these records is not just the insight of men. Indeed, he goes further; he says that they never intended to write, they never set out to write, 'prophecy came not in old time by the will of man'. It is not man deciding to write what he thinks, it is more than that. It is not like a man writing an article in the newspaper.

What then is it? The great claim that is made is this, that these men were taken hold of by the Holy Spirit. The Holy Spirit came upon them and took hold of them and gave them a message, carried them along, drove them along as they wrote and put it down on record. And that, of course, is exactly and precisely the claim that is made by the prophets themselves – these are the very terms that are used – 'the Word of God came unto them', or 'the Word of the Lord came unto them' – 'Thus saith the Lord'. They do not say, This is what I think, but 'Thus saith the Lord'. The other phrase is, 'the burden of the Lord', referring to the message that the Lord has put upon them, the thing that has come to them from the Lord, the constraint of the Lord that is making them write – these are their terms. And what substantiates that still further is the thing of which I have already reminded you, namely, the statement made by the Apostle Peter in his first Epistle, to the effect that there were times when the prophets themselves did not understand the things they were writing. Far from it being their own thought and idea, this is what he says: 'Of which salvation the prophets have inquired and searched diligently, who prophesied of the grace that should come unto you: searching what, or what manner of time the Spirit of Christ which was in them did signify, when it testified beforehand the sufferings of Christ, and the glory that should follow. Unto whom it was revealed, that not unto themselves, but unto us they did minister the things . . .' There, then, is a further proof that it was a message that was given. But we can go even beyond that. We are told definitely and specifically that these men were not only called by God through the Holy Spirit, but that sometimes they were called against their own will and against their own desire. You remember how often Jeremiah, poor Jeremiah, raises his objections. Have you read chapters 15 and 20 of his Book? Read them again and notice how often he says, I do not want to give that message, I know it will lead to trouble and I shall become unpopular – I shall probably be thrown into prison. But God is speaking and God has said, 'You must give it, you are bound to speak this word.' God called him against his will; he did not want to speak. How often has that been true of the prophets – this call of God, not their own will. It has been laid upon them; they have literally been driven by God the Holy Spirit, as that ship was driven in the Adriatic.

In other words, we have set out by Peter in this very explicit manner the great New Testament and Old Testament doctrine of revelation. The claim is made here that God has been pleased in His infinite compassion and condescension to speak to men. The claim is made for this Book that it is absolutely unique, that there is no other book in the world like it. All other books are the production of man; they are the result of man's will, man's understanding, man's insight. But here is a Book which claims that it is the record of God speaking. And it claims this with regard to the message – revelation – and also the way in which the message was recorded – inspiration.

This is the second great fact on which we stand, and on which we decide that the whole of our life must be lived in terms of this Book. It is not human thought and understanding, with men trying to predict and prophesy what is going to happen. Here we find that the eternal God has been pleased to make known unto men certain things that are of vital importance. The teaching of the Book, in other words, is that, because of sin, mankind cannot arrive at a knowledge of God, but that, in spite of that, God has been pleased to grant this knowledge to man. This is not the time to study in detail the doctrine of inspiration, but we can put it like this – the Bible teaches us that God, who is inconceivable to man, has been pleased to reveal Himself to man in two main ways. First there is a general revelation in nature and in creation and, if you like, in the process of history. But in addition to that, there are special forms of revelation. God revealed Himself sometimes in the old dispensation in what are called Theophanies – appearances amongst men. You read about the 'Angel of the Lord', the 'Angel of God' – those are the Theophanies, the appearances of our Lord in human form – not incarnation but appearance. Then God at times revealed Himself by addressing the people in words and in actions, at other times in miracles. But above all I would emphasise the fact that God has revealed Himself by speaking to certain chosen servants, and by revealing His message to them and by enabling them to record it – that is the claim for the inspiration of the Bible. We see that God guided men like Moses. Moses recorded facts. You remember how the Epistle to the Hebrews tells us, 'Through faith we understand that the worlds were framed by the word of God' (Heb. 11:3). Now that was a fact that was revealed by the Spirit of God to Moses. It was not Moses' imagination or idea or discovery; it was revealed to him, and he recorded it together with all the other facts in his books. The same is true of prophecy and prediction. Coming events are communicated to the prophets by the Holy Spirit of God.

The doctrine goes even further than that. It does not merely tell us that the man was inspired, it does not merely say that the Truth was inspired; it goes further than that and announces that the very recording itself was inspired. Not only was the man taken hold of, he was carried along, he was borne along. We believe that the words of Scripture are inspired by the Holy Spirit. Does that mean, says someone, that these men were but amanuenses? Does it mean that they were just taking down what God dictated to them? No, we do not believe in a mechanical doctrine of inspiration, because you cannot read the Scriptures without noting the variation in style. When you read a certain passage you know that it has been written by Paul; you recognise Paul as you read it. In the same way, when you come to passages written by Peter, you say, 'Obviously that is Peter.' Anyone can recognise the style of John. Personality has not been effaced. The doctrine means that these men were so controlled by the Holy Spirit that they were safeguarded from error; they were guided not only to a knowledge of the truth, but in their expression of the truth. Their own personality was given free play, but it was controlled by the Holy Spirit, and that guaranteed this ultimate result. Now this of course is one of the most amazing and miraculous things of all. We claim it is the Word of God. In this Book we have the only account of God that man has. What can we know about God truly except what we are told in this Book? You can reason, if you like, through nature and you will arrive at a Creator. You will never arrive at a Father and loving God; you will never know God as the Father of our Lord Jesus Christ. It is only as God has revealed Himself and His character and His holiness in this Book that we really know anything about Him.

But not only that, God has here revealed His own thoughts concerning man, and life, and the world. Here we are told how man came into existence, how all man's troubles are the result of sin, what God has done about sin, and what God is going to do about sin. Here is a map of history. Here is a philosophy of the ages. Here we are told what is going to happen in the days that lie ahead – and that, you will remember, is Peter's immediate point here. He has been telling these people about the return of Christ, about the Second Coming. How can I know that this is going to happen? Well, my ultimate and only answer is this. I find it is stated in this Book, and I believe that this Book is not the imagination of man, but God the Holy Spirit speaking through man. As I read it I am confronted by the fact of Christ: I am confronted by these inspired, authentic records, and I believe what I believe about Him because I find it here; and I therefore believe when I am told that He is coming again. I either accept this Book and its verities, or else I base my life and view of the future upon the thoughts and ideas and insights and understandings of men. And as I am confronted by these alternatives, I say for myself that I am driven to believe this Word, which is not of man's will, but which is the product of men moved, borne along, inspired, carried along, driven and guided by the Holy Spirit. Here is a Word which in truth and in fact is the Word of God Himself. It is not private interpretation, it is not human understanding; it is God speaking. Let him who is wise hear the Word of God.

11

Fulfilled Prophecy – the Message of Christmas

'We have also a more sure word of prophecy; whereunto
ye do well that ye take heed, as unto a light that shineth in
a dark place, until the day dawn, and the day star arise in
your hearts:'

Chapter 1:19

The Apostle here, I would remind you again, is giving what we may
well call his apologetics. He is comforting people who are in trouble
and difficulties. He has been reminding them of the central and
cardinal tenets of the Christian faith, and then he, as it were,
proceeds to confront a question like this – a question that was asked
in the first century of Christianity, and is still asked – How can we
know that these things are true; what foundation, what basis have
we, what confidence, for believing and accepting these things? Here
the Apostle gives a series of replies to that question. The first was,
that 'we have not followed cunningly devised fables' – the Apostolic
testimony and witness. 'We have seen and heard,' said Peter, 'we
were with Him on the holy mount.' There is that apostolic witness
and testimony to the things that they saw in His life and miracles, and
especially that which happened on the Mount of Transfiguration.
And then you will remember that we have considered the other great
element in our confidence – the great fact of revelation, with special
emphasis upon the inspiration of the Scriptures. We considered
verses 20 and 21 in which Peter is concerned to remind these people
of the very nature of prophecy and of Scripture in general, that it is
God speaking, that these are not ideas woven in the minds and
imaginations of men, but that it is all a result of God's intervention,
God's action, God graciously revealing and manifesting Himself
unto us.

That, however, is not all; for now we have this further statement to consider: 'We have also a more sure word of prophecy', or 'we have also a word of prophecy made more sure'. What exactly does the Apostle mean by this? This is a further argument, he says, a further source of comfort. Now let us consider for a moment the exact exposition of the words. What is more sure? What is the comparison that he is making? There are various suggestions that strike us at once. Is the Apostle saying that the word of prophecy is more sure than cunningly devised fables? We need not stay with that – cunningly devised fables have no basis at all, they are sheer invention and imagination, they have no actuality, no real existence. So that if the Apostle were merely saying that prophecy is more sure than cunningly devised fables, he would not be establishing anything. To show that something is better than that which is non-existent is not to pay it a compliment; indeed, it is not to praise it at all.

Well then, is the Apostle here saying that the word of prophecy is more sure than the apostolic witness and testimony? At first sight that offers itself to us as a suggestion. He has been giving his account of what they saw on the Mount of Transfiguration, and how they heard the voice, and then he says, 'We have also a more sure word of prophecy', as if to suggest that this prophetic word is something which is firmer and more sure than that which they had seen and heard. And yet it does seem to me, and I think most expositors would agree, that this again is not the right explanation of these words, because there is a sense in which nothing could be greater or fuller than that which they saw on the Mount of Transfiguration. They were there looking at the Son of God transfigured. They actually heard the direct voice from heaven which of necessity is something that cannot be compared even with the same voice speaking through the medium of the inspired prophets. But what seems to me to exclude entirely that explanation as a possible one is that Peter says, 'we have also'; in other words, he is not merely referring to the people, he is including himself and the other apostles, and he says that 'we', 'the apostles', who actually did hear that voice speaking from heaven and who did see Him transfigured, we have a word of prophecy made more sure.

There is only one adequate explanation of the words and it must be this. He is not comparing the word of prophecy with what he has already been describing; what he is really doing is to compare the word of prophecy as it was given in ancient times to the people then living, and that self-same word of prophecy in the light of what has taken place. It is the word of prophecy itself that has been made more sure. It is not that it is more sure than something else, but that it itself has been made more sure because of its fulfilment and because of its substantiation. And thus, the Apostle says, these are the foundations on which we rest and base our all. We did see Him, we did hear the voice, but in addition to that, we have got this other amazing and extraordinary thing. The prophets spoke of old and said certain things were going to take place. To them and to the people to whom it was spoken that was an amazing and wonderful thing. But to look at and to meditate upon the very fulfilment of those things is obviously still more wonderful. Now that is the argument which is often used in the New Testament. You will find it used by the author of the Epistle to the Hebrews in chapter 11 where, having given his long list of all the saints of the past and the heroes of the faith, he argues that all those walked by faith; the fulfilment of the promise was not given to them as it is now given to us.

In this way the Apostle, here, is emphasising how it is that the coming of our Lord and Saviour Jesus Christ, and all He did and said, is the fulfilment of prophecy. I want to call your attention to that; that is the way, I think, in which we can with the greatest benefit approach Christmas Day and the days that come before it. Whenever we think of the birth of the Son of God, and His coming here on earth, there is no more profitable way of doing so than to take it, as Peter puts it here, in the light of its fulfilment of prophecy. As the Apostle argues, there is nothing more strengthening to faith than to do this very thing. We do indeed consider the apostolic witnesses and testimony, and we have no hesitation in accepting it; but in addition to that, let us remember how everything that we associate with Christmas is, in a New Testament sense, a direct and complete fulfilment of the prophecies, and therefore provides us with a confidence that cannot be shaken in these dark and difficult days.

Let me then put it in the form of a few propositions.

First, *Christ and His coming are the fulfilment of the Old Testament prophecy.* 'We have the word of prophecy made more sure.' In other words, we are entitled to say that the Old Testament really can only be understood in Jesus Christ. The Old Testament is a Book which in one sense is without meaning until you look back at it with Christian eyes and in the light of the fulfilment and carrying out of what is there predicted. That, of course, is the right way to read the Old Testament; it is to grasp as you read it that it is a Book of promises, a Book of shadows, a Book of types. Everything in it is temporary; there is that note to all the things that are set down. The incidents which it records are undoubtedly actions in and of themselves, and they have their own importance and significance; but each one suggests very much more than it says – there is a feeling that it is all a kind of temporary legislation, that we are in a period of interregnum, we are looking onward and forward. The whole of the Old Testament is a Book of types and expectation, seeking and waiting and looking for something. Now the great statement which Peter makes here is that Christ in His coming upon earth is the fulfilment of all and everything that is there stated. You will remember how the apostle Paul puts the same thing in his own language, and in his own way when he says, 'All the promises of God in him are yea, and in him Amen'. There are the promises; here is the yea, the answer, the amen the substantiating, the fulfilling of everything that God hás said through His Old Testament prophets. Here is one of those great keys to the understanding of the Bible which again helps to demonstrate the amazing unity and wonder of the Book. Christ is the centre of the Book; everything in the Old Testament looked forward to Him, everything in the New Testament looks back to Him. He is the centre of history. He is the focal point in the whole movement of humanity from the creation to the end of time. It is in Him, in His Person, that you find gathered up together all the promises of God. They, every one of them, have their yea and amen in Him, and in Him the word of prophecy is made more sure – by His coming and by His every word and all His actions.

But look for a moment at the detailed nature of that fulfilment; for this again is something that is truly astounding and amazing. And we can do nothing better as we thus approach Christmas Day than to remind ourselves of the very detailed nature of this fulfilment. As we do so we shall once more be reminded how this Word must of necessity be the Word of God. Even if it were just a matter of a few general statements with a kind of general similarity and correspond- ence with the New Testament it would be very wonderful. But here it is not just a question of ideas that seem to have a general fulfilment; there is a detailed fulfilment which can only be explained in terms of the fact that the men who wrote these prophecies were writing under the inspiration of God. This is a further proof of the contention that no prophecy of the Scripture is of any private interpretation, but that prophecy came not in old time by the will of man, 'but holy men spake as they were moved or driven, or carried along, or borne along, by the Holy Ghost'.

Let us now make a very rapid and cursory survey of this detailed fulfilment. The details are of great value as they are set out in terms of the tribe and family from which our Lord came. There is that Child born in Bethlehem. To what tribe does He belong? The answer is, 'The tribe of Judah'. Of which particular family of that tribe? The answer is, 'The house of David'. Now you remember in the Old Testament it had been predicted and prophesied that it was out of the tribe of Judah and out of the house of David that the Messiah, the Deliverer, would come. Away back many centuries before, as far back as a thousand years before the birth, and even prior to that, the promise had been made that He would be of that tribe and house. And here in Bethlehem where the Babe is born is the dual verification of that promise.

Then, what about the time of His coming? This is a point of great interest and importance if you approach the birth of Christ merely from the standpoint of the philosophy of history. It is generally agreed that there was no time in the history of mankind when the coming of the Son of God, the Messiah, was less likely than the very time when He came. If men had had the choice that would never have been the time, for it was actually the time when the sceptre seemed to be departing from Judah. But that was precisely what had been prophesied and predicted hundreds of years before, that in the days to come, when the sceptre seemed to be departing out of the hand of Judah, then the real King and Ruler would come. And if you read the contemporary history you will find that this was the position of the Children of Israel when our Lord was born. Or take it again in terms of the prophecy of the prophet Daniel. Read the ninth chapter of the Book of Daniel with its prophecy about the seventy weeks, and there you will find again, down to the minutest detail, a statement beforehand of the exact time of His coming. This extraordinary process, this accuracy, this foretelling by prophecy even down to details, is most astonishing.

Then with regard to His mother. You will remember the prophecy that foretold that a virgin should bear a child. I know that probably the immediate and most direct reference of this refers to an event in history at that time, yet you cannot confine it to that. There is a dual element, an immediate fact and a remote fulfilment – 'a virgin shall bear a child'.

Again consider the place of His birth. You remember how it was given to the prophet Micah to add that detail; that He should be born in Bethlehem. You will remember the visit of the wise men to Herod when, in the fulness of time, our Lord was born. Because Herod did not understand what they reported, he consulted the authorities, and they replied that Christ should be born in Bethlehem, according to prophecy. Now as you look at your Old Testament, you see constantly unfolded to you this extraordinary thing – how God gave to one, one fact, and to another, another fact. It is only Micah who mentions Bethlehem, but God gave him that particular fact and detail, and the exact place of His birth was thus foretold.

Now think of our Lord's words – the words He spoke. If you read from the sixty-first chapter of the Book of Isaiah you will find there that the prophet prophesies and predicts that the Messiah will speak certain words and do certain things. Then cast your mind to that occasion in the synagogue at Nazareth when our Lord had gone into the synagogue as was His wont. There He was given the Scriptures to read and He read out of the sixty-first chapter of Isaiah, and having read thus, He said, 'This day is this Scripture fulfilled in your ears.' The very words He spoke, His method of speech, His manner of teaching, down to the minutest detail – all these actions were predicted and prophesied.

Then think of His works and His miracles. We read in the thirty-fifth chapter of the Book of the prophet Isaiah, of how He would open the eyes of the blind and unstop the ears of the deaf, and the lame man would leap as an hart, and the dumb would sing; and then you come to the New Testament and you read the account of His doing these very things. You remember John the Baptist in his period of uncertainty in prison sending his two disciples to Jesus to ask, 'Art thou he that should come?' and these two men are told to go back and 'tell John again the things which ye do hear and see; the blind receive their sight, and the lame walk, and the deaf are made to hear,' etc. Here John is referred right away back to that thirty-fifth chapter of Isaiah.

Not only that, you remember the fifty-third chapter of Isaiah with its prophecy of the Servant of the Lord bearing our sicknesses and our diseases, and you remember how Matthew, in describing some of our Lord's miracles of healing, refers back to that very prophecy, that He would 'bear our sicknesses'.

Let me remind you briefly of how His entry into Jerusalem was predicted by the prophet Zechariah, how he mentions the ass and the foal of an ass which would be connected with that triumphant entry, and of how He would be sold for thirty pieces of silver. I need scarcely remind you of how His sufferings are described in detail, not only again in that fifty-third chapter of Isaiah but especially also in the twenty-second Psalm – how the very fact that His hands and feet were to be pierced is there prophesied and predicted – how everything is forecast down to these minutest details. They had all been predicted hundreds of years before they happened. The fact that He should be buried in a particular place, that His grave should be made with the wealthy, was prophesied. And when the time came He was buried in the tomb of Joseph of Arimathea. Both his resurrection and the Day of Pentecost, were foretold. You remember how after His ascension He sent the Holy Spirit according to His promise, and when the people in confusion began to ask, What is this?, back came the reply from Peter, 'This is that which was spoken by the prophet Joel.'

All these instances, and there are many others, show how, down to the minutest detail, He by His coming, and by all that He has done and said, has made the word of prophecy more sure; he has fulfilled it, he has substantiated it.

But let me say something about *the glorious nature of this fulfilment*. It is wonderful in detail, but look at its glory as a whole. In the coming of Christ, in the birth of our Lord, in His life and all His activity here on earth, God kept His word. God has honoured His word given to the fathers in ancient times. To see this as one reads the Bible opens one's eyes to the unique glory of the Scriptures. You read these promises given by God so long ago to His ancient people, and as you go through your Old Testament you begin to see how God has kept His word. Some of those people cried out in their agony, 'How long, Lord, have you forgotten to be gracious?' We read the words of the promise, but look at the situation. Is God forgetful, has He forgotten to be gracious – what of the promises? When that Babe was born in that stable in Bethlehem, the great pronouncement that was made was this – God has kept His word. God has proved that His promises are true. Everything that God has ever promised is here being fulfilled. It is a great declaration of the immutability of the counsel of God, that God's word is fixed and absolute and eternal, that God has here fulfilled the oath that He Himself took in order that we might have such a consolation.

But let me try to show you the glory of it all in this way. God, we see, has carried out all the promises that He ever gave with respect to man and his salvation. For, after all, that is what we have in the Old Testament. The Bible is the history of man in his relationship to God, so that we can describe it, if you like, as the History of Salvation. It is the history of the entire human race from the beginning to the end. Now God made man and He made him perfect, and man had perfect communion with God. But sin came in and that communion was broken. Man brought upon himself the wrath of God and all the misery that has followed. What is going to happen to man? Here the Bible comes in with its great message. Its whole business, its whole story, is to tell us what God proposes to do about fallen man. So God began immediately after the Fall to make promises, and they are promises with respect to man and his salvation. Now in the birth of Christ, and all that follows, all those promises are carried out and fulfilled. Let me just remind you of some of the main ones. From the very moment, as it were, that man fell, God illumined the darkness by giving a precious promise. The serpent had entered God's perfect creation and he had beguiled man and caused man to fall, and thereby had offended God also; but God in His infinite grace at once gave a promise, 'The seed of the women shall bruise the serpent's head.' There you are away back four thousand years before the birth of Christ. The promise given was that the seed of the woman should bruise the serpent's head. That was the first promise of God – the original promise. And when the Babe was born in Bethlehem the promise was carried out – the seed of the woman had arrived and He proceeded to bruise the serpent's head.

Another great promise was the one of which we are reminded in the third chapter of Acts, how Moses said, 'A prophet shall the Lord your God raise up unto you of your brethren, like unto me'; that was something to which the people under the old dispensation looked forward through the centuries. They called it 'the coming of the

Prophet'. That is what John the Baptist meant when he asked, 'Art thou he that should come?' They were looking for the Prophet, the Leader, they were waiting for someone who in a much greater sense than the delivery from Egypt, should lead them out of bondage. Moses said, in effect, I have led you out of the bondage of Egypt, I have taken you through this passage from Egypt to Canaan; but this is just a picture of another Prophet who shall come, who shall be greater than I; He will lead you out of the bondage of sin and the slavery and serfdom of iniquity. And here in that Babe of Bethlehem you have the Prophet, the Teacher, the Leader of the people, the One long expected and looked for.

In the same way it was promised that an offering would one day be given that would be sufficient to cover sin. In the Old Testament dispensation there is a great deal written about offerings and sacrifices, about the blood of bulls and of goats, about the offering of a lamb and so on. And yet it is all of a temporary nature. As the author of the Epistle to the Hebrews puts it, 'for it is not possible that the blood of bulls and goats should take away sins'. All is temporary. A great offering is necessary, a great final sacrifice that will really be efficacious, that will satisfy God. So there, running right through the Old Testament, you have the types and the shadows of a great offering that is ultimately to be made; and it is only in Christ that that offering was made. 'This Man' offered Himself once and for ever and has made the final sacrifice. In exactly the same way the Old Testament foretells that a great High Priest should come to represent us before God and commend us to God. You remember that Aaron was allowed into the 'holiest of all' once a year, and he went in fear and trembling, but here at last is the perfect High Priest, touched with the feeling of our infirmities, yet without sin. And having entered into the holiest of all with an offering and a sacrifice – His own blood – He represents us for ever and is continuing an eternal ministry, and so He 'can save to the uttermost all who come to God by him'.

Then there was the promise of a new Covenant. God made a covenant with man through Moses. It was a covenant of law which no one could keep. But God said through the prophet Jeremiah, 'A new covenant will I make with you', not like the old covenant – it will not be an external law, but I will write it in your hearts and minds – a new covenant. And where is the prophet that can mediate such a covenant? No man is worthy of it; even the angels are not sufficient. Here, however, in the Babe of Bethlehem is the Mediator of the New Covenant, the One who ultimately can give the Holy Spirit and who will put the law of God into our minds and hearts and give us life. He can take out the stony heart and give us a heart of flesh wherewith we can love Him.

Above everything else, however, there was the promise of the coming of a kingdom. Running right through the Old Testament is this idea of a great king who should come and reign, who should conquer all the enemies of the people and establish a kingdom of righteousness and of peace. And where is He to be found? He is to be found only in one place. There He is, a Babe in a manger in Bethlehem – the King of kings, the Lord of lords. There the wise men come and do their obeisance and offer their offerings, and they acknowledge Him at once. He has conquered all enemies, Satan, death, hell. Every evil thing is vanquished – He is King universal, almighty, and He shall reign from pole to pole and His kingdom shall be without end. The Son of God, the King everlasting.

Thus you see that God has fulfilled, has carried out, His every promise. Let me say a final word. *What do I deduce from this word of prophecy which is made more sure?* There are some obvious and inevitable deductions. Salvation clearly is in Christ and in Him alone. He has fulfilled all the promises. It is in Him that God is saving mankind. God promised to save mankind – here He does save mankind – Christ is the fulfiller of all promises. There is no other Saviour, there is no other way. 'There is none other name under heaven given among men, whereby we must be saved', says this self-same Peter in preaching after the Day of Pentecost. The Babe of Bethlehem fulfilled the promises. He is the only Saviour, the only way to God, the only hope of deliverance – He and He alone is the Saviour. He is the Prophet, He is the High Priest, He is the King.

What else? From all these things we may deduce this. That as His coming and all He did and said is a fulfilment of all that God has promised, so that very fact in itself is surely a guarantee that everything else that has been promised will be likewise fulfilled. Everything that had been prophesied and predicted and promised with respect to His first coming was carried out literally. But there is more to come. Peter is talking here about the Second Coming; and though the Second Coming may sound as strange to us today as His first coming did to the Old Testament people, let us work out this inevitable logic. Though they did not expect Him, He came; though many ridiculed the idea, it did not prevent His coming; and though these things may seem as impossible to us, what has happened is proof that they will also come to pass.

Lastly, let me sound a note of comfort and glory and joy. Because the birth of Christ, the Incarnation and all that followed is something that makes the word of prophecy more sure; something that tells me that God has kept His word and that God has fully carried out His own plans and promises and purposes on earth, then I draw this deduction: God's Word is something that I can always trust. There are great and precious promises, 'exceeding great and precious promises' in the Word; promises to you when you are taken ill; promises to you when you are bereaved; promises to the widow, promises to the fatherless and the orphan; promises to others who are passing through the deep waters; promises to those who are in anguish of soul and knowing not what to do or which way to turn; every conceivable condition in which you and I can ever be is covered by promises. My dear friends, believe them, take them to your heart, prove that God always honours His promises. He never fails to keep His Word; every promise He gives you is a promise you can believe and act upon. Therefore, when I read His Word again and I see promises such as 'I will never leave thee, nor forsake thee', 'Lo, I am with you alway', I will believe them, I will accept them. I say the coming of Christ substantiates all and proves all. He has given His word, and His word can be relied upon; and therefore I will take Him at His word. Blessed be God! 'Thanks be unto God for His unspeakable gift.' Thanks be unto God for the One in whom all the promises of God are yea and are amen without a doubt or a peradventure.

12

The Gleam in the Gloom

'We have also a more sure word of prophecy; whereunto
ye do well that ye take heed, as unto a light that shineth in
a dark place, until the day dawn, and the day star arise in
your hearts.'

Chapter 1:19

I want to deal especially with the exhortation in this verse –
'Whereunto ye do well that ye take heed, as unto a light that shineth
in a dark place, until the day dawn, and the day star arise in your
hearts.'

The Apostle in these words gives to the Christians to whom he was
writing what is, in a sense, his ultimate piece of advice. He was
anxious to help them and to comfort them and cheer them, and he
has been reminding them of the great centralities of their faith. Here
he comes to this 'word of prophecy' which, in reality, means the
whole of the Old Testament Scriptures. The prophecies are to be
found, as we have seen, right through the entire Old Testament, and
his exhortation to these Christians is that they should pay very great
attention to them – 'ye do well that ye take heed'. 'To take heed'
means, of course, to give careful, earnest, believing attention. Hold
on to the prophecies, says the Apostle in effect, study them diligently,
spend your time with them, be governed by them, meditate always
upon them.

That is not only his final advice to these people, it is at the same
time a most remarkable claim for the Bible, for the Word of God;
because the Apostle, you observe, gives a number of reasons why
they should take heed to this Word. We have already considered
some of them – may I just remind you of them. He reminded them
that it is the Word of God and not the word of man. The whole

prophecy of the Scripture is of no private interpretation. It does not originate or arise in the mind of man, for the prophecy came not in old time by the will of man, but holy men spake as they were moved, borne, carried along, driven, by the Holy Ghost. So that is one good reason for taking heed, for paying great and reverent attention to one's study of this Word. It is the Word of God and not the mere theories and ideas of man. Then we have seen, and particularly in our last study, that another very good reason for taking heed to this Word is that in so many respects it has already been fulfilled. We have 'the word of prophecy made more sure'. If you cannot believe and accept it as the Word of God because of its inherent character, look at its fulfilment, look at everything that has happened in the Incarnation; see there a verification of those detailed prophecies which have gone before. Very well, he argues, the inevitable logic is this, that because so much of what has been prophesied and predicted has been fulfilled, the remainder is certain to be verified also. So we pay heed to it because of what has already been fulfilled and verified. But also, he says, you must pay heed to it and pay attention to it because of what it says.

And now we come here to this further reason which the Apostle gives us for giving heed and paying attention. 'Whereunto ye do well that ye take heed' – why? – because it is like 'a light [or lamp] that shineth in a dark place, until the day dawn, and the day star arise in your hearts'. Now that is a very remarkable claim – a claim which, in other words, can be put like this: that the only light which any man has in this world is the light of Scripture. There is no other light, and Scripture to man in this world is exactly like a lamp shining in a dark cavern, in a gloomy, squalid, dark place. So he urges and exhorts them to pay great attention to this Word, to take heed and to consider it diligently, because it is indeed the one and only hope, and the one and only light which can possibly illumine the darkness. The Apostle is referring particularly, of course, to the Old Testament Scriptures, but what he says of the Old Testament is equally true of the New Testament and its prophecies and predictions. The claim is made by the Old Testament writers of a unique inspiration, and what we claim for the Old we claim for the New; so that the whole Bible as we have it is really covered by the Apostle's exhortation in these words.

Now as we come to look at this extraordinary claim there are some

two or three preliminary considerations which seem to me to be of
very great importance, and I cannot proceed to deal explicitly with
this statement without noting certain things. I would note, first of all,
the *realism of the Bible*. For myself, if I had no other reason for
believing this to be the Word of God, its realism would, for me, be
more than sufficient in and of itself. Whenever I read the Bible I feel it
is true, because it does not hesitate to state the facts. It states them
bluntly, it states them openly. I always tend to be more than
impatient with all the attempts to paint life in a romantic, rose-
coloured manner; one just knows that it is not true. It is a great thing
to have a Book that you can trust. It is a great thing to read a Book
which is not just out to pay compliments and to make you feel what a
fine and wonderful fellow you are. The Bible is realistic; it tells us the
truth about ourselves. It conforms to the demand that was made by
Oliver Cromwell of the man who was going to paint his portrait.
You remember that he wanted to be painted 'warts and all', nothing
must be left out. The Bible is exactly like that; it gives us a picture of
man and life and the world as they are. The amazing realism of the
Book! It exposes the weakness of its greatest heroes; it shows us the
blemishes in the most outstanding characters. It does not attempt to
give us a cheerful and rosy picture of life for the sake of pleasing us; it
is realistic and gives us a picture of life as it is.

And the second thing which of necessity follows from the first is
the *profundity of the biblical view of life*. It does not just look at life
on the surface; it does not merely look at it in certain aspects and
appearances. The Bible with its profound psychology is always
dealing with life beneath the surface. The Bible is never misled by
mere appearances. 'Man looketh on the outward appearance,' it
says. And how true that is, and that is the reason why man is so
constantly misled by appearances. Let me illustrate what I mean.
Imagine the difference between preaching on a text like this today,
and let us say forty years ago. There was a sense in which men would
have ridiculed a statement like this, with its description of 'a light in a
dark place', in 1906. How confident we were then; life appeared to
be successful, we seemed to be solving all our difficulties and to be
moving up from some primitive and undeveloped period to the
Edwardian period, to the twentieth century that was going to usher
in a paradise on earth. That was the view then, and, of course, a text
which talks about the world being a dark, squalid, gloomy place did

seem at that time to be utterly ridiculous to the savants. They talked then about the pessimism of the Bible and the pessimistic doctrine of sin. But it does not seem quite so much beside the mark today. Men have always tended to look at life on the surface, and it is because so many have done so that the world is optimistic and confident and is entirely misled. Now the Bible was equally certain in 1906 that this world is a gloomy, squalid, dark place; the Bible is not misled by superficial changes and appearances. It knows the heart of man. The Bible has always said that 'the human heart is desperately wicked and deceitful; who can know it?' It has gone on saying that in spite of the optimism of the Victorians – 'There is no peace, saith my God, to the wicked', and 'evil men . . . shall wax worse and worse'. It is because the Bible is profound that it does that; it is not misled by any changes on the surface. It sees things as they are and down in the hidden depths.

Perhaps another way of saying all this would be to say that the Bible always states the truth, and nothing so truly impresses anyone who reads the Bible at a time like this as the obvious truth of the biblical view of life and of the world and of man. For myself again I find it increasingly difficult to understand how it is that everyone is not being driven in these days to believe the Bible. Is not the blindness of mankind rather amazing? Here is the old Book that has gone on saying certain things throughout the centuries. It has been scoffed at and ridiculed: its pictures of life have been blasphemed by the optimistic and the confident. And yet we see today that what this old Book has always been saying is nothing but the literal and sober truth. How can man fail to believe it? Is there any book that explains life as it is at this moment save this Book? Its prophecies are being fulfilled round about us; its diagnosis is being verified before our very eyes. The truth of the Bible! How we should thank God whenever we pause to review our lives in this world that, to use again the language of this Apostle, 'we have not followed cunningly devised fables' throughout the year. How we should thank God that He has been pleased to give us a revelation of His view of life and of man and of the world, an understanding and insight, a diagnosis! How we should thank God that whenever we come back to it we come back to consider something that has been proved to be true! All these are reasons for paying very great heed unto it, for giving time to it and giving attention to it. Here surely are reasons for deciding as we face the future that we shall spend more of our time with this Book. If we are anxious to understand the times in which we live we must come back to this Book. We must study its whole view of life and history, of the destiny of the individual and of the race. We must take heed, and study it, and grasp its fundamental principles.

What then is its teaching? We can summarise it under very obvious headings as suggested by the Apostle himself. What is it the Bible tells us about life as we see it today? How do things stand at this moment, not only individually but nationally and internationally? What of the outlook, what of the times?

The first thing the Bible does is to get us to realise *the gloom of the world* – 'as unto a light that shineth in a dark place'. 'Dark' here means squalid, gloomy. Now that is the biblical definition and description of this world; it is a dark, gloomy and squalid place. This is something which is absolutely vital and essential to the under-standing of Christian doctrine. I have no doubt that there are some at any rate who say to themselves when they hear something like this – 'What a terribly depressing doctrine! I come to a place of worship in order to be cheered and comforted, and here I am being told that the world is a squalid, gloomy place. How depressing!' But actually this is a very interesting statement, and a most important one, for to have a right understanding of life in this world is one of the first steps in Christian doctrine. In the last analysis a man proclaims whether he is a Christian or not by his view of this world. Now there is no question as to the biblical view. You have but to read the Bible in almost any place to find that its view of the world is precisely what is said in this verse. Every attempt, therefore, to minimise the sin of the world and of mankind is to be un-Christian; every attempt to deny the biblical doctrine of man and sin and of the Fall, and of all the results of the Fall, is again to deny the Gospel itself. It is only those who accept the biblical diagnosis of the world who are likely to accept the remedy of the Bible for man. And what the Bible still tells us about the world is that it is full of woe, a place of darkness. Surely there never was a time when it should be easier for man to accept the biblical diagnosis than it is at this present time. Let us look at people, let us be realistic. Look at life, look at the world, take a view of the political and international situation. Is there anyone who would describe it as being bright and full of light and hope and optimism? Just look back across the past few years at the series of conferences that have been held, the attempts to produce order out of chaos resulting from the war, nationally and internationally. There is nothing but gloomy darkness – it is there, it is obvious. Take your newspaper, look at any article in any of the journals; they are admitting it and confessing it – it is there. Look at the social conditions, look at the increasing lawlessness and the increasing manifestation of sheer selfishness. See this in the increasing prevalence of strikes, official and unofficial. The spirit of lawlessness is abroad socially. Look at the constant tendency for people to argue that what they are inclined to do is the right thing to do – taking the law into their own hand, going slow, not doing their work, only doing the minimum.

Then look at the situation morally. Is it one about which we can be happy, which we can describe as being bright and hopeful and optimistic? Look at the overwhelming increase in divorces, look at the immorality and the vice, the increase in drinking and gambling and drug taking. Look at the money spent on these things. Look at men crowding into pleasure; hear them shouting in their excitement; see the things that appeal to men and women today in the midst of a world situation which is almost appalling. Look at the lightness and the frivolity, the failure even to be deeply concerned, the desire to have more and more pleasure, just to get away from it all and to enjoy ourselves for the hour and the moment. And then at the back of it all, and hovering over it all, the terrible possibilities associated with atomic power. We are all perfectly well aware of these things. That is our world as we see it at this moment. Is there any thinking person, I ask, who would still be foolish enough to dispute the description given of the world in this text? It is a dark place, a gloomy and squalid place. We seem to be travelling, as a race, through a dark cavern, where there is no light to be seen. We feel the stagnation and the chill, we hear the water dripping. There we are, travelling apparently endlessly through the cavern, hoping that we are going to come out at the other end, but seeing nothing but gloom, squalor and darkness, misery and wretchedness. 'In a dark place,' says the Apostle. Now that is the biblical view of life in this world right the way through. It says that this world, as the result of sin, is like that; and to refuse to recognise this fact or to attempt in any way to minimise it, is to deny one of the first principles of the Christian Gospel.

But let us go on to the second assertion of the Apostle. It is that

there is no light to be obtained anywhere, except in the Scriptures.
Now here, once more, is a proposition that is absolutely vital and
essential. There is no light in this dark, gloomy, squalid place apart
from the Gospel. I exhort you, says the Apostle here, to take heed to
the word of prophecy because it is like a lamp, a light in that dark
cavern – it is the only light. Now here again I am constrained to point
out that this second proposition, exactly like the first, has been
constantly disputed during the last hundred years. Men have
objected to this gloomy, biblical view of the world. They ridiculed
the conception of sin. Ah, they say, that was Puritanism – the fathers
believed in that kind of thing; but man is not like that. And they
disliked the preaching of sin and the call to repentance. Now in
exactly the same way men objected to this second statement that
there is no light whatsoever apart from the light of the Gospel and the
Scriptures. For myself, I find it very difficult to decide which of the
following two men has done greater dis-service in the past hundred
years or so to the Gospel and the message of the church – the man
who denied the biblical doctrine of sin, or the man who lost his head
in believing that social improvements and political enactments could
solve the problems of the human race. As I look back I thank God
that I, at any rate, shall not have to bear the responsibility of many
leaders in the Christian church who seemed to give the impression
that things which were really going to solve the problems of the
world were Acts of Parliament and the advance of Science. I always
feel that those who became immersed in the social Gospel, and the
so-called preacher-politicians, will have to bear a very great responsibility. How many of our fathers turned from the pure preaching of
the Gospel and the power of the Holy Spirit to action that can be
taken by man! How many began to worship the statesmen and the
politicians rather than God! All that has been characteristic of the
last hundred years. They believed there was a light there within the
grasp and reach of man himself. But the Bible has always said that
there is no light apart from the light which the Bible itself gives, and
here again we see the biblical doctrine being verified round and about
us and among us.

Let us look at the question quite directly and realistically. Is there
anything that can explain the cause of the present situation today
apart from the Bible? Read the books and the journals, listen to your
modern philosophers. They cannot explain the present situation. For

they have been brought up on a theory and view of life which believed in man's inherent capacity to save himself and his world. It was a theory which taught that by an inevitable evolutionary process man was already automatically advancing and progressing. And that by means of education and knowledge this advance would be still more accelerated. It was inevitable. Nothing could stop it, and the twentieth century was going to be the crowning end in man's story. Read the speeches of the great Victorian statesmen and you will find that everybody was confident that the world was going forward. If you believe that, how can you explain the world as it is today? How can you explain the two world wars? How can you explain the degeneracy and decadence of the period between the wars? It is inexplicable. There is no light on the cause of the state of the world apart from the light of the Bible.

And then when we come to consider the power to deal with and to change the situation, the same thing is still more noticeable. I never make a practice or custom of quoting modern popular writers who are not Christian, but there are times when their testimony is of value. I was reading recently a review of a book by a certain Lewis Mumford, called 'The Condition of Man' – a very able and remarkable book, a book that in many ways I believe it is right for Christian people to read and study for its description of our age and our period. And yet I must agree with the criticism passed upon that book by Dr Joad who, reviewing the book, said this: 'It is a wonderful diagnosis,' but (he said) 'you go and ask Mr Mumford for a solution and he just hasn't a solution to give.' He tells us we must organise, we must have conferences, we must try to federate. 'Well,' said Dr Joad, 'we can all say that and we are all saying that, but we all have a feeling within us that it is not going to work; it has all been tried before, but it does not seem to answer, it does not seem to be a solution.' Again, if you read the new book on philosophy by Bertrand Russell, you will find he says the same thing. He confesses quite frankly that philosophy cannot deal with the problems of mankind. He does not know the answer; he can describe the situation, but he cannot solve the problem. There is no hope and no light in the world today apart from that which is found in the Scriptures. Can conferences solve the problem? Can education make men live a decent and good life, can it give them a new understanding of the dignity of work, and of the sanctity of certain solemn vows?

We all know perfectly well that it has already failed to do so.

What hope is there for this dark, gloomy, squalid world today? The answer is the old answer of the apostle Peter here. There is no light apart from the light of Scripture and the light of prophecy. But, thank God, here there is a definite light. It is still like a lamp in a dark cavern, it is the only thing that gives us a glimmer of hope. What has it got to say? Let me summarise it in a few words.

It tells us that *the only hope of the world lies in God's action with respect to the world.* The hope of the world is not in anything inherent in man, neither does it lie in any action that man himself can take. The hope of the world is in God's programme and plan for the world. That, of course, is the great theme of prophecy – you see it in the Old Testament and in the New. What is it? Well, we can put it like this. It says that the world is what it is because of man's disobedience, because of man's sin, because of man's rebellion against God. It is the inevitable consequence of that. Do what we like and what we will, there is the fact. God said that if man sinned he would be visited with a curse; and the curse fell and is still upon us. This being so, what is there that can be done, what is it that can give us any light and hope? The only answer is that God is concerned, and God has outlined in this Book exactly and precisely what He proposes to do, and what He has been doing. God initiates His plan and purpose of salvation. In the Old Testament He starts the process. He takes a man like Abraham and turns him into a nation. That nation falls upon evil days and finds itself in Egypt. God brings them out and takes them into the promised land. He goes on with the process, and gives them judges and kings. Then He sends prophets to tell them that the Messiah, the Deliverer, is going to come. Look at the Old Testament, read it through. Is there any hope in the Old Testament dispensation, apart from the light of this prophecy, that the Messiah, the Deliverer, is going to come – Someone who will bear the sins of men, the One whom God is going to send into the world? What light would there have been in the ancient world were it not for the lamp of prophecy? It was the one thing that sustained these people. They could not understand the times, their enemies defeated them, everything seemed to be going wrong, but there was always a glimmer of light, the light of revelation, the light of the coming of the Messiah – the only hope! And then, 'in the fulness of the time', He came. Well, says someone, if that is right, are you correct in saying that this world is still a dark, squalid, dank and gloomy place? According to the New Testament that is still the state and the position. Although the Messiah, the Son of God, came into the world, the world rejected Him. He did not, by waving a magic wand, change the entire appearance and condition of the world. Not at all! The process of salvation is this. The Son of God has made the atonement, He has reconciled man to God, and what is happening in the process is that God is now calling a people out of the world. The world remains sinful and dark and gloomy, the world is still in the condition it was in before the Messiah came. You have only to look at life today and to read the Old Testament and you find you still have the same problems. Here is still rebellion against God, still the same falling to the same vices, still living on the animal level – exactly the same! It is still a kind of dark, dank, squalid, gloomy place; but this is what is happening – God is calling out a people, God is rescuing and redeeming His own out of it.

Not only that, the light is still there, the lamp is still shining. And what does it show? Here is the final statement. This process is to go on 'until the day dawn, and the day star arise in your hearts'. What does that mean? The biblical statement is that this process of calling men out of the world into the kingdom of God is to go on until Christ, the Messiah, the Son of God, shall again return to this world. He will come as a King. He will come as a Conqueror. He will take hold of everything that is sinful and evil and wrong and He will destroy it. Sin and evil will be removed, will be taken right out, and everything that emerges from, and belongs to, sin and evil will likewise be destroyed. So that everything that makes the world dark and gloomy and squalid will be taken away. And there shall be 'new heavens and a new earth, wherein dwelleth righteousness'.

But, says someone, I cannot believe all that, it sounds like a fairy tale. The only answer to the people who have that objection is very simple. You either believe the Gospel message or else you remain in utter gloom and darkness and hopelessness. There is no light apart from that. The world has been seeking for light ever since the beginning. That is the meaning of all the fluctuation in the rise and fall of great empires. There is a period of apparent light and then a dark era; and then another period of enlightenment and then another dark era. That is the story of the world; it remains dark, there is no light. But the light and lamp of prophecy still goes on shining. It tells us that God is intervening in the affairs and in the life of this world; that as certainly as He sent His Son as a Babe in Bethlehem, He will send Him again as a mighty King and Conqueror, and all enemies will be finally destroyed, and the world will be made perfect and good, and all who believe in Christ shall reign with Him and shall enjoy eternity in His Holy Presence. That is the biblical light.

Is that kind of statement light to you? Is that a message of hope to you? Are you seeing life like that as you look at the international position, as you look at our problems here at home, as you look at your own life, as you see the gloom and the darkness and the squalor? Do you thank God for the lamp of prophecy, for the light of Scripture, for the light of truth? That is what decides whether we are Christian or not – that we accept this biblical view of life and of the world. It means that we submit to Christ, that we accept His view of life and that, ceasing to look for light anywhere else, we look only unto Him. 'A light that shineth in a dark place, until the day dawn, and the day star arise in your hearts.'

13
False Prophets and their Teachings

'But there were false prophets also among the people,
even as there shall be false teachers among you, who
privily shall bring in damnable heresies, even denying the
Lord that bought them, and bring upon themselves swift
destruction. And many shall follow their pernicious
ways; by reason of whom the way of truth shall be evil
spoken of. And through covetousness shall they with
feigned words make merchandise of you: whose judgment now of a long time lingereth not, and their
damnation slumbereth not.'

Chapter 2:1–3

Of all the chapters which are to be found in the entire Bible, this
second chapter of the Second Epistle of Peter is among the most
terrible. For threatening, for warning, for the idea of doom and
disaster and destruction, there is nowhere in Holy Writ itself,
anything which surpasses this particular chapter. Now the Apostle
here is helping these Christian people to face the future – that is why
he writes like this. He is looking to the future and he is looking to
their future. He has already told them in the previous chapter that he,
now an old man, has been told by our Lord that he has not very long
to live. He knew the time of his departure was at hand, and here is
concerned about the flock that he is leaving behind. He looks into the
future, and here he prepares them for that future. He does so in what
is a thoroughly typical and characteristic New Testament manner.
He warns them; his message is primarily one of warning. He has
already in his letter reminded them of the great truths on which they
stand, impregnable truths which can never fail, and, having
reminded them, he now proceeds to warn them.

Now that is very typical and characteristic of the New Testament;
that is exactly its way always, everywhere, of preparing men and

women for the future. If one does not believe its central message, then there is no book on earth that is more depressing than the New Testament. If we do not accept that central core of the Gospel concerning our Lord and Saviour Jesus Christ and God's purpose through Him, then, I say, it is impossible to find any statement anywhere with respect to life that is so utterly pessimistic and depressing as the New Testament. That is the point of departure as we consider a chapter like this. This New Testament picture of life is that it is the scene of a mighty, terrible, spiritual struggle and conflict. Read anywhere in this Book, read the words of our Lord as recorded, read the sermons of the first preachers as you find them in the Acts of the Apostles, read any one of these Epistles you may choose, starting with the Epistle to the Romans, and going right on through to the Book of Revelation; everywhere you are given a sense of crisis, a sense of judgment. Life in this world, according to this Book (and the same thing is equally true of the Old Testament) is the scene of a mighty, terrible conflict between two vast powers. And they are both spiritual powers – God and all His forces on the one hand, and Satan, the Devil, and all his forces on the other. And, according to this Book, what happens in this life and in this world is that these two mighty powers and forces are both engaged in trying to win the suffrage of man, trying to attract man, trying to win man to their respective sides. This terrible, mighty conflict is going on. The result is that there is never any easy optimism to be found in the New Testament; there is no vague general superficiality. All along, its message is one of preparing us for this conflict, of enabling us to realise the nature of the conflict. It will not allow us to escape; indeed, its great theme is that the one great danger is that we allow the world in various ways to make us forget it.

The typical message of the New Testament is the one we find in this chapter – it is minatory, threatening, couched in words of warning. Indeed, the Bible, and the New Testament in particular, would contend that this world is not only dangerous for all men, but it is even dangerous for Christians, and these messages were written very specifically for Christian people. The argument of the New Testament put by Peter in this Epistle, as in his First Epistle, is that 'judgment begins at the house of God, and if the righteous scarcely be saved, where shall the ungodly and sinner appear?' That is his argument, that even for those who are Christian the world is a dangerous place because of the evil powers and forces that are arrayed against us, which are at all times trying to draw us away from God. Therefore, you Christian people, he says in effect, be on your guard, observe, take heed, watch and pray! These are his words, and they are the great watchword of the New Testament. In other words, he would have us realise and understand that the fight can be so hot and difficult that there will be times when even Christian people will begin to feel almost hopeless and will wonder what is taking place, and will be tempted to listen to the innuendoes of the Evil One.

Now the only way to guard against that, according to this Book, is that we should realise that this is going to happen, and that we should prepare ourselves for it. Knowing what is going to take place, we should be fully armed and therefore never be taken by surprise. But, and it is to this I want to refer particularly, the forces of evil that are arrayed against us are never quite so dangerous as when they speak to us as *false prophets*, or *false teachers*. The forces of evil have an almost endless variety of ways in which they deal with us; but according to the New Testament they are never quite so subtle and dangerous as when they appear amongst us as prophets, false prophets who would represent themselves as true and able to guide us and show us the way of deliverance and escape. Now you observe that Peter says here that this was the case in the Old Testament. The Bible has a term which is used in the New Testament to describe the Jews – 'the people' and Peter says, – 'There were false prophets also among the people [under the Old Dispensation], even as there shall be false teachers among you.' Now this is the situation as it applies to us. There were false prophets and teachers in the early church; there are still false prophets and teachers; and if we are to understand the times in which we live, the first thing we have to do is to realise that the greatest danger confronting us today is the danger that arises from false prophets and false teachers. Therefore there is nothing more important for us than that we should be clear in our minds as to how to differentiate between the true and the false.

There is no need to describe the difficult world situation in which we find ourselves – everybody is aware of it. We are aware of difficulties and problems. The whole question for us is how we are to face what is happening and going to happen. Now the greatest of all dangers on that particular point is the danger that arises from false teachers and prophets, those who would come to us apparently in the name of God, and yet are nothing but the messengers of Satan. That is the thing that Peter tells these first Christians they must be aware of – they must be careful to observe and to act in this matter of discrimination. Today we are confronted by precisely the same condition. Look at the multiplicity of advice being offered, look at the theories being propagated, look at all the solutions that are being offered, and all the clever people that are writing and telling us what ought to be done. The whole art of life is to be able to discriminate between the true and the false, and then to reject the false utterly and to cleave to that which alone is ultimately true. In view of this let us listen to the help and advice that is given to us here by the Apostle, for he tells us of a way in which we can very clearly differentiate between the true prophet and the false. What has he to say about it?

Let us consider first of all the negative tests which he suggests to us. There are certain wrong ways of estimating the truth or falsity of a prophet and his teaching. What are these? Well, the first wrong way of deciding whether a teaching is true or not is to *allow its newness or its modernity to determine whether it is right or not*. There is no need to stay with this because it is the most obvious of all the fallacies, and yet there are people who are obviously victims of it. It is another way of saying, 'Anything that is new must be right.' This fatal belief in inevitable advance – just taking it for granted that because we are living in the twentieth century we must, in these matters, know something which men living in the last century could not – how common an assumption it is! The New Testament always gives the lie direct to this particular fallacy. Peter puts it like this: 'There were false prophets also among the people, even as there shall be false teachers among you.' That is New Testament philosophy of history – as there were, even so there shall be. In other words, the world remains the same, and there is nothing so pathetic as the belief that because we are living in the twentieth century we are in a different world from the world inhabited by our forefathers. The answer of the Bible is that since the fall of man this world has remained exactly and precisely the same. Of course there are superficial changes, but they are utterly irrelevant. Men dress in a different way, men travel in a different way, but we are not discussing superficialities, we are discussing man's problems with respect to life. And when you look at it in that way you find at once that the world remains exactly the same. There were false prophets, and there will be. So that if we fondly imagine because we are living in the twentieth century that we are in a superior position to face the problems of life, then we are doomed to failure and disaster. The problem is still the same. Man is still tempted by the Devil not to believe in God and not to obey God – that has been going on ever since the fall of man and it is the central problem now. I trust therefore that there is no one who still harbours the particularly fatuous and futile fallacy that because we live at this particular moment, and because of recent new ideas, we are in some specially advantageous position to meet the problems and battles of life.

The second test with respect to the wrong way of testing the false prophets is *the fallacy of always assuming that if the teaching is popular it must be right.* 'Many shall follow their pernicious ways,' says Peter. False teachers are going to arise amongst you, he says, and they will attract a crowd – 'many shall follow their pernicious ways'. Surely this fallacy hardly merits any prolonged attention, but I have to refer to it because one still hears the glib phrases, 'Everybody believes it', or to put it negatively, 'No one any longer believes the Bible; no cultured, educated person believes; look at the masses outside the church.' Therefore it is assumed that Christianity must be wrong because the crowd is always right! That position is so childish and so foolish that it is hardly worthy of serious consideration; but

> *Truth for ever on the scaffold,*
> *Wrong for ever on the throne*

is as true for our age as for any time in the history of the world. 'Many shall follow their pernicious ways.' What is the lesson of the New Testament and of the Bible on this matter? Go back to the Flood for an answer – you will find the whole world was wrong and only eight people right. The many were against God at the time of the Flood; only eight people were saved. Is a thing true because everybody says and believes it? Then go on to the story of Sodom and Gomorrah – what do you find? Exactly the same thing; the many, the mass, were all on the wrong side. Lot and his family alone were rescued. That is the teaching of the Bible. It has always taught the doctrine of the remnant – the many, the popular, the crowd all going in the wrong direction and just the small remnant remaining true. To me one of the saddest features, even of modern religious life, is the tendency to estimate truth in terms of results, popularity, crowds, movements. It is an utter denial of the biblical teaching. You cannot estimate spiritual truth by polls; the counting of heads is not a biblical way of discovering whether teaching is right or wrong. You do not take a census and ask people to fill in certain details. 'To the law and the testimony'! Popularity and numbers are a very false test of truth.

But let me go on to something which is still more serious. *The fact that the message is taught even by the church is no guarantee that it is true.* Listen. 'There were false prophets also.' Where? In the world, in the nation, outside Israel? No, amongst 'the people' – even as there 'shall be false teachers'. Where? In the world, in the unbelievers outside the church? Not at all! 'Among you.' Now this is not an isolated text. If you read the twentieth chapter of the Acts of the Apostles you see Paul bidding farewell to the leaders of the church at Ephesus. He tells them exactly the same thing. There is scarcely a New Testament Epistle that does not warn the Christians against false teachers amongst themselves in the church. The mere fact that a message is preached in and by the church is no guarantee that it is true. There are such things as false professors in the church, false Christians, people who imagine they are Christian but who are not Christian and therefore preach and teach a false message. This, I say, is the most serious matter of all, and here we have to be particularly wary at the present time.

For I think you will agree that the prevailing tendency is not to talk about and write about the truth itself. The whole emphasis at the moment is that we should all be getting together and forming great organisations. The concern is not so much as to the truth of the message, but to gather ourselves together into one great community. The tendency today is to minimise truth in favour of organisation, and men are telling us with unwearied reiteration that the greatest tragedy of the world is the disunited church. But the tragedy, the greatest tragedy, as I understand the New Testament, is not the disunity of the church, is not the fact that the church is divided into groups and denominations, is not that we are not all in one organisation, but that all the sections are preaching a false message and there has been a departure from the truth of God as it is in Christ Jesus. If we were all brought together and formed into one organisation, that is no guarantee that the message preached would be true. There are false teachers; there were in the Old Testament and there are and always have been in the church. There is nothing quite so sad and pathetic as the way in which certain church members seem to think that whatever is preached in the denomination to which they belong must be right; and yet the whole time the New Testament tells us that this is no proof of truth. We cannot assume that any man that stands up in the church is a true prophet. He may be a false teacher and prophet. So that if we glibly assume that because the 'church'is preaching something it must be right, we are in the greatest danger possible of being led by false prophets. Belief in the infallibility of the 'church' is not confined, unfortunately, to Roman Catholics.

Those are the wrong tests. How do we test in a positive manner? Peter says, Go to the Bible! Consider the marks of the false prophet. Their characteristics are all there and are always the same. Read them in the New Testament. See them also in the subsequent history of the Christian church. The type never varies or changes. What are these characteristics? The first, says Peter, is that he *has not been called* – he has not been called by God. He is a false prophet, not only false in what he teaches, but false in his appointment. He is no prophet at all. You notice here again that he is obviously contrasting this type of individual with the kind of prophet he has been describing in the previous chapter. There, he says of the true prophet something like this: 'Knowing this first, that no prophecy of the Scripture is of any human origin [it is not of private interpretation or theory or idea] for prophecy came not in old time by the will of man, but holy men of God spake as they were moved by the Holy Ghost.' There is the true prophet. He does not spin out his own theories or elaborate his own ideas. He is a man who does not will to speak or decide to speak; he is a man taken hold of by the Holy Spirit. He is given a message, he is moved, carried along in stating it. 'But there were false prophets also among the people, even as there shall be false teachers among you.' What is the characteristic of the false prophet? First of all – he has not been called. He is unlike the true prophet. The false prophet speaks of his own will; he elaborates his own ideas. He has no real authority, he has no ultimate sanction. In other words, the false prophet is always a man who is giving expression to his own theories and ideas.

In saying that, I am describing the last hundred years. How true it is! Think how philosophies have replaced revelation during that period. What is philosophy? Human ideas! On the other hand to believe in revelation is to say, I believe the Word of God. But that has been put on one side, and man's philosophy is what has been popular – human ideas. Let me mention some of them. Take for example the theory of the evolution of man. We are told that our first fathers were apes. Is there any proof of that? It is nothing but pure theory, yet it has been accepted, it has been taken as an utterly established fact. There isn't a vestige of proof behind it. That is what the false prophet always does; he evolves a theory and then presents it as fact. He has no sanction or authority – that is why he is false.

What else? Take psychology. Men in the mass believe that psychology has utterly exploded Christianity and religion. What is it? Nothing but a theory. Look at the different schools of psychology, how they cancel one another out. And yet on these mere theories and suppositions we are asked to reject the Bible and disbelieve the Gospel. This wonderful theory states that by application of psychology we can rid ourselves of all personal ills and all national and international ills; and yet, alas! we often find that the very people who propagate this theory, themselves fall victims to the very things they claim to cure. And then, what of the statements that have so often been made, that miracles are impossible, statements given by many as a reason for not believing the New Testament? Have they ever been proved? Take again all the talk about comparative religions, and the confident claims of so-called assured results of the higher criticism, so many of which have been destroyed by archaeologists. It has all been theory; and in the name of these theories and suppositions, and without any divine sanction and authority, men have been denying the Gospel, and have given themselves to a belief in these theories. But what makes it still more false is that, often, all that kind of teaching has been given in terms of this Book. Surely the ultimate difference between the true prophet and the false one is this, that the true prophet preaches the message of the Bible, and the other preaches what he thinks the Bible ought to be saying and teaching. That is the first characteristic of the false prophet; he is not called, he has no real authority and sanction.

In the second place, the *false prophet has not a true message*. What are the characteristics of his message? Well, says Peter, many shall follow their pernicious ways, and 'through covetousness shall they with feigned words' – clever words, smooth and easy words – 'make merchandise of you.' That is their teaching. The second characteristic of the false prophet is that he is always comforting. He never criticises, never makes us feel uncomfortable. He always tries to say what we want him to say. And then, says Peter, he is also covetous; he always desires popular applause. Also, he comes 'with feigned words'. He never makes you feel you are a sinner, he never makes you feel you are lost, he never makes you hate yourself and the sin that is in you. He is always telling you in one way or other that you are wonderful, if only you were given decent circumstances. 'Feigned words'!

But, still more seriously, the ultimate way of testing a message is this. The false prophet and teacher denies the Lord that has bought him – 'denying the Lord that bought them' and there are more ways than one of doing this. Sometimes they deny the Lord that has bought them by just leaving Him out altogether. They purport to give a Christian message, and yet the name of Christ is never mentioned. God is mentioned, but Christ the Lord is not. They deny Him by leaving Him out. Sometimes they deny Him by not making Him absolutely central, vital and essential. If Christ is not in the centre, He is being denied. He is either in the centre or He is nowhere. Again, they may deny Him by denying His Person, by regarding Him as a man only, as a great teacher, a wonderful example, but denying His Deity – denying Him as God-Man, the 'theanthropos', in all the glory and fulness of His blessed Person. Or they deny Him most of all and most seriously by denying His atoning work, by denying the fact that if He had not gone to the cross every man would remain doomed and under the wrath of God, by denying that this is the only way to God, by failing to see themselves as hopeless, damned sinners who are only saved because He bore their sins in His own body on the cross – denying the centrality of the cross! 'denying the Lord that bought them'. Whatever teaching a man may have to offer to you, if the Christ on Calvary's Cross is not the central pivot at the heart of it, I say he is a false prophet and a false teacher. And no one can give hope, either to the individual or to the world today, who is not centred absolutely upon that atonement. He is a false prophet and teacher.

But lastly, according to Peter, false prophets and teachers *are false in their lives and living*. They haven't a true calling, they haven't a true message; neither have they a true way of living – a true life. And many shall follow their 'pernicious ways', or if you prefer the translation of the margin, their 'lascivious ways'. That is always true; false teaching always leads to false living.

During the last hundred years we have been told that the evangelical Gospel was adequate for giving men a personal experience, but that it did not deal with ethics, it did not deal with social conditions. It brought men to a personal conversion but it did not really uplift the masses and the race. So they began to preach a so-called ethical Gospel. What has it led to? It always has the same effect. Look at the state of society in these days, with all its immorality and vice. If the message is wrong, the life will always be wrong. A false view of life always leads to wrong living and a lower ethical standard, even though you preach ethics. You cannot separate these things. Holiness must never be separated from the Cross. You cannot put the New Testament doctrine into compartments and have a special movement for each. They all go together. There is no holiness unless it comes from the crucified Christ. The doctrines of life are inseparable.

Very well, there I have brought you face to face with some of the characteristics of the false prophet and teacher. If these tests had been applied as diligently as they should have been during the last hundred years, would the Christian church be as she is today? Would society be as it is today? Would the world be as it is today? Oh, the tragedy of forgetting the tests of God's Word and elaborating our own superficial so-called philosophical tests! We should ask ourselves some questions, and I suggest to you that they are these. First, what is my view of the world today and of its future? How do I view it? Do I view history in the light of this Book or in the light of popular philosophies? Do I see this world as the seat of a mighty spiritual conflict? Do I see it heading up to an ultimate cataclysmic crisis, the time of it unknown but the fact inevitable? The second vital question is this – What is Christ to me? Where does He come into my scheme of things? Is He absolutely vital? Am I depending utterly upon Him? Do I say with honesty, 'Simply to Thy cross I cling', and 'Helpless, look to Thee for grace'? Have I an ever-deepening view of the holiness of God and of my own sinfulness as I compare myself with what I was a year ago? Can I honestly say that I see the holiness of God more than I have ever done before, and my own sinfulness more deeply than I have ever done before? Am I therefore driven more and more back to Him, the Lord that bought me, and who will hold me until ultimately He presents me perfect, spotless, without blame and blemish in the presence of God with exceeding joy?

14
False Teaching and its Consequences

'But there were false prophets also among the people, even
as there shall be false teachers among you, who privily
shall bring in damnable heresies, even denying the Lord
that bought them, and bring upon themselves swift
destruction. And many shall follow their pernicious ways;
by reason of whom the way of truth shall be evil spoken of.
And through covetousness shall they with feigned words
make merchandise of you: whose judgment now of a long
time lingereth not, and their damnation slumbereth not.'

Chapter 2:1–3

This chapter deals, as we are reminded by the third verse, with the
whole subject of the havoc wrought in the Christian church by false
teaching concerning the nature of the Gospel. I am ready to admit
that I approach this chapter once more with a good deal of
disinclination. It is, as I think all must agree, one of the most terrible
and terrifying chapters in the entire Bible. Anyone who enjoys
reading a chapter like this must surely be abnormal. It is a chapter
which has much in it that is unsavoury and unpleasant; and I say, left
to one's own choice, and one's own likes and dislikes, this is the kind
of chapter that one would avoid. I say that in order that we may
remind one another in passing of the importance of taking the whole
Bible, and the importance of being systematic in our reading and
studying of the Bible. Anyone who does not follow a system of Bible
reading which takes one through the whole Bible is certain never to
read a chapter like this. People who only read their so-called
favourite chapters, and who pick out the sections that they like and
which help them, would never spend much time on this second
chapter of the second Epistle of Peter. And yet we must remember

that if we believe at all in the doctrine of the inspiration of Scripture, this chapter is as inspired as is the eighth of Romans or the third of John, or any one of our favourite Psalms. It is the Word of God, and we are to take and consider the whole Word of God. We must take those parts which do not appeal to our natural man and realise that they have their lessons for us which are as definite and as certain as those other parts which make a greater natural appeal to us. I say, therefore, that this chapter has to be faced; and this is perhaps another justification for expository teaching – preaching which is concerned to expound the Word of God and not merely to express the ideas of the preacher, preaching which is not merely topical and intended to suit the popular palate and conditions prevailing at the moment. This shows us the importance of a systematic consideration of the Word of God and its message.

Now here, I say, we are driven to this because of the very fact that Peter ever wrote the chapter and wrote it at such length. He seemed to be concerned to make his point so clear that he elaborated it and gave all these grim and unsavoury details in describing the kind of person whom he is considering. Peter felt that this subject was of such vital importance that he could not possibly take anything for granted. You will remember that the Epistle of Jude bears a very striking resemblance to this chapter. There are certain verses which are almost identical, and the authorities have debated throughout the centuries as to which was dependent upon the other. That really does not matter – the point is that both realised the importance of the subject. You will find similar warnings and exhortations in the other Epistles, and in the Book of Revelation in particular. You will find it also in the first Epistle of John. The Apostles were tremendously concerned about this matter, and they left nothing undone in their endeavour to warn these first Christians about preserving the purity of the faith and 'contending for the faith that had once and for ever been committed to them' – to defend it and to make certain that it should never become adulterated. That is the theme.

There is nothing that is more important at the present time than for us to consider again very carefully everything that the Apostle has to say here. I hinted in the previous chapter that it would surely be very difficult to find a more accurate and perfect description in detail of the world as it is today, and of the church in the world, than that which you find in this very chapter. Personally I know of no more perfect summary of the last hundred years than what you find here. Here is a picture, in other words, of a world steeped in godlessness immorality, vice, looseness and lawlessness. That is the picture. You see here the kind of moral conditions prevailing in the history of the world at the time of the flood, in Sodom and Gomorrah, at the time when our Lord came into this world, and subsequently in the so called Dark Ages. Does it not seem evident and obvious that we are descending into such a condition at the present time, if we have not already made the descent? Look at the world around and about us. Look at its apostasy from God, its living to the flesh and that which is foul and ugly, and, especially, all the lawlessness that is characterising the life of mankind at this present time. Here is the church, hesitant, doubtful, seemingly uncertain of her own word and message, afraid, concerned about herself and her own future as an organisation, and yet apparently impotent as she faces this world – impotent in the sense of having no message of condemnation and no call to repentance and a return to God in Christ. Now that is the situation.

It seems to me that we have outlined here the very condition in which we find ourselves at this present time. Put quite simply and bluntly, you and I, my friends, find ourselves living in one of the really difficult periods, indeed in one of the most difficult periods in the whole history of the church. Contrast our position today with that of our fathers, even going back twenty to thirty years: contrast it with those who lived sixty or seventy years ago. Then the whole life of the country was different; Christianity and religion were in a sense popular; men and women gathered together in the House of God and Christian teaching influenced the whole life of the nation and even the life of Parliaments. Then the Gospel of Christ really did count, and was at any rate respected even by those who did not practise it. But we no longer live in such a day and period. The masses have turned their backs upon the Gospel and we find ourselves a comparatively small remnant facing such a world. Now that is the situation. It is a time of exceptional difficulty. It is not an easy thing to be a Christian today. It never has been, but it is unusually difficult at a time like this. And perhaps the difficulty that presents itself to us above every other difficulty is that of having to make a stand, even within the church herself, for that which we believe to be the real and true Gospel. It becomes difficult for this reason. The whole tendency at the present time is for men to speak in this way. 'Here,' they say, 'is your world as you have described it. Christian people have become a small company. Now surely the one thing that matters above everything else at a time like this is that we should all stand together.'

I have referred to the Ecumenical Movement, this idea of a great world church. The argument for it is that because we are small in number we must sink all individual differences and distinctions and preferences. It is a time, we are told, when we should close the ranks, when we should avoid being over-punctilious, when we should avoid especially the tendency to insist that everyone should dot his i's and cross his t's exactly as we do. We are told that we should not be arguing about differences in teaching and doctrine. 'Let all who claim the name of Christian, however vaguely, stand together and present a united front' – that is the argument that one hears so constantly. In such a situation it is not easy to contend for the faith, it is not an easy thing to fight for that which you believe to be the Gospel and which alone you believe to be the Gospel. It is a very difficult thing at such a time to stand for truth, and to say that truth matters even more than unity, and that over and above this question of numbers and a common stand, is the purity of the faith and an honest declaration of the Word of God as we are given to see it.

Now that is in a sense the very problem with which Peter deals here. His whole argument is to the effect that, if we are to do what God would have us do, we must set truth ever in the first position, and that even though we may be reduced to a handful we must still contend for the faith. For our one and only concern must be for 'the truth once and for ever delivered to the saints'. Here he tells us how that is to be done. He gives us great encouragement. Thank God for it, but before we can go on to that encouragement we must again return to Peter's own analysis of this false teaching – the false teaching in the Old Testament times and the false teaching of the new era. The first thing we have to do is to recognise the true and the false. We considered that in general in the preceding chapter, but I want to consider it further and in greater detail now. I say once more that I would prefer to teach the Gospel in a more positive manner. But it is not for the preacher to choose his text. It is for him to expound the Word of God; and as Peter goes on reiterating these statements, it is our business, if we are to be honest expositors, to follow in his footsteps.

According to Peter, the first thing we have to determine and realise, is *the cause of this condition*. What is it that leads to the world becoming so immoral and godless and foul? What is it that leads to this even within the church herself at times? What is it, in other words, that leads to a godless world and to apostasy in the church? Why is the world as it is? Why is the church as she is today? What is the matter? Why is there this lack of life and power and vigour in the Christian church as she faces the world today? Well, according to the Apostle, the answer is that it is always due to false teaching. The cause of the trouble is invariably a failure to conform to the law and the testimony and the teaching of God. Now that, according to Peter, is not a matter to be deduced; it is a fact. And he proves it by producing evidence from history. You remember his evidence. He takes first of all the case of the Flood. You remember the descriptions that are given of the world immediately before the Flood – the godlessness and the licence, the utter moral confusion. Go back to the Book of Genesis and read the account of that world for yourself. The world was so full of terrible things that God destroyed it by the Flood – God judged and condemned it. But the question is, What was it that brought the world into such a state? What was it that led to such a condition? There is only one answer to the question; mankind had departed and had fallen away from God and from his teaching. God had told man how he was to live. God had always given man a law, but men had flouted the law of God, men had turned their backs upon God, men had laughed at the name and thought and suggestion of God. It was because they had turned their backs upon God and were living according to their own ideas that the world ever entered into that state which produced the Flood by way of judgment. Apostasy from God and consequent lawlessness were the causes that led to the Flood.

Then Peter hurried on to his second instance and illustration. I need not remind you of the unsavoury details in connection with the Cities of the Plain. Read chapters 18 and 19 of the Book of Genesis and you will find all about them – the terrible moral pollution, the ugliness and the foulness of the life of those cities. Yes, but I ask again, What was the cause of it? And again the answer is exactly the same. These were people who had turned their backs upon God; they had forsaken the teaching, they had given up the way of the law and were living according to their own desires and lusts. Still the same answer! Or take any other period of moral degradation in the history of the Children of Israel and you will always find it is the same explanation. Whenever they turn from God and His teaching, they always sink morally to the very dregs and to the very depths. And if you take the story of the early church you will find the same sequence there. As soon as they began to depart from the pure Gospel of Christ it showed itself in their moral living and in their daily life. And as you take the subsequent history of the church you will always find exactly the same thing.

What of our age and generation? Can anyone dispute that this is still the same? There is only one explanation of the state of society in this country today, and the state of the whole world, and it is that mankind during the last hundred years has been turning its back upon God. Whether we like it or not, it is an invariable rule. It always follows, as the night follows the day; when men cease to worship God and to live by this Book and to believe the Gospel of Christ, down goes morality and everything good with it. Though you may have the best education system the world has ever known, though you may have passed Acts of Parliament designed to deal with moral and social conditions, though you may have catered for every eventuality, when God is forgotten, you immediately return to a condition such as obtained at the time of the Flood and in Sodom and Gomorrah, and which obtains largely even at this time. Whether we like it or not, that is the solid and solemn fact. It is the turning away from the pure doctrine that ultimately leads to moral, political, social and economic chaos.

But it is interesting to observe how this process of decline and of degradation generally takes place in stages. That is where this whole teaching is so important, because of the subtlety of the process. It never happens suddenly. You never get the result following immediately after men and women have started turning away from God. There are always steps and stages. That notable professor of theology, Emil Brunner of Switzerland, has I think, put this in a perfect way when he says that there are generally three stages. The grandfather believed the Gospel and he lived a life that was in conformity with that teaching. The son ceased to believe the Gospel but he still conducted his life according to the ideas of morality that were given to him by his father. The third generation ceases to believe not only in the Gospel but also in the moral and ethical view of life based upon and derived from the Gospel. By today you and I are surrounded by the grandchildren of the Victorian grandfathers; and by today we have found that morality cannot exist apart from the Gospel. The very category of morality is being denied today. But the deterioration takes time to take effect.

Then surely another very interesting point about this whole question is *the relationship between false teaching and loose living.* From the standpoint of mere mechanics it is very difficult at times to see which of the two comes first. False teaching always leads to false living; yes, but false living always tends to produce false teaching. Let me put it like this. We are told here by Peter in prophecy that 'many' shall follow their pernicious or 'lascivious' ways. Why is it that the many are always so ready to listen to false teaching? What has made man during the last hundred years so ready to believe the theory put forward by Charles Darwin as though it were a solemn fact? Why is man so ready to read articles or reports of sermons in which someone has denied the miraculous and the supernatural? Why is it that the many are always ready to follow various false teachings? Surely there is only one adequate answer to that question. It is because the false teaching makes it easier for them to live the kind of life they want to live. It is because, if they can get rid of God and the miracles and the supernatural, they will be able to live the life they want to live without being condemned by their conscience. It is, in a sense, the immoral life that calls for wrong teaching. There is a strange inter-action between these things – it is the apostate state of man that always encourages false teaching. The false teaching, in other words, panders to man as he is fallen from God; and man welcomes the teaching because it excuses the life that he lives.

There then we see the cause of the condition; and unless we are aware of the fact that it is this falling away from God that accounts for our world as it is today, we have not even begun to understand the modern situation. Now having seen that, let us go on.

How is all this to be avoided? Here Peter gives us very detailed instructions. The thing we have to do is to realise the character of false teaching. We must examine it, we must sift it, and investigate it, and this is the thing that so many find difficult. It is not an easy thing for a man to be different from others, it is not an easy thing to stand on your own against the vast majority of people. Man by instinct and by nature does not like to be the odd man out. It is very much easier to go with the crowd, and to conform to all that is popular. But that is the very thing against which the Bible warns us. We may have to be like Noah, standing alone and having the whole world laughing at us. We may have to be like Lot in Sodom. We may have to stand as some of those first Christians had to stand. We may have to stand as some of the Protestant Fathers had to stand; we may even have the church condemning us. No, it is not easy, and yet it is the very thing which we are exhorted to do. We must not believe everything we hear, we must examine it by the Word of God. We must be contenders for the faith; not that we appoint ourselves as spiritual detectives, but that we realise the importance of standing for the truth. How can we do this? How can we recognise that which is false? Here are some details that fill out the principles already laid down. Here are some of the general points.

It is right to observe that false teaching is always subtle. Peter puts it like this – 'There were false prophets also among the people, even as there shall be false teachers among you, who privily shall bring in damnable heresies.' That word 'privily' is very important – that is how he emphasises the subtlety of it. Now as we go into these details it is important that we should bear in mind what has been happening during the last hundred years. The subtlety of the process is emphasised by the apostle. Do not expect, he says in effect, that the false teachers will suddenly stand among you and say, 'I am a false teacher and I am going to say something that is entirely opposed to anything you have ever heard.' On the contrary – 'privily' – in a very subtle manner. See, they will say, I am a preacher of the Gospel, I am one of you and I am going to preach the Gospel to you. They will even use the language of the Gospel but they will give a different meaning to it. That has been happening during the past century. Men have called Christ Saviour, but they have meant by Saviour 'a Great Example'. They have used the very terminology of the New Testament, but they have evacuated the meaning of the New Testament terms. That is where the whole danger comes in. The terms are still used and employed, but they confuse the meaning in this insinuating and subtle manner. The poison of error and heresy has been introduced – 'privily' – using the language but giving it a different meaning.

Another characteristic of this procedure is, according to Peter, *that it is irreverent.* Reference to this is made in verses 10 and 11 –

'presumptuous', 'self-willed'. There he is describing partly the irreverent attitude of these false teachers towards the truth. Instead of preaching the Bible as the Word of God with reverence, instead of using this as a unique Book which in a sense a man must only preach with humility, instead of preaching the Person of the Lord as realising His unique Deity, these false teachers preach these things without a spirit of reverence. They deny that this is an entirely unique Book, and they do not hesitate to use human language with respect to it. They do not hesitate to dismiss and expurgate certain parts of it. They speak of our Lord as but a man. There is an absence of reverence, there is an absence of a godly approach. There is little of the respect and awe which these things deserve. 'Irreverence', says Peter. And again, let me remind you of the past hundred years and the story of the so-called higher criticism.

But not only that, the Apostle tells us that *this kind of teaching is dishonest* − 'Which have forsaken the right way, and are gone astray.' These false teachers are going to be dishonest, says Peter; and I am not exaggerating when I suggest that this very prophecy of Peter has often been fulfilled during the last hundred years. There have been men who have taken ordination vows in which they have said they believe this to be the Word of God, and the unique Word of God, and have then proceeded to say it is not the Word of God. They have sometimes promised under oath and vow that they will not engage in certain practices that had been condemned by their own church, and they then proceed to do those very things. Can such conduct be described in any language save that of dishonesty?

Those are some of the general characteristics of the false prophets and false teaching.

But let me go on to a more particular question, to a more detailed analysis of the teaching itself. What are the characteristics of the teaching? Well, according to Peter, *it always takes a superficial view of sin and evil*. To go back again to verses 10 and 11, 'presumptuous are they, self-willed', 'they are not afraid to speak evil of dignities. Whereas angels, which are greater in power and might, bring no railing accusation against them before the Lord.' Now what does it mean to speak evil of dignities? There can be no doubt that he is referring to the way in which these teachers speak of evil powers, about the Devil and about the forces of hell and evil. He says that even the angels do not bring railing accusation against them, but these people do. Isn't it amazing to notice how accurately Scripture has prophesied what has happened. Have you observed the way in which men have joked about the Devil during the last hundred years? The Bible takes the Devil terribly seriously, but the Devil has become a joke in the last century. The Bible takes evil spirits and evil powers desperately seriously. 'We wrestle not against flesh and blood, but against principalities, against powers, against the rulers of the darkness of this world, against spiritual wickedness in high places.' But men today ridicule evil powers and spirits. The Devil has been dismissed, he is nothing but a joke – 'speaking evil of dignities'. Let us beware, my friends, lest we allow the world in its irreverence to influence us. False teachers always take an inadequate view of sin and evil; indeed, for a hundred years or more men have not really believed in sin. They have recognised certain laxities which they claim can be corrected by education and culture.

The other characteristic of the false teaching is that *it is empty* – see verses 17–19. 'These are wells without water'; in other words, the false teaching has no light, has no knowledge, has no real instruction. It does not give us any power, it therefore has no effect upon life. Let me put it in the form of a challenge. Think of all the books that have been written in the last century criticising the Bible. Think of the new theology of which we have heard so much – the new teaching that was going to correct these ancient myths and these mere magical beliefs, the new gospel that was going to be a social gospel, an ethical gospel, this marvellous new higher criticism of the Bible that was going to abstract the truth, and that was going to lead to such amazing results. Let us ask simply, What has it led to? What do we know about truth that our great-great-grandfathers did not know? How much better is our world? What has it really produced? Well, it is interesting to note that the latest scholarship with respect to the Old Testament is now telling us that we must no longer spend our whole time on criticism; we must now try to get at the ethical teaching and the message of the Old Testament. The very authorities themselves are now granting that the higher criticism has largely played itself out, and that we must get back to the message of the Bible. 'Wells without water, clouds that are carried with a tempest.' Think of the wells that men have been sinking in the last hundred years; look at names like Wellhausen and others and the marvels they were going to produce. They have led to nothing but a spiritual barrenness, and two world wars, 'wells without water, clouds carried with a tempest.' They never work – 'they promise liberty but they themselves are the servants of corruption. They are but 'great swelling words of vanity' which lead to nothing whatsoever but corruption and despair.

So we are to avoid this false teaching – we are to recognise it for what it is and avoid it. Why should we do so? 'Because,' says Peter, it is 'damnable' – they are 'destructive heresies'. They have the elements of destruction within themselves, they destroy the very men who believe them, and they are going to lead to still more terrible destruction.

But perhaps the most vital reason of all why we should avoid such teaching is that it *brings the truth into disrepute*. Because of whom, says Peter, 'the way of truth shall be evil spoken of'. Alas and alack, that it has been so often men who have claimed the name of Christian who have undermined the belief of others in this very Book. Alas that it has so often been the church herself that has caused men not to accept it as the Word of God, but rather to believe in something which is merely social and human teaching. The truth has been brought into disrepute. The vast majority of men and women are outside the church today because they somehow have got the notion that the church herself does not believe in this Book, that the church herself is uncertain about the Gospel. That is why you and I must be careful to avoid such teaching, such heresy. Men and women of the world are looking at us, and, as the times may become darker, they will look at us increasingly. Let us make certain that we know the truth we believe, let us make certain we know Him whom we have believed. Let us make certain of the faith, so that when they come to us and ask for a word, we shall be able to give it without hesitation, knowing 'the Word of God, which liveth and abideth for ever.'

15
The Examples of Noah and Lot

'And spared not the old world, but saved Noah the eighth
person, a preacher of righteousness, bringing in the flood
upon the world of the ungodly; and turning the cities of
Sodom and Gomorrha into ashes, condemned them with
an overthrow, making them an ensample unto those that
after should live ungodly: And delivered just Lot, vexed
with the filthy conversation of the wicked: (for that
righteous man dwelling among them, in seeing and
hearing, vexed his righteous soul from day to day with
their unlawful deeds:)'

Chapter 2:5–8

The words of our text compel us to consider the whole position of the
individual Christian at a time of religious declension, not to say a
time of apostasy and spiritual confusion. That is the particular theme
of these verses which we are going to consider together. They are a
kind of interpolation, or, if you like, a digression, in the great central
theme which occupies the attention of the Apostle throughout the
body of the chapter. This theme is a large one, and in dealing with it,
the Apostle, incidentally, holds up as examples these two men –
Noah and Lot – and by means of them gives us invaluable instruction
with regard to the place and position of the individual Christian in a
time of appalling religious declension, and of spiritual muddle and
confusion.

Now there is nothing, I think, that is more important for us at this
time than to consider this particular instruction. There is a rule
which one can find everywhere in the Bible from the beginning to the
end, and which is abundantly confirmed by the subsequent history of
the Christian church, to the effect that the fewer the number of
Christians the greater correspondingly is the importance of the
individual Christian. That obviously needs no demonstration. The

importance of the individual is a principle which was inculcated during the Second World War, and obviously it becomes heightened and exaggerated when the total number of such individuals is small. Every man, therefore, counts and counts tremendously. And it does seem to me more and more that this is one of the first things we have to realise at this present time, confronted as we are with a situation that is in so many ways reminiscent of what is here described by the Apostle. This exhortation to the first Christians is as appropriate and as apposite today as it was then.

Fortunately for us he puts his teaching in terms of a picture, a picture of these two men who stand out so prominently in the history of the ancient world – Noah and Lot. We are all familiar with the story of these two men. You remember that Noah lived in that terrible period before the Flood. The account of the religious and moral declension of that time is given in very graphic phrases in the Book of Genesis. The world had so turned its back upon God that, in a sense, it had gone beyond hope, and God said, 'My Spirit shall not always strive with man.' The conditions that then prevailed were appalling, but in that society there was this man, Noah. Now it is important that we should consider together how this man conducted and comported himself, surrounded as he was by iniquity, and faced with evil of such dimensions that eventually it led to the judgment of the Flood.

Then you will remember the story of Lot and the cities of the plain, Sodom and Gomorrha. We notice the tenderness and the gentleness of Scripture as we read the story of Lot. In the Book of Genesis you may very well not feel inclined to describe him as 'just' Lot, for he was a man who chose to go to the plain of Jordan because it was more profitable, and in spite of the sinfulness of the cities of the plain, he chose to live there. Yet you notice that the Apostle here says very little, if anything, about the folly which led Lot to do that. What he rather emphasises is how Lot conducted himself in that atmosphere – 'delivered just Lot, vexed with the filthy conversation of the wicked'. Go back to chapters 18 and 19 of Genesis and there you will find the account of society as it was in those days – the terrible moral degradation, the foulness and the ugliness that characterised the life, all the departure from God and His holy ways, and everything to which such departure always leads. There it was; and in that society there was this man Lot and his family; and what Peter is anxious for us to consider is how that man conducted himself, how he reacted to that environment, what effect the situation had upon him. That is the theme we are considering here, and, as we claim to be concerned about these things, I suggest again that there is nothing which is of greater importance to us than that we should grasp the principles that are here enunciated.

There are two main principles. The first thing we are told very distinctly is that the Christian is always severely tested by such a life. According to the Apostle one cannot live the Christian life in a small minority without undergoing such a severe test. There are many reasons for this. *The very fact of the smallness of the number is a severe trial and test.* You notice the interesting words in which Peter brings out this point, 'And spared not the old world, but saved Noah the eighth person.' Well, what does the 'eighth person' mean? It obviously does not mean that there were only eight persons living at that particular time or eight persons from the beginning of the world. It means that Noah was the eighth person in the sense that there were only eight persons saved out of that ancient world. You will find that Peter in his first Epistle in the third chapter, after describing the Flood, says exactly the same thing –'few, that is, eight souls were saved by water' . Here, therefore, the word 'few' – represents eight, and this is just another way of saying that there were only eight persons who were righteous. You notice the contrast – 'spared not the old world, but saved Noah the eighth person, a preacher of righteousness, bringing in the flood upon the world of the ungodly'. That is the contrast – the whole world was ungodly apart from these eight persons.

Then you remember how exactly the same thing was true in the case of Sodom and Gomorrha. You remember the amazing account that is given in Genesis of Abraham as it were pleading with God and asking Him to spare the cities. Abraham mentions various numbers of people – 'Will You spare them for fifty righteous people?' 'I will,' said God. Then having reduced the number in stages, 'Would You spare them for ten?' said Abraham thinking perhaps of Lot's family. 'If there were only ten – yes, even for ten I will spare the cities,' said God. And you remember, that in the end the only people who were saved were Lot and his family. All the citizens of the plain were ungodly and unrighteous – the only people who maintained the testimony and the witness, the only people who were trying in any sense to live a godly and just life were Lot and the members of his own family and household. Now that, I say, in and of itself, constitutes a very severe trial. If we had been living sixty or seventy years ago, and even more recently, our problem would be very different from what it is at the present time. Then, religion, in a sense, was popular, and men and women believed it was the right thing to go to God's House. It is not a very difficult thing to be religious at a time like that; but it is very difficult to find yourself, not only in the minority, but in a very small minority. It is not an easy thing, whatever else you may say about it, for one man only in a barrack room to get down on his knees to pray to God. There may be some theorists who would say it ought to be an easy thing to do – well, whether it ought to be or not, it is not easy in practice, and the Bible does not say it is an easy thing. It is not an easy thing for one person only, or for one or two, in a college or hospital or any institution, to live the godly life and to be true to God when the majority are doing something different. Still more difficult is it for one member only in a family to stand and stand alone. The smallness of the numbers in and of itself means that we are severely tested. There is an instinct in us that makes us dislike standing out in this way and being the odd man out. It is a very easy thing always to go with the crowd. You remember our Lord said, 'Strait is the gate, and narrow is the way, which leadeth unto life, and few there be that find it', and 'Wide is the gate, and broad is the way, that leadeth to destruction, and many there be which go in thereat'. There are large numbers of people who really do not want to go with the crowd, but the mere fact that there is a crowd carries them away; they are afraid to stand alone.

But that, of course, is not the only thing. It is a time of testing also because of *the conduct of the world with respect to those who do stand thus, small in numbers, on their own*. Here again these stories in the Book of Genesis are very valuable. We can imagine the sarcasm and the ridicule which Noah had to endure and face; and in the same way one can see that Lot and his family would have had to endure precisely the same thing in the cities of Sodom and Gomorrha. There is no need to elaborate this – to the extent to which we are truly Christian we are bound to experience it. The world will not have it, and its ways and methods of showing its dislike are almost endless – the ridicule, the contempt, the sarcasm! If you should happen to be the one Christian in an office, or in your particular circle, or in your institution or college or wherever else it may be, you have but to enter the room and you will find the others looking at one another. They say nothing, but they just look, and you feel the ridicule, the contempt and the scorn. Then sometimes it takes a more active form, and a more positive attack is made, when you are questioned and queried and asked how any intelligent person can really believe this sort of thing now – 'Surely you do not believe the Bible to be the inspired Word of God?' You will be laughed at if you accept the history of the early part of Genesis. You will be regarded as being a fool. The world is actively condemning this Book and saying that it is played out and exploded. And I say once more that it is not an easy thing to face such a situation. Any man who is at all sensitive, any man who has any degree of intellect, though he knows that what he believes is the Truth, dislikes being the butt of sarcasm and scorn and derision in this way. The world is doing its utmost to attack the few who still stand for the things of Christ; and because of these attacks, I say, the position of the individual Christian is made extremely difficult.

But I want to show that one is tested in a much more serious sense than all this. Look at the verses that are found at the end of this chapter. 'While they promise them liberty, they themselves are the servants of corruption: for of whom a man is overcome, of the same is he brought in bondage. For if after they have escaped the pollutions of the world through the knowledge of the Lord and Saviour Jesus Christ, they are again entangled therein, and overcome, the latter end is worse with them than the beginning. For it had been better for them not to have known the way of righteousness, than, after they have known it, to turn from the holy commandment delivered unto them. But it is happened unto them according to the true proverb, The dog is turned to his own vomit again; and the sow that was washed to her wallowing in the mire.'

The point I am emphasising is the terrible and terrifying truth that is contained in this statement. Here we are told very clearly that every profession of Christianity is not of necessity a true profession. Peter's whole point, in a sense, is this. There are people in the Christian church who claim to have believed the Gospel. Yes, but a time of trial like this is going to test them, is going to sift them. And those who have not got the real thing are going to go back. They never have been changed, the dog was always a dog, the sow, though washed, 'shall return to her wallowing in the mire'. Religion may have a temporary effect upon us, the Gospel of Jesus Christ can work temporarily in us. So that the test of whether we really are children of God is whether we stand true in spite of the tendency of the world to go the other way. A time like this is a time of unusually stiff, severe testing and, unfortunately, what the Apostle says here is being witnessed upon all hands. When religion was popular, people crowded out places of worship, and it was comparatively easy to be a Christian; but when the majority turn their backs upon it, the people who have only a loose hold very soon lose that hold. Those who really have not the root of the matter in them cannot stand persecution. They are like those people depicted by our Lord in the parable of the sower, who receive the word with joy, but because they have no root or depth in themselves, in time of trial or persecution the seed which had sprung up withers away. Not often has there been a time, and certainly not for many centuries, when the profession of Christianity and truth has been so severely tested as it is today. It is not popular to be a Christian today. There was a time when it would help a man to get a job, and when it would help a man to get on in his profession; but today it is almost a hindrance. To be a Christian is almost as if you are some doubtful kind of person. It is not popular, there is no glamour about it – and this is how it tests us. The man who holds on tenaciously to the Gospel today, does so because he really believes it, and because he knows it to be God's Truth.

Let me move on to the second principle, which is, that *the Christian is always a man who stands out, apart, at such a time*. And that is obviously the great point about Noah, as it is about Lot. Noah and Lot were men who stood out as being altogether different from the prevailing tendency of their age; and what is true of Noah and Lot, is, of course, true of all true Christians at every similar period in the long history of the Christian church. Think of certain of those Waldensian brothers in the Middle Ages, how they stood out; think of how the Protestant Reformers stood out; think of how the Puritans stood out and especially in the reign of Charles the Second. When you read of that licentious king upon the throne, and of how society followed his lead, see how the Puritans stood out by contrast. Think of the first Methodists – they were called Methodists as a term of abuse, hurled at them for the very reason that they lived a different life. It has always been the case. Christian people at a time like this have always stood out distinctly as men and women different, separate, apart.

Now this is not a debatable matter; it is something that is absolutely inevitable if we really believe that a Christian is one who has become a partaker of the divine nature, if we really believe that a Christian is one who has been born again by the Spirit of God from above. If we believe that God has made this person anew, he is bound to stand out; he cannot be like those who have not been born again and who are not the recipients of the divine nature. What always amazes and shocks me is that anyone making a profession of Christianity should be surprised at this or should object to it. The one person I frankly cannot understand in the world today is the type of Christian who is afraid of being called narrow. I can quite easily understand a person of the world who objects to that. I expect nothing better of him. He does not claim to have been born again, he does not see himself as a partaker of the divine nature. He sees himself as a man of the world. But what I cannot understand is a person who claims all that is meant by being a Christian and who, at the same time, is afraid of being too good or too holy. That is a contradiction in terms – it is muddled thinking, and it is indeed a very significant confession. The fact is that the true Christian, because of what he is, must of necessity stand out in society; and it is because of that, of course, that Christians have ever had an influence and an effect upon the world.

Have you read the story of the great Tertullian? He was a very able and intellectual man. He was converted by what he saw in the first Christians – they were not like other men, they were Christians. It was this that impressed him. He saw that these men, rather than take the oath which they could not take seriously, and rather than deny Christ, were ready to be thrown to the lions in the arena. 'Look at them,' he said, 'there must be something in this, there must be something in this belief if it can make a man do that. They are prepared to give up everything, even life itself.' And that led to his conversion. Is it not one of the greatest tragedies today that it is almost impossible to tell who is a Christian? Is it not one of the greatest tragedies, that we Christians are so amazingly like the men who have never made such a claim – like them in appearance, like them in conversation, like them in interests, like them in habits, like them in our reactions to events? Do we stand out as the first Christians did? Do we stand out as the Puritans did? Are we like the Waldensian brethren of the Middle Ages; are we like those first Christians? The tragedy is that the difference between us and the world is almost imperceptible. At times it is worse, for some even make a positive attempt to be like the world. Even within the church this is too often evidenced, and people think of the church as a place which is just for cultural entertainment and even other forms of entertainment. The church, in an attempt to make herself popular, organises dramatics and dances so as to be as much like the world as possible, instead of standing out like Lot and Noah. And it is not only true of the church in such social matters, but even in her evangelistic meetings she often does the same thing. She attempts to be like the world and to give the impression that, though we are Christians, we are not so very different. In exactly the same way you see this when you come down to the realm of the conduct of the individual Christian.

Well, now, that is something that is utterly contrary to the Bible, where we read that the Christian is a man who stands out, a man apart. However, he stands out and is a man apart, not in any false sense, not in the sense that he just has nothing to do with the world at all, that he refuses to take part in local politics, or national or international politics. It does not mean that he becomes a monk or a hermit. Neither Noah nor Lot were men apart in that sense. Well, what does it mean? It means he is a man, as James puts it, whose 'pure religion and undefiled...is... to visit the fatherless and widows in their affliction and to keep himself unspotted from the world'. It does not mean going out of the world; it means being in it, but not of it.

How does it work out? Surely the teaching is that we must not allow ourselves to be influenced and affected by the world either in its mind and outlook and mentality, or in its conduct and behaviour. You notice the significant word that Peter uses. He uses the word 'entangled' – 'if after they have escaped the pollutions of the world through the knowledge of the Lord and Saviour Jesus Christ, they are again entangled...' Oh, the subtlety of it all! The greatest danger of all is always the danger of compromise, the danger of allowing the world to dictate to us what we should think and what we should say and do. Now that is the thing against which we have to fight. You remember how John puts it in his first Epistle – 'Love not the world, neither the things that are in the world.' What are they – 'the lust of the flesh, and the lust of the eyes, and the pride of life'. That is the characteristic of the world always. That was its condition before the flood and in Sodom and Gomorrha, and it is still the same today. That is the worldly outlook, and we must never allow it to contaminate us. We must avoid it as the very plague itself, and, far from being governed by the world and its outlook and its mentality, we must be governed solely by our love of God, by our concern about His kingdom, and our relationship to our Lord and Saviour Jesus Christ.

The second thing is that we must be troubled by and concerned about the state of the world. Peter puts this very clearly – he tells us that even Lot was distressed, that he 'vexed his righteous soul from day to day' with 'the filthy conversation of the wicked'. Now that, being interpreted, can be put in this form. We must first and foremost regret the state of the world; we must bemoan it; we must be revolted by it. This comes to us as a very personal and a very simple and direct test. Let me put it in one illustration. Is it right or wrong for a Christian person who has received the divine nature to be amused by the constant jokes which the world makes about drunkenness and immorality and vice? According to the Bible's teaching, we ought to be vexed about such things, we ought to be revolted; we ought to hate the very garment spotted by these sins. I say we ought to be worried and troubled about it. I go further and suggest that the teaching of this Book is that we *must* be burdened about it. It is not enough just to condemn it; it is not enough to say, 'How terrible it is!' The reaction of these men was that they prayed about it. It became a burden on their souls to such an extent that they cried out to God; they asked Him to have mercy and to intervene. That is how the Christian behaves at such a time. These things trouble him and vex him and distress him. Can we honestly say that we are burdened about the state of the times in which we live? Do these things press upon our souls, do they make us pray to God for revival and for reawakening?

And, finally, we are to preach righteousness to such a world. We are to warn it; to tell it of the judgment that is coming because of its sin; we are to plead with men to see their danger and escape from it. And, above all, we are to give them an example of the Christian life and the Christian character, and of loyalty to God and His Truth. And indeed it may be that we shall be called upon to suffer. We may yet have to suffer for our faith in this country, as they have had to do in other countries. We may have to choose between the Pope or some other authoritarian power and loyalty to Christ. We may have to choose between life itself and loyalty to Christ. We must so grasp our faith and be properly grasped by it, that if ever we are confronted by such a choice we shall gladly die for His Name's sake and consider it a supreme honour to lay down our lives for One who laid down His life for us.

There, briefly are the principles that are taught here. I end with a question. Are we like Noah and Lot? The world today is amazingly like the world of those days. Is it easy for people to tell that we are Christians? Are we different, do we stand out? Are we, by being what we are, a rebuke to modern society? Above all, are we burdened about it all? Do we grieve for God's honour and God's glory? Do we grieve for the souls of men hurtling themselves thus to destruction? Are we praying about it and doing our utmost to hasten the coming of a true revival and religious awakening? That is the challenge of Noah and of Lot to the modern Christian.

16

The Sovereignty of God

'The Lord knoweth how to deliver the godly out of temptations, and to reserve the unjust unto the day of judgment to be punished:'

Chapter 2:9

These words form the conclusion of an argument which starts at the beginning of the fourth verse where we read, 'For if God spared not the angels that sinned, but cast them down to hell, and delivered them into chains of darkness, to be reserved unto judgment...' Then the Apostle goes on to deal with the cases of the Flood and Sodom and Gomorrha, and after all that, 'The Lord knoweth how to deliver the godly out of temptations, and to reserve the unjust unto the day of judgment to be punished.'

We must keep on reminding ourselves that the object which the Apostle has in mind in writing this letter is to help and encourage and comfort Christian people, who are face to face with a time of terrible difficulty and indeed of threatening and increasing apostasy. His method of doing so, as we have seen before, is one which is typical of the biblical teaching everywhere. First of all he warns them against the false prophets and the false teachers. Then, as we saw in our last study, he follows that word of warning with a word of personal exhortation to Christian people in such a situation. They not only needed to be warned against the dangers threatening from the outside, they must be reminded of what they themselves had to do. There we saw that he calls us to the type and kind of life that was lived by Noah before the Flood, and by Lot before the destruction of Sodom and Gomorrha. Now this is a difficult task, and the Apostle, therefore, after that personal exhortation, following a method that is invariable in the Bible, goes on to a word of encouragement, a word of consolation, a word of cheer, a word that is calculated to stimulate us to this great task to which we are called. And in this ninth verse we have the very essence of that comfort and encouragement.

Now there can be no doubt at all that for Christian people faced, as these first Christians were, with such problems and difficulties and trials, the greatest danger always is that of giving way to a sense of despair because of a feeling of utter hopelessness and futility. That is perhaps the greatest danger of all afflicting us at this present time, living as we do in the modern world which is so similar to that in which the early Christians lived. The power of evil seems to be so great. We are a small band, and apparently decreasing steadily year by year. The power of evil seems so great, so highly organised, so deeply entrenched in life. The whole world seems not only against what we believe, but against God in outlook and in practice. We are made conscious of this as we walk about the streets of our cities; but we see it in villages in the country as much as in the towns. There is this obvious departure from God and from religion, not only in practice but in theory and in idea – the blasphemy and the dismissing of God. Then in books and in articles, in papers and journals, the whole outlook seems to be against the things of God. Therefore, the danger is that many, seeing all this, are tempted to give way to a sense of utter discouragement and a feeling of complete hopelessness. Now that is the very danger against which the Apostle is trying to guard. Seeing the great majority apparently and increasingly against God, many people are tempted to listen to the false teachers, and to go after them and follow their pernicious ways. How is it that we can be saved from thus falling away? What encouragement have we to continue standing for God and truth whatever the world may be doing, and even though we may become but a handful such as were found before the Flood and before the judgment of Sodom and Gomorrha? What is it that can encourage us to continue in that position, come what may? That is exactly what the Apostle gives us in this ninth verse.

What is his message? Let us first of all point out what he does not say. Let us observe that he does not say that everything is going to be all right. Peter does not tell these people just to hold on a little bit longer because circumstances will soon be changed and they will no longer have problems to confront. He does not say that – that is something we must never be tired of repeating. The Bible does not offer a wonderful world just round the corner. The Bible never indulges in light and easy optimism; it does not help us by telling us that our troubles are only temporary and that soon all this evil and sin will be removed and banished. That, indeed, is the very opposite of what the Bible does say. That is the false idealism and optimism and humanism that have been so popular during this past century; and you and I have had, whether you call it our fortune or misfortune, to live at a time when we see all such false, light optimism utterly uprooted and exposed in all its superficiality. Peter does not say that things are going to be all right and that circumstances are going to change quite soon.

Neither does the Apostle tell these people that what they have to do is to go out preaching and to tell the world that it is either 'Christ or chaos'. I deliberately put it in that form because that is the kind of phrase one hears frequently at the present time. I was asked to address a meeting quite recently and that was the subject a good friend suggested for my address. I asked him what subject he wished me to speak on and he said, 'Well, we think the great thing to say to the world at this time is that it is either Christ or chaos.' There are many variations of that – 'rebellion or revelation' – you are familiar with them. Now I say that the Apostle does not say that either. He does not tell these people that unless the world soon turns to Christ all is going to end in chaos – that is not his message.

How then does he comfort and strengthen and encourage these people? To put it in a phrase, he introduces them to the doctrine of the sovereignty of God, which he works out from three different standpoints. Now again I am constrained to point out that that is the very essence of the biblical method. The Bible always gives us comfort and encouragement by means of doctrine – never apart from doctrine. Take that great eighth chapter of the Epistle to the Romans. It is one of the most theological, doctrinal passages to be found anywhere in the Bible; and yet there is nothing more comforting, more consoling and more encouraging. The argument is this: 'Whom he did predestinate, them he also called: and whom he called, them he also justified: and whom he justified, them he also glorified.' Doctrine! and apart from that doctrine, the Bible has no comfort and consolation to offer us. Well here, I say, is the great doctrine of the sovereignty of God which the apostle works out along three different lines.

The first is to remind us of *the power of God*. Listen. There is the whole world, as it were, going against God and against religion – what of it? Here is the answer – 'The Lord knoweth how', or if you prefer it, 'The Lord is able, the Lord has the power . . .' That is the first thing, as it is always the first thing in the Bible. And it is always the thing with which we must start. This is first and absolute. The Lord God is the Almighty. Now it is for that reason that I deprecate so strongly this tendency today to talk about 'Christ or chaos'. That is a phrase which suggests that there is a kind of possibility that God may be defeated, and that Christ may be defeated, which is an utter denial of the great central doctrine of the Bible from beginning to end. If you want to use a phrase including 'Christ' and 'chaos' I suggest a better phrase for you. Instead of talking about 'Christ or chaos' we should speak about 'Chaos and Christ'. If the world reduces itself to utter chaos, still God is above it and God is more powerful than it, and out of that very chaos He can produce His own purpose. We must never put Christ and chaos as possible alternatives. We must ever start by reminding ourselves of the *power of God*. In spite of chaos, God remains – whatever men may or may not do, whatever they may do with the earth, whatever they may produce in the world, still the Lord reigneth. And there is no sense in which His power can be affected even to the slightest extent. 'Ah, very well,' says someone, 'that is all right as a theoretical or abstract statement, but it does not seem to me to be working out in practice, because if God is as powerful as you have just been saying, why is the world as it is? Look at the power of evil, look at what is happening in the world round and about you; can you still say that God is Almighty, that God is on the throne, that God is controlling everything while the world is as it is?' Now it seems to me that this chapter which we are considering together really supplies the answer to that question, for in an indirect way it deals with the whole question of the problem of evil.

What does it teach with respect to this problem of evil? First of all, that, obviously, God permits evil. This is a great mystery, and yet it is something which is taught in the Bible. God in His own inscrutable wisdom and counsel has chosen to permit and to allow evil. Were it not that God had given this permission, evil would never have come into existence at all. Now it is no use asking why God did that, why a holy and all-powerful God should permit evil. We just do not know, and it is no part of the Christian position to say that we understand the mind of God in an exhaustive sense. We do not know – the problem of evil remains a mystery, but there it is! We do not understand the origin of evil but we do know that it has come into being and that God must have allowed it. Why did the Devil originally fall? what made Lucifer, that star of the morning, stand against God and rebel against Him? We do not understand it, but the fact is that it was allowed. In the same way, the angels that are referred to by Peter were allowed to follow Lucifer. The holy, great God, for His own purposes allowed evil to come into this perfect world which He Himself had made. This is the first proposition. God permits or allows evil.

The second step of the argument, which is equally clear, is that God, having permitted evil, does not give it free scope. He keeps it within bounds and within limits. Now that, in a sense, is the great argument of the Book of Job. You remember how Satan appeared before God and made certain remarks about Job, and God gave him permission to try Job. But all the time God was in control, and Satan was not allowed to go beyond a certain point. Not only that. Why are there States and Governments and magistrates and all these other powers? The answer of the Bible is that 'the powers that be' are all ordained of God and that they are designed to set a limit to the effects and results of evil. Were it not that these powers had come into existence, the whole world long since would have hurtled itself to destruction. But God having permitted evil, then puts a limit on it, and keeps it within bounds, and has a certain check on it.

Another way in which we see this principle working is in the fact of revivals. Have you observed the character of the history of the church? The church starts in a great outpouring of the Spirit. Gradually that time passes away, and religion becomes apparently dead, and the whole world becomes godless and irreligious. Then God revives His work, and the result of the revival is that evil is checked and controlled. The countries which have experienced revival become better; the people, in general, live a better life, the standard of morality is raised and certain reforms come to pass. Then after a while that again seems to pass off and the country again reverts to a state of godlessness and irreligion, and it looks as if everything is going to end in destruction. Then God sends another revival. I suggest, therefore, that revivals and the history of revivals, are a very clear proof in and of themselves of the fact that God controls evil and keeps it within very definite bounds.

It may be, however, that the clearest way of all in which I can prove this contention is to remind you of the great theme of Peter in this chapter, namely, that there are periods of special judgment in the history of mankind. Take, for instance, the story of the Flood. This is the fact: the world was made perfect, then man sinned, and gradually sin began to develop and spread until the state of the world had become almost unspeakable. We are told that 'every imagination of the thoughts of his (man's) heart was only evil continually'. Evil seemed to be getting entirely beyond all bounds, and then God said, 'My Spirit shall not always strive with man.' Evil had reached such a point that God decided to pour out His wrath in judgment upon it; and He condemned the world and brought an end to it, save for that one family of Noah. Then the world starts off again and after a while men again become irreligious, and you see this centred in the case of Sodom and Gomorrha. Those cities had become so foul that God, as it were, decided once more, in His own inscrutable counsel, that a revival was not what was needed. He must judge and punish and destroy, and He did so.

Then look at the Children of Israel in their long story. In spite of their rebellion and sin, God sends His messengers to them and raises up His prophets. The prophets appeal to them, sometimes they listen and there is a temporary reform and things are a bit better; but gradually the people slip back again, they continue in sin, and then things become so bad that God deals with them in judgment. He raises up the Chaldean army which comes and destroys the city of Jerusalem and smashes the temple and carries the people away captive. The judgment of God put an end to that period of sin. And so it has continued since then.

As you look at the history of the Christian era you will observe the same phenomenon. There was a very great and powerful Christian church in North Africa at one time, but it is not there today. There have been instances within Christendom of where churches have fallen into such a degree of apostasy that God, has, as it were, come to the decision that they cannot be revived, and He judges and destroys them. They vanish out of existence. All this is but a proof of the fact that God sets a very definite limit and control upon evil. This, once more, of course, is a great and profound mystery. We do not understand it, but the fact that it is so is beyond doubt. God seems to allow evil to develop and expand up to a certain point, until it seems to have become supreme and all powerful; and then, at that point, God acts and intervenes and shows that He is there over and above it all, and that He controls it thus in judgment. So we emphasize once more that chaos can never be more powerful than God. God, in a sense, never manifests His power so much as when He intervenes in an utterly chaotic condition. That is the first manifestation, therefore, of the sovereignty of God, the power of God.

In the second place, the sovereignty of God manifests itself in terms of *righteousness and of justice*. This again is a very important matter because there are many people who are in trouble at this point. It is a very old trouble and you will find it stated perfectly in the seventy-third Psalm, where the Psalmist, looking at the ungodly in their prosperity, asks, Is God being fair? 'Verily I have cleansed my heart in vain.' I have been living a good life, but these godless people seem to be flourishing while I suffer. Is that right? Now Peter emphasises the righteousness and the justice of God and says that they are as absolute as the power of God. This again is something that is shown everywhere in the Bible. Here is the principle. Nothing is more certain than the fact that God punishes sin and evil and unrighteousness. Let me remind you how He does so – it is all found in this chapter.

Part of the punishment of sin comes immediately. A sense of guilt and shame is nothing but a part of the punishment of sin. You cannot sin without feeling unhappy and miserable – that is a part of the immediate punishment. Sin generally carried with it also a revulsion of feeling. Man generally hates the wrong thing which he has just done. That is a part of the feeling of remorse. Sin also always leads to muddle, to discord, to unhappiness and to wretchedness. Go back to the Book of Genesis and read the account of society before the Flood. What a terrible muddle it was in, what an unhappy state! Look at the people in Sodom and Gomorrha, with all the apparent wonder and glamour of the life of those cities which had attracted so many from the country, and yet see the bestial and ugly and foul life it was. And look at the times in which we are living. The world laughs at religion, it scoffs at Christianity, it says we are just as well without it. But the newspapers do not seem to suggest that. Look at all the separations and divorces, look at all the murders, look at the strain in people's faces. It is not a happy life; it is a miserable life. The world is in its present chaotic condition simply because that is an essential part of the punishment of sin. Perhaps the best exposition of this matter is to be found in the second half of the first chapter of the Epistle to the

Romans where we are told that God 'gave them over to a reprobate mind'. The result was all the foulness and filth which characterised the life of men and women at the time when Jesus Christ came into this world first of all. The Bible has always reminded us of this – 'the way of transgressors is hard'. Put your finger into fire and it will be burned. The Prodigal Son is perhaps the outstanding illustration of this. What a wonderful life that seemed just for a while; but it always leads to the swine and the husks, to the misery and wretchedness. Sin is punished by God immediately.

But God's action doesn't stop at that. You notice that Peter, in speaking of these heresies, describes them as 'damnable heresies' and (v. 1) that those who are carried away by them shall bring upon themselves 'swift destruction', he says. The punishment of sin always continues. It continues, according to Peter, not only in this life but in the next life also. This is what he says in our text (I give the Revised Version rather than the Authorised) – 'The Lord knoweth how to deliver the godly out of temptation, and to keep the unrighteous under punishment unto the day of judgment.' Did you notice that the same word is found in the fourth verse: 'If God spared not the angels that sinned, but cast them down to hell, and delivered them into chains of darkness, to be reserved unto judgment?' Now that is the biblical teaching. A man is punished for his sins the moment he has sinned, and while he continues living in this world. Then what happens after he dies? Well, after death the unjust and the ungodly are reserved in a state of punishment until the day of the final judgment. It is a terrifying and terrible thought, and yet I suggest to you that if you deny that doctrine you are denying the whole of the Bible from beginning to end. That is what makes this life of ours such a serious matter; that is what makes the business of preaching such a desperately serious matter. That is why light and flippant evangelism is, to me, in many ways, a denial of the New Testament Gospel. If a man goes out of this life and world in an ungodly state, he goes 'into chains of darkness' and is reserved in punishment for the final judgment. In other words, the final step in God's punishment of sin is the Day of Judgment – reserved in punishment unto the Day of Judgment. There, I need scarcely remind you again, is something that you will find running right through the Bible. There is to be a final judgment of the world, and not only a final judgment of the world, but a final judgment of all created beings everywhere – angels, principalities, powers, sin, evil, hell, everything. 'The wrath of God is revealed from heaven against all ungodliness and unrighteousness of men'. The Lord knows how to do this, says Peter. Do not be frightened by the power of evil; do not be frightened by the Devil and his cohorts and all his legions; do not be frightened by what you see round and about you – 'The Lord knoweth how to reserve the unjust to the Day of Judgment to be punished.'

But our third and last principle to illustrate the doctrine of the Sovereignty of God is *the love of God*. Thank God for it. The sovereignty of God manifests itself in its power, it manifests itself in its righteousness and judgment, yes, but it also manifests itself in His love. And this is something which is as certain as the two previous principles. As God has the power to deal with sin, and as God has the righteousness and the justice to deal with it, so He also deals in love with those who belong to Him in spite of their sin. 'The Lord knoweth how to deliver the godly out of temptations.' This is one of the most comforting and consoling doctrines which is to be found in the Bible. How does God do this? Well, let me point out again that He does not do it in the sense that He promises us that we shall avoid all troubles and suffering and trials and tribulations. That is not promised in the Bible. There are so many who seem to think that that is what the Bible says, and because they get troubles, they turn their back on God and follow the false prophets. But that is not promised. We are not told that Noah and Lot did not suffer anything. They suffered a great deal. Indeed, the Bible tells us that we may have to suffer death for Christ's sake. We are not told we shall be put in a kind of glass case where nothing shall ever touch us – that is not the promise. What then, is the promise? The promise is that God will never allow sin and evil to harm us in any vital sense. Our Lord once put it like this: 'Fear not them which kill the body, but are not able to kill the soul, but rather fear him which is able to destroy both soul and body in hell.' Now the world can do certain things to us, but it will never be allowed to harm us in any vital sense. The Lord knows how to deliver us from all that. How does He do it? He does it by delivering us from the power and the polluting effect of sin and evil. He does it also by enabling us to rejoice even in the midst of evil and tribulation. He enables us indeed to be 'more than conquerors'. Thus it comes to pass that we can turn these things that are against us into victories, and they but minister to our comfort and to our strength.

But the final and supreme promise is this: God knows how to save us from the ultimate judgment and destruction which is going to fall upon sin and evil and everything that is unjust and unrighteous. That is the great message of this chapter. The Flood, and the fate of Sodom and Gomorrha, are but a preliminary indication of the final judgment, and in the judgment, finally, everything and everyone who is opposed to God shall be committed to everlasting and eternal destruction. Now the promise that is given here is that God will save the godly out of all that. We shall not be enveloped and overwhelmed in that ultimate last destruction. He knows how to deliver us out of it. In other words, that I may summarise the teaching of the chapter, we can put it like this. There are two kinds of people in this world always, and there have always been only two kinds of people – the godly and the unjust – those who are like Lot and Noah, those who are God's people, and those who are against God. The fate of these two groups of people is already fixed and determined. If we are godly we shall be delivered out of all that final destruction; if we are ungodly we shall be involved in it. People may say that they dislike this doctrine. Indeed many today are fond of saying something like this: 'That is all right, you needn't think you are going to frighten us, we know too much nowadays to believe that kind of thing. You might have succeeded in alarming us like that fifty years ago.' I am not concerned to frighten, but I am here to preach and to announce the Truth. And I would ask one simple question: What knowledge have we, of which our fathers were ignorant, which in any way invalidates this doctrine? Can anyone disprove this teaching that is the solemn pronouncement of the Bible from beginning to end? The godly are to be delivered out of the judgment, the ungodly will be overwhelmed by it. The separation of these two groups is clear from Genesis to Revelation.

The one thing that matters, therefore, is that we make certain we are amongst the godly. What are the marks of the godly? Simply, they are these. We must believe on, and confess, the Lord who has bought us. We must be the exact opposite of that which is told us in this chapter of these false teachers and these false prophets – they denied the Lord that bought them. We must believe on Him, we must confess Him, we must acknowledge that apart from Him we are lost and have no hope whatsoever, and that we are relying entirely upon the Lord Jesus Christ.

The second mark of the godly is that they can see that the world is under judgment. They can see that the mind of the world is opposed to God, that the world is at enmity with God. Therefore, obviously, they separate themselves from it: they refuse to be governed and controlled by it; they refuse to live its kind of life. In other words, they live to the glory of God, their supreme ambition is to please Him, to extol His great and Holy Name, and to tell others about Him and to do their utmost to bring these others to Him. The Lord, with all His almighty power, knows how to deliver the godly out of all temptations. However hard and difficult the times may be, however trying your situation may be in the particular place in which you find yourself, stand firm, my friend. Remember the power of God, remember the righteousness and the justice of God; above all, remember this amazing love of God. He will never allow you to suffer beyond a certain point. 'God is faithful, who will not suffer you to be tempted above that ye are able; but will with the temptation also make a way to escape, that ye may be able to bear it.' And He will deliver you from the final destruction that will certainly overwhelm all who are opposed to Him.

17
The Vital Importance of Biblical History

'This second epistle, beloved, I now write unto you; in both which I stir up your pure minds by way of remembrance: That ye may be mindful of the words which were spoken before by the holy prophets, and of the commandment of us the apostles of the Lord and Saviour: Knowing this first, that there shall come in the last days scoffers, walking after their own lusts, and saying, Where is the promise of his coming? for since the fathers fell asleep, all things continue as they were from the beginning of the creation. For this they willingly are ignorant of, that by the word of God the heavens were of old, and the earth standing out of the water and in the water: Whereby the world that then was, being over-flowed with water, perished: But the heavens and the earth, which are now, by the same word are kept in store, reserved unto fire against the day of judgment and perdition of ungodly men.'

Chapter 3:1–7

We must now consider the argument which is contained in the first seven verses of this third chapter of the Second Epistle of Peter. We must take the seven verses together because they form a complete and entire argument in themselves.

The sequence in the argument worked out by the Apostle in this letter is something like this. You remember he introduced the whole subject of the second coming of our Lord and the final judgment in the sixteenth verse of the first chapter. Then in the second chapter he has been reminding us of the certainty of God's ultimate punishment of evildoers and of the rescue of the godly, and he has been considering the position and attitude of the false teachers who were opposed to that doctrine. Then, having exhorted Christian people to stand up to the times, and to comport themselves as Christian people should do in such an age of apostasy and sin, he gives them the word of comfort and consolation that we considered in the previous chapter – 'The Lord knoweth how to deliver the godly out of temptations and to reserve the unjust unto the day of judgment to be punished.'

But then at that point he seems to imagine, and indeed not only to imagine, he definitely predicts and prophesies, that certain people will appear who will put this question. 'Where is the promise of his coming?' 'It is all very well,' say these people, 'to make an announcement like that; it is all very well to exhort us to suffer as Christians' – for many of those first Christians were persecuted, they were tried very severely – 'it is all very well to exhort us to stand steadfast and to continue. But on what grounds are we to do so? It was all right,' they would say, 'for the first Christians; when you preached that doctrine to them you told them that the Lord was going to return, but now all this time has passed and nothing has taken place at all. "Ever since the fathers fell asleep all things continue as they were from the beginning of the creation." What is the point,' they say, 'of asking us thus to stand and to continue and to go on when all the signs and all the appearances are utterly opposed to that which you are preaching?' That is the argument with which the Apostle proceeds to deal and never, perhaps, was there a time when this argument needed to be considered more than at this present hour. Here is the case to put against those who are described as scoffers, or, if you prefer it, as mockers – the people who ridicule the Gospel and its promises, and especially all that the Gospel has to teach us with regard to the course of history and the final outcome of life in this world. The position today, of course, is not only similar to that which obtained at the time when the Apostle penned these words; there is a sense in which it is still more accentuated. All the appearances seem to be against what is taught here in the Bible, and all this opposition is greatly reinforced today by various so-called scientific teachings, which seem to fly flatly in the face of the teaching of the New Testament Scriptures.

Now what has the Apostle to say to all this? Let me summarise his statements. His first statement is this, *that this whole matter is fundamentally and finally a matter of faith and a matter of acceptance of the teaching of Scripture.* The Gospel tells us that there is to be a definite end to this world, and Peter goes on to tell us how that end is to take place. He tells us that world history is heading up to a great climax and final judgment. That is perhaps one of the most difficult things which we are asked to believe. There are large numbers of people who are very ready to accept the Gospel in general, with regard to its doctrine of forgiveness, and with regard to its doctrine of the atonement; there are many people who are prepared to accept the doctrine of the cross; but they find this whole idea of the second coming of our Lord, or the return of our Lord in judgment, and the destruction of the world, and the new heaven and the new earth, particularly difficult. They find it strangely incredible. Everything, they say, seems to be against it. It is very difficult for the natural mind to accept such teaching.

Peter's reply to them is that ultimately it is not a matter of reason, it is not a matter of argument. He bases his whole case primarily upon the Scriptures themselves. 'This second Epistle, beloved, I now write unto you; in both which I stir up your pure minds by way of remembrance; that ye may be mindful of the words which were spoken before by the holy prophets' (that is to say, the Old Testament prophets). In other words, in this letter, as indeed in all central matters of the Christian faith, we either accept the revelation or we do not; and the Bible itself tells us that revelation is something which is definitely beyond reason. That is perhaps the great watershed that divides men into two groups at this moment – those who are prepared to accept the revelation of this Book and those who reject it. Peter refers to those who reject it as scoffers. What he means is that these people come to revelation and ask their questions and are concerned about reasons, whereas the very category of revelation suggests the supernatural and the miraculous. It suggests something that is in reality beyond the mind of man and which the power of reason unaided can never attain unto. Now the whole idea of the Bible with respect to life in this world is put in that form; creation itself is a miracle, it is making things out of nothing, it is this manifestation of the power of God. Now the natural man, of course, finds it very difficult to believe that, and that is why, during these last hundred years particularly, he has been rejecting that teaching. He feels that you must start with something, that everything must evolve out of something. Hence the theory of evolution. But of course that still leaves unsolved the original matter. Where did that come from, what is the origin of that primitive matter itself? There, in a sense, even that theory is forced back upon some original bit of creation, though men are not prepared to grant it. The theory of evolution apart from the activity of God as Creator leaves unsolved the problem of original matter.

Now that is just one illustration of the whole case as it is given by the Bible. The Bible asks me to believe things which to the natural mind often seem to be quite ridiculous. You get instances of that in the Bible itself – this warning with respect to the flood which Peter deals with here, the case of Sodom and Gomorrha, and various things that happened to the Children of Israel. The Bible is frankly supernatural, it is frankly miraculous, it asks us to accept such things without the slightest hesitation. The whole prophecy with regard to the coming of our Lord, to the natural mind seemed utterly fantastic. Nothing seemed more ridiculous to the rationalistic Jews of that age than that this Carpenter of Nazareth should be the Messiah, the Son of God. The whole thing to them was ridiculous, and they scoffed at Him and mocked at Him and jeered at Him. Now that is exactly what these other people did, and will do, says the Apostle, with regard to the doctrine of the end of the age, the return of Christ, the destruction of the world and the bringing in of new heavens and earth. They ridicule the whole thing and they say, 'Where is the promise of His coming? Look at life and the world, how can you say these things are heading on to what you have described? Everything continues as it has always been.' And the first answer to that is that you either base your whole outlook upon human reason and understanding, upon what you can fathom and follow out, and you yourself can reason out, or else you frankly say, I believe this to be the Word of God, and because this is taught in the Word of God I accept it and I subscribe to it. This doctrine of the end of time and the final judgment is as integral a part of the teaching of the Bible, as is the first coming of Christ, and as is every other cardinal doctrine of the Christian faith. It is essentially a matter of acceptance of revelation and submission to the authority of the Word of God. But, says Peter, this central statement can be buttressed and supported by various other subsidiary statements. And he mentions them.

The first thing is that Scripture *comforts us and strengthens our faith by prophesying unto us the coming of these scoffers.* 'Knowing this first, that there shall come in the last days scoffers, walking after their own lusts.' Now that to me is a matter of great comfort and consolation. It works in this way – the greater the scepticism today with regard to these things, the greater in a sense is the proof of the fact that the biblical teaching is a revelation from God. Men today by scoffing at this doctrine are simply confirming the biblical prophecy. That, I say, is something which is of very great value and importance; and it is for that reason chiefly that I am never tired of criticising and denouncing that view of the teaching of the Gospel and of the New Testament, which would have us believe that the New Testament predicts a world which is gradually going to improve and to get better and better until at last it becomes perfect. Now if we do accept that false view, well then it is extremely difficult to understand the times in which we live. If man is automatically improving, if the world is automatically improving, then I say it is extremely difficult to understand the modern world. Now there are many people today who are troubled by that – there are even many Christians who are shaken in their faith. They say, 'Look at the majority of people; they do not believe the Gospel, the Gospel has been preached now for nearly two thousand years, don't you think it ought to have a stronger hold upon the people if it is the Truth of God? Shouldn't it be the case, as the Gospel has been preached century after century, that its doctrine should be so engrafted in the heart of man that by today the whole world should have become christianised and Christian?' And holding that view, and finding the masses of the people outside the church, and finding the leaders of the people in many countries, not to say most, opposed to the Gospel or ignorant of it, their faith is buffeted and they wonder whether the Gospel is after all the power of God unto salvation. Now the real answer to that is something like this: that the very state of the world today is a confirmation of the Gospel teaching. The Bible nowhere says the world is going to get better and better. The Gospel predicts that the last times will be perilous, there will be these scoffers, the world will ridicule the Gospel. Do you remember the question put by our Lord – 'When the Son of man is come, shall he find faith on the earth?' The whole prediction of the New Testament is that somewhere, before the final end of history, there will be a terrible apostasy, the world will be full of these scoffers who will ridicule the Gospel. I say, therefore, that rather than allow ourselves to be depressed by the present state and situation, we ought to see in it one of the most striking and extraordinary confirmations of the New Testament teaching. Here is a fact, then, which helps me to believe that this is the Word of God – it seems to know man, it seems to know the world in a more thorough manner than does any other teaching. The very terrible nature of the times itself is a confirmation of the Scripture.

But then he goes on to expose still further the state and the condition of these scoffers, and he *does so again by simply reminding us of certain facts.* This is what the scoffers say, said Peter: 'Where is the promise of His coming; everything seems to be as it has always been; how can the doctrine be right?' How does he expose the foolishness of that attitude? He does so by reminding us of certain facts, and I want to emphasise again the importance of facts.

There is a movement today, a certain theological movement, which at first sight seems to be a return to the Bible, but which on close examination reveals itself as a sort of spurious movement in that direction. The originators of this movement bemoan the fact that the so-called higher criticism of the Bible, and especially of the Old Testament, has arrived at a deadlock, at an impasse. We have been so criticising the Bible, they say, that we have nothing left; we have been dividing up the Books and the phrases, and even dividing up the sentences, and we have lost the message. Now we must come back to the Bible. But what they really mean is that we must come back to what they call the 'message' of the Old Testament. They say they are still not going to reject the higher criticism, but, they tell us, they are prepared to accept the message of the Old Testament. They reject many of the facts of the Old Testament – they do not accept the early chapters of Genesis as history, they reject the story of the flood, they do not believe the story of Sodom and Gomorrha. They cannot believe such things as these, for their scientific knowledge makes it impossible. But they tell us that there is a kind of religious value in it all and that they are willing to take hold of the religious principle and teaching, while they reject the facts as such and regard them as myth.

Now that is the very opposite of what the Apostle argues in this chapter. You notice that here his whole case is based upon the acceptance of the facts. If we do not accept the fact of the Flood, then Peter's argument collapses. His whole argument is based upon these facts. And there again, speaking for myself, I find myself in exactly the same position. Miracles are not meant to be understood, they are meant to be believed. There are things I cannot understand in the Old Testament but as I find them to be an integral part of biblical history,

I believe them. For, as I understand this Book, the salvation of God is something that is given in action. God does not save by words; God saves by deeds. And you notice how our Lord accepts the Old Testament history. He refers to the Flood, He refers to Sodom and Gomorrha. He believed those things. How can I believe that He is the Son of God and yet believe that He is so mistaken with regard to facts? My very belief in His Person insists on my accepting these facts of Old Testament history. Very well, having accepted them, Peter works out his argument like this. He shows how this false assertion of the scoffers has already been falsified on many occasions. He picks out one perfect argument, the argument from the Flood and the same argument from Sodom and Gomorrha. He says that these scoffers are ignorant. In other words he reminds us of this story. There in that ancient world, when the men had given themselves over to sin and evil and iniquity, God gave a message to a man called Noah. He told him He was going to judge and destroy the world; He told him, therefore, to build an ark and to save himself and his family, and to warn the people. Noah began to do so, and you remember how, for a hundred and twenty years, he warned that generation of the flood and of the destruction that was coming. What was the response? Well, we can imagine that the world at that time thought it was the greatest joke they had ever heard. They thought this man was a lunatic, they scoffed at him, they mocked him, they jeered at him. This idea that the world was going to be drowned! 'Look at the stability of creation,' they said, 'look at the mountains and the valleys, look at the hills, everything remains as it is, and you are telling us that all this is suddenly going to be destroyed.' How confident they were that this man was a fool. And yet, in spite of their scoffing and jeering, it happened. Their insolent confidence and their arrogant assurance were entirely unmasked and falsified.

As you read your Old Testament you will find the same thing running right through it. Do you remember the searching words of the prophet Amos about those who were at ease in Zion? He saw the destruction that was coming and he went and warned the people; but they laughed at it all. They said, 'This man is trying to frighten us, it is ridiculous.' They were at ease in Zion, but that did not help them when the destruction came, swift and sure, upon them. Indeed, it is one of the great messages of the Old Testament to show us how men and women with their natural rationalistic ideas refused the revelation of God, utterly ridiculed these warnings, and then were overwhelmed by the events. And as you read the New Testament you will find our Lord and Saviour Jesus Christ repeats and reinforces the same message: 'And as it was in the days of Noe, so shall it be also in the days of the Son of man. They did eat, they drank, they married wives, they were given in marriage, until the day that Noe entered into the ark, and the flood came, and destroyed them all. Likewise also as it was in the days of Lot; they did eat, they drank, they bought, they sold, they planted, they builded; but the same day that Lot went out of Sodom, it rained fire and brimstone from heaven, and destroyed them all. Even thus shall it be in the day when the Son of man is revealed.'

But then Peter goes on to point out how *these people are deliberately and wilfully shutting their eyes to the facts.* 'This,' he says, 'they willingly are ignorant of.' The ignorance was wilful, because they knew that what people of old had regarded as impossible had already actually happened. Peter's argument on the facts is this. As God destroyed the old world, so God will destroy the present world. The scoffers say this is impossible. But the scoffers of old said the same thing. Nevertheless the facts of history stand out against them as a solemn warning, and for man not to believe it is just to shut his eyes to history, and to blind himself to that which has already happened.

Then the last argument. The ultimate trouble with such people, says the Apostle, is that *they forget the power of God.* He puts it in these words: 'This they willingly are ignorant of, that by the word of God the heavens were of old, and the earth standing out of the water and in the water.' This is a reference to the creation of the world. The world was without form and void, it was in a formless state, and it would have remained like that but for one thing – the power of God. God said, 'Let there be light' and there was light. That is the kind of God in whom we believe. The whole thing looks impossible to us, but the power of God is such that He had but to say, 'Let there be,' and there was. That is the God that is behind the universe. In exactly the same way the ancient world was there in apparent eternal stability, and God commanded the flood. And the waters came down from the heavens and rose up out of the earth and the ancient world was destroyed. Very well, he says, 'the heavens and the earth, which are now, by the same word are kept in store, reserved unto fire against the day of judgment and perdition of ungodly men'. That is the final trouble with the scoffers; they forget the power of God. The world seems very stable, it seems fixed and immovable; but we must remember that the God who made and controls it and the entire cosmos is this Almighty God who can bring things into being out of nothing, and destroy them in a moment, the God who can handle the world and play with constellations as if they were but atoms. It is this Almighty God who has reserved this world for punishment. As He has made it once and destroyed it, so with the same word He can destroy it again. He is 'reserving it unto the day of judgment and perdition of ungodly men.'

Therefore the appeal of the Apostle to us is simply this. We must preserve what is called in the first verse 'a pure mind'. – 'I want to stir up your pure minds' – and he means by that, a mind which is unadulterated by false teaching. He means the mind which is the very opposite of that of the scoffers. The scoffer is the man of the world, the man who, as Peter puts it, follows his own lusts, the clever man who thinks that he can ridicule the whole of religion and who talks so confidently about 'science' and the principle of uniformity. He says it is monstrous to be asked to believe in miracles and in interference with the natural laws. But note the words of the Apostle: I exhort you to keep your minds pure, clean, and unadulterated by such scoffing and teaching. Christian people, in other words, are called upon to adopt an attitude and position that to the world seems to be utterly ridiculous. To believe these things today is as monstrous to the natural man as it was to the unbelievers of Noah's day. And yet if we accept the Bible as the Word of God, if we believe in this as revelation, we must believe that it is an essential part of the teaching. The whole world is being divided into two groups, the godly and the ungodly; judgment is coming, swift, certain and sure; and what will determine our eternal and everlasting fate is which of these two positions we are in. We must not bring natural reason to this; we must accept the Bible as the Word of God, the revelation of God, and live a life which is in conformity with it. The pure mind, not the scoffing, mocking mind of the natural man who rejects the revelation of God, is what we need. God grant that our minds may thus be pure, and utterly free from all modern suggestions and teachings which would have us reject the clear teaching of the revelation of God in His Holy Word.

18
God and Time

'But, beloved, be not ignorant of this one thing, that one day is with the Lord as a thousand years, and a thousand years as one day. The Lord is not slack concerning his promise, as some men count slackness; but is long-suffering to us-ward, not willing that any should perish, but that all should come to repentance.'

Chapter 3:8–9

So far in our study of this chapter we have seen that in this world we are confronted by two possible positions: we can either accept the ideas of men and their philosophies, their attempts to understand history and to explain history and to forecast the future of the world – we can either do that, or else we can believe that the Bible is the Word of God; that these prophets, to whom Peter refers, and these Apostles were men specially chosen by God, given by Him a message, and an understanding beyond human reason, and that here in this Book we have God's account of the world and history. We must be in one of those two positions. That is the argument that Peter is working out, and you remember how, in doing so, he takes past history and shows how the scoffers are utterly mistaken. He points out how there have always been such people – before the Flood and before Sodom and Gomorrha. How confident and arrogant and assured they always are, but they have been proved to be wrong, not only by what has happened, but also by the way in which God has finally acted after a long delay. Peter ended on that great note by reminding them of the power of God.

But now, here, in these two verses he goes a step further forward. For it is not only the scoffers who are concerned about these questions; God's people themselves know what it is to be affected by doubts and uncertainties. They believe the Gospel, they accept the

Gospel and yet, as they look at the world, it does not seem to conform to what the Gospel says. Thus it comes to pass that most of these New Testament Epistles were written in order to strengthen the faith of God's people and to comfort them. For though God's people are not like the scoffers, though they do not put their questions in the same way, they very often put the same questions. You will find in many of the Psalms such questions as, 'Hath God forgotten to be kind?' In other words, the difference between God's people and the scoffers is in the way in which they put the questions rather than in the nature of the questions. For instance you will find many times in the New Testament itself that God's people have become discouraged. The members of the early church, at least many of them, seemed to have believed that the Lord would return immediately. They began to wonder, therefore, what was taking place – why hadn't God done this? why didn't God send Christ?

Well now, the position is very much the same still as we look at the modern world, as we see its godlessness and its irreligion. It is not surprising that at times we should feel like asking questions – why does God allow this? why does God tolerate it? If God has the power, why does He allow this to go on, why does He not intervene and interfere, why does He not overwhelm His enemies? He has promised to do so, why doesn't He? That is the kind of question which the Apostle now deals with in these two verses. Here we have his answers to the church and to the Christian; not his answer to the scoffers, which we have already considered.

We can divide up his answer most conveniently under two main headings – the general answer, and the particular answer. There are certain general points here, says Peter, which we must always bear in mind. The first is that *we must never be too curious about 'the times and seasons'*. I need not stay with that, because this warning about being over-concerned about dates and times and seasons is found repeatedly in the Bible. In general, the Bible tells us that we must have a great concern about the End; that we must be looking for, and waiting for, this great event which is going to wind up history; but we must never be too concerned as to the particular time, as to when it is going to happen. That seems to be the way in which the New Testament approaches this whole subject – we are to be always looking unto and waiting for and expecting the coming of the Lord, but the moment we begin to calculate and to fix when it is going to happen we involve ourselves in difficulties and troubles. Hence the warning not to be concerned about times and seasons and dates.

I do not want to stop with that now, but it is a most illuminating and interesting study to read history on this subject and to see how even good and devout and godly men have fallen into this particular trap. There were people centuries ago who felt certain that the coming of the Lord was going to take place in their time. It has always been something that has come very naturally to some people to identify certain of the symbols – Napoleon as the anti-Christ for example. When they have tried to fix times and seasons, men have always fallen into that error. We know how there were people who were certain of the significance of the war of 1914–1918, while in the last war, too, men and women were guilty of this particular fallacy and made the same identification in connection with Mussolini and Hitler. Now the answer is, that we must always expect the Lord, and yet never try to fix and determine exactly the time of His coming. For the Bible says that it will be sudden and unexpected, and known to no one.

But perhaps the most important general principle which Peter lays down here can be put like this, that *we must always remember that we cannot by our very nature and constitution understand fully the mind of God*. We are upon earth; we are finite. Not only that, but our minds have also been twisted and perverted as the result of sin. One of the first things we have to realise, therefore, is that we always start with this limitation as we begin to meditate upon God and His ways and His works with respect to man. 'For my thoughts are not your thoughts, neither are your ways my ways, saith the Lord. For as the heavens are higher than the earth, so are my ways higher than your ways, and my thoughts than your thoughts' (Isaiah 55:8 and 9). That is the great principle which we find everywhere in the Bible, and we can put it in a practical form and manner. Whenever I am troubled as to God's ways, if I cannot quite understand what is happening, if I feel that something altogether different ought to be happening; if God's ways with respect to me personally or with respect to the world and mankind seem odd and strange, the first thing I should say to myself is that I must always remember that the trouble is probably in my mind, because God is so infinitely above me, and His mind eternal and so different that I must not expect to be able to understand. If we begin to approach these problems on the assumption that we can understand the mind of God as we understand our own mind, there, at once, is an initial fallacy. Indeed the one thing that is quite definite is that we must start with the realisation that there is this infinite qualitative difference, as the modern theologians put it, between God and ourselves – that God is in the heavens, we are upon earth. We cannot see things as He sees them.

That, then, being the general principle, let us see how Peter works it out in particular and in detail. The first point which he makes is *God's relationship to time*, which he works out in the following terms.

In the first place, Peter tells us that *God is altogether above time*. 'Beloved, be not ignorant of this, that one day is with the Lord as a thousand years and a thousand years as one day.' That is the principle; God is eternal, God is above time. We must never think of God as being involved in the time process or in the flux and movement of time and history – God is altogether above time. It is almost impossible for us to grasp such a thought and such a concept, and yet it is a very vital principle. We, being creatures of time, of necessity think in terms of time. God is altogether above and beyond and outside it, so that when we are thinking of the purposes of God, it is always dangerous to exaggerate this time element. God Himself, being eternal, is right outside it. To Him a thousand years are but as one day and one day as a thousand years. In other words, He does not live at all in the realm, or in terms of, the time process.

However, we do not stop there, obviously, because we must go on to this second statement: *though God is above time, God does act in time*. That is equally necessary. It is God who started the time process. God, by creating the world, began the movement of history. He Himself is outside it and above it, but He set it going. Now in that sense I suppose that the argument of the famous Deists of 200 years ago can be used as long as we do not misuse it. God is like a man making a watch or clock – He Himself is outside it, He exists without it, He is not a part of it. The watchmaker makes the watch, he winds it up, he sets it going, he is outside the process but he initiates the process, he sets the hands in motion. That may help us a little to understand the relationship of God to time. But, according to this biblical teaching, God set the process going and He keeps it going. We can even go further than that – God is controlling time and God's actions are all worked out on a very definite plan and according to a very definite scheme. You cannot read the Bible without seeing that quite clearly and quite definitely. God made the world, and at a certain point history began. But man sinned and fell. Then God intervened. Again it seemed as if the process was going on apart from God, but then God intervened again. You notice all along how He did things – it all happened 'in due time' – that is a biblical term which is constantly employed. So we see that although God is above and beyond time, He still controls and acts in time. He has set the time process and the historical process going and then He comes into it; if you like, He enters into it from the outside. That still does not make God a part of the time process, but it does show His control over it and His interference with it, according to His own eternal will and counsel.

That brings us to a concrete statement of the nature of what we may call *divine chronology*. God acts and plans and schemes, He interferes and enforces. When does He do so? What is it that determines when God intervenes? That is the question that concerns people. Our trouble when we begin to think of time, of chronology, is that we think of clocks and calendars, of weeks and months and years. But a study of the Bible makes it abundantly plain and clear that God's chronology must never be thought of in this way. It is always, rather, a matter of moral conditions. Let me give you some quotations from Scripture to prove what I mean. In Genesis 6:3 we read, 'And the Lord said, My spirit shall not always strive with man.' Now what was happening there? Well, the world had sinned and the moral conditions were getting worse and worse. God was speaking, God was upbraiding, He was condemning, and calling to repentance; but men paid no heed. So He makes this statement: the point will arrive when I will cease to strive with you and I will act. That is not a point on a calendar, it is that the moral conditions would become such that God then would act. Or take the statement in Genesis 15:16, 'For the iniquity of the Amorites is not yet full.' God will only act when the iniquity is full. Take again the words from the New Testament: 'I will send them prophets and apostles, and some of them they shall slay and persecute; that the blood of all the prophets, which was shed from the foundation of the world, may be required of this generation.' The prophets had been killed centuries before, but the punishment comes when the iniquity has reached a certain level. Then take the phrase, 'until the times of the Gentiles be fulfilled', and 'this gospel of the kingdom shall be preached in all the world, and then shall come the end'. When is the end going to come? It is obviously not a certain date on a calendar, it is when the Gospel shall have been preached to all nations and amongst all people – 'then cometh the end.' When did Christ come into the world? 'When the fulness of the time was come' – when the conditions were such that God said: This is the time. Again, 'in due time Christ died for the ungodly'. When will the end of the world be? It will not be until the fulness of the Gentiles has come in, until God has gathered out His people from amongst the Gentile nations – it will not happen until then. Now that is the biblical teaching on divine chronology.

Let us therefore get rid of all these ideas of dates and calendars, and let us realise that what determines God's intervention in the time process is the matter of moral conditions. What is much more important than any particular date is the moral state and condition of the world today; for Scripture makes it very plain that before the end there will be a terrible apostasy. But we must be careful, for men have often said before, 'This is the last great apostasy'. We must not again try to fix the exact time of the end, but we should be made to think, as we see the falling away from God and the arrogance and the active godlessness and irreligion. We should be made to think of these things because we are told that just before the coming of our Lord and Saviour Jesus Christ, the moral conditions will be such that there will be this great apostasy and sin and iniquity will be revealed. Let us therefore, keep our eyes on the moral conditions rather than on the dates, because that is what seems clearly to be the teaching of the Bible with respect to the nature of divine chronology.

Peter then moves on to the second principle, which I am just going to note. It is *the principle of God's righteousness*. Having pointed out that although God is thus outside the time process, He nevertheless interferes in it, Peter goes on to say, 'The Lord is not slack concerning his promise, as some men count slackness; but is longsuffering to us-ward.' Let me put it like this. When we are troubled about these things, we must not only remember that we cannot understand the mind of God, that this whole question of time is not to God what it is to us; we must also hold tenaciously and without wavering to the principle that God is righteous. In other words, whatever else may be the explanation of the things that trouble us, it is not anything unworthy in the character of God. When we see the world as it is today, or as it has been in previous ages, and God does not seem to act, the temptation, suggested to us by the Devil, is to ask, 'Is God unconcerned that the ungodly are thus being allowed to flourish?' Now I say there is only one way to answer that, and it is to say, 'The Lord is not slack.' Whatever else it is, it is not any unrighteousness in God. It is not that God is unconcerned. We can be certain and sure at this moment that what God has said, God will perform. His promises are absolute, they are sure, they are certain. God's righteousness is something that cannot vary, it is one of those absolutes which I must never attempt to quibble about. What God has said, God will perform, and we can be sure that the ungodly and the unrighteous shall be brought to judgment, shall be brought to punishment. 'The heathen rage and the people imagine a vain thing; yet have I set my king upon my holy hill of Zion.' That is the biblical answer.

Christian people, let us comfort ourselves as we think of that great principle. Because we are Christian we may be called upon to suffer at a time like this. The world may laugh and mock, and it may seem to be very successful as it does so, but as certainly and as truly as we are alive at this moment, the unrighteous and the ungodly will have to answer for their every word, and those who have been faithful to the Lord will receive the 'Well done, thou good and faithful servant'. The Lord is righteous, the Lord is 'not slack', there is no slackening in God, there is no moral slackness; the utter, absolute righteousness of God remains. Let us hold on to that whether we understand what is happening or not.

Then lastly, there is this wonderful principle of God's *long-suffering*. 'The Lord is not slack concerning His promise, but is long-suffering to us-ward, not willing that any should perish, but that all should come to repentance.' This is a difficult statement. It is a difficult statement theologically, and it has led to much argument and disputation. If I may say so in passing, it is generally one of those stock quotations which are always brought forward whenever people are discussing election and predestination. But to look at it in that way is rather to miss the point which Peter is making. It seems to me that Peter's point is this, that a part of the explanation of what seems to us to be a delay is God's long-suffering. This we can be certain of, that God does not wish that any should perish (I did not say 'will', I said 'wish', for the word translated 'will' should really be

translated 'wish'). Whatever God wills inevitably comes to pass –
there is a difference between God willing and God wishing a thing,
and what Peter says is that God does not wish that any should perish
but that all should come to repentance. God takes no delight in the
death of the ungodly; that is why, Peter says, He delays His action.
That is something which we can illustrate from Old Testament
history. Did you notice the times before the flood – how God seemed
not to act for one hundred and twenty years? There was Noah
preaching to those people. Why didn't God destroy them at the
beginning, you ask? Ah, that is the long-suffering of God. God by thus
holding back His hand does not wish that the ungodly should perish.
God always warns before He strikes, and if you read your Old
Testament history again from this standpoint, it will amaze you more
and more to notice the extraordinary patience of God. Look how He
waited before the destruction of Sodom and Gomorrha. Look
especially at His patience with the children of Israel when they laughed
at Him and insulted Him and turned their backs upon Him. God sent
them that succession of Prophets – the long-suffering of God! Oh, let
us not ask our questions as to why God delays. It is this amazing
patience and long-suffering of God.

Then look at it in terms of the centuries that passed before Christ
came – why that long apparent delay? To me there is only one
answer: it was God, as it were, showing the ancient world how it
could not save itself apart from His action. Man always claims that
he can put himself right – God gave the nation a law and said, If you
can keep that law it will save you. They felt confident they could do
so and God gave them all those centuries just to show them that they
could not. It is this long-suffering of God that leaves the world
without an excuse or a plea. And that, according to the Apostle Peter,
is the explanation of why the Lord has not returned before this
particular point in history. The world is being given a chance, an
opportunity; Christ is preached, the Gospel is offered; all these years
are passing and the offer is being made. So it works out like this.
When the end shall come, and when the final judgment shall take
place, all men and women who have ever lived shall be raised to
stand there before God in judgment, and then this delay will in itself
be the one thing that will finally condemn them. The world will be
left without an excuse. God will be able to say, 'The Gospel was
preached, Christ was offered to you and throughout all these long

centuries I waited, I delayed, I gave you the opportunity.' The righteousness of God will be revealed. The world will be left without a vestige of an excuse. Thank God that there has been this delay. Where would you and I have been had it not been for it? The long-suffering and the patience of God! 'The goodness of God leadeth thee to repentance,' says Paul. And again at the end of this chapter we find Peter saying once more, 'Account that the long-suffering of our Lord is salvation.'

That then seems to me to be the Apostle Peter's answer to the Christian who is troubled about the conditions, and who sometimes is tempted to query and question with regard to the delay. Remember that we are dealing with God and not with man. Remember His eternity. Remember His relationship to time. Remember the utter righteousness and holiness of God. Remember His love, His mercy, His compassion. We are in time, and let us confess it, we are far too much like James and John. You remember our Lord sent them one day to prepare His way for Him. They went into a city of the Samaritans who would not receive them, and you remember how James and John said unto our Lord, 'Shall we call down fire from heaven to consume and destroy them?' If you and I controlled this world, no doubt it would be like that – we would bring in immediate judgment. But the reply was, 'Ye know not what manner of spirit ye are of, for the Son of man is not come to destroy men's lives but to save them.' 'The Lord is not slack', but He does not wish that any should perish, but that all should come into this blessed knowledge of salvation.

Let us then submit unto God and His absolute wisdom, and especially to His love and mercy, His long-suffering and compassion. The ways of God are certain and are sure. We cannot understand them now, but in His own good time we shall understand all things.

19
The Biblical View of History

'But the day of the Lord will come as a thief in the night;
in the which the heavens shall pass away with a great
noise, and the elements shall melt with fervent heat, the
earth also and the works that are therein shall be burned
up.'

Chapter 3:10

In these words the Apostle continues his consideration of the subject
which has been his theme from verse 16 in the first chapter. In writing
to these Christian people to encourage them, to help and comfort
them, above everything else he holds before them what is described
in the New Testament as the 'Blessed Hope'. In other words we are
dealing here with the New Testament view of the course of the
world's history. It is a central theme in the New Testament. You find
it in every Book somewhere or other. It is in the Gospels – our Lord
was constantly speaking about it. It stands out prominently in every
New Testament epistle, and is of course exclusively the theme of
some of the books.

Now it is a subject which is clearly engaging a good deal of
attention at the present time. I do not mean that the New Testament
view itself is engaging attention – I mean this whole question of
history. There is quite an unusual interest being taken in it during
these days and that, of course, is something which is inevitable and
perfectly natural in view of the experiences through which we have
passed. The problem of history is becoming increasingly the first
problem of philosophers and of all who are concerned, even
indirectly, with the whole question of life and its meaning. In many
ways it is the big theme of this twentieth century of ours. We have
experienced such shocks, things have happened which have been so
unexpected, that ideas which had been taken more or less for granted
in the previous century, and at other times, have been made to look

even somewhat ridiculous. Owing to the world wars, and owing to the uncertainty of life between the wars, and to the present uncertainty, it is not unnatural that people who think at all should be facing this question, in considering the history of this world – Is there any purpose in it? Is there any object in it all? What is it going to lead to? What lies ahead of us? These are the questions that are being asked. No longer are people content just to live without wondering what is going to happen. The idea of the eternal stability of the world seems to have been shaken and there is a feeling, as a result of all our experiences, that we should apply our minds to this whole question of history. We all desire to know if there is an objective, if there is a directing purpose. And that, in turn, will affect the way in which we live our life. Now that is the theme with which the Apostle deals here so clearly.

Perhaps our best way of considering it together will be to consider it in the light, and against the background, of some of the modern popular ideas with respect to this subject. Let me just note, therefore, some of the commoner views with regard to the history of the world that are current today.

The first is the view which, in spite of everything that has happened, still believes in the *idea of inevitable progress*. This was the typical, most popular, 19th-century view of life and of the world and of history. History, according to that view, which was first propounded clearly by the German philosopher Hegel, is a gradually advancing process, it is the working out of a great principle. There are apparent contradictions, says this view, but they all ultimately blend together. You have your thesis, and then the antithesis, and the two operating together produce the ultimate synthesis. According to this Hegelian view, all history shows nothing but the working out of this great and grand and developing process.

Some of our own poets were very fond of this philosophy. Tennyson in many places gives expression to it – the great idea that there is a magnificent principle of progress being worked out, until eventually you will arrive at some glorious millennium. He sang about the time soon to come when we should see 'the parliament of man and the federation of the world', and of 'knowledge growing from age to age'. The characteristic Victorian optimism, as we tend to describe it today, was based upon that theory and upon that outlook.

There are many sub-divisions of this which need not delay us, but we may note that the Marxist view of life, the communist view of life, is just a variation of this idea of inevitable progress. According to that view there are forces, material forces, struggling against one another and producing this ultimate synthesis – employer and worker, and the division between the two, these two inter-acting. That is the explanation of history. They claim that they can thus explain all the wars of the past, all the advance of civilisation and all the scientific advances. All this is really produced as the result of the inter-play of these two forces. And the whole time the process is going on, and continuing, and developing. Each one is superior to the previous one, and it goes on interacting until you arrive at a state of perfection which, according to that view, is the classless state of society. That is one view which, I say, is still held by large numbers of people. It is astonishing to see how often it comes out in newspaper articles and in the speeches of the politicians and others, and in the writings of certain popular writers – this belief in the inevitability of progress and of development.

But then there is another view, and it is a very much older one, the view which regards *history as being a matter of cycles*. That was the view which was held by the ancient Greek philosophers. They said history is nothing but a turning round in cycles. There seems to be an advance, and you imagine as you are going up one side of the curve, that you are going on and advancing and rising for ever; but it does not work like that. You find you are simply going round in circles. You get to a certain point, then you get to a level, then you begin to come down. Those who held this view would point out how history shows the rise of civilisations, how they came to a stage in which they flourished and blossomed, and then declined and disappeared. These people remind us of such civilisations in China and in Egypt and in other parts of the world. You see it in the history of empires and great states – the gradual rise and gain in power and influence and importance; they go on and on until they reach the point beyond which they do not advance, and then, down they go. History, we are told, is a matter of cycles, you just go round and round. Now that is a fascinating idea. You get it in a sense, in the Book of Ecclesiastes – 'there is no new thing under the sun'; what is, has been; what is to be, has been already.

It is astonishing to discover in how many respects in life there is so much evidence which seems to support this view. In the realm of science, for instance, I remember a man who after much patient research work made a discovery which as far as he knew was absolutely new. He had been making experiments, and he had found something. He was very pleased about it, and was about to write out his report. But being a wise man he thought he had better search all the literature on the subject first to make sure it had never been discovered before. After spending three weeks in such reading, he was disappointed to discover a little footnote at the bottom of a page, in very small print, which pointed out that the ancient Egyptians had discovered something which was almost identical with that which he himself had discovered after all his painful, wearying research. I remember the man saying, 'What is the point of research on anything? I believe that everything we can ever find has really been discovered before.'

Again, in connection with the wonderful treatment of diseases with penicillin, I was interested to read in a magazine recently, that quite clearly the ancient Chinese, thousands of years ago, had been using the very self-same thing. They did not know what it was, they did not call it penicillin, but they were doing the very same things. Now that is the kind of evidence that makes certain people believe in this cycle view of history. It is a matter of fate, they say, a matter of chance; there are certain blind forces operating here in life and at the back of everything. No one understands them, no one controls them, the world has been just spinning round like that always, and always will. That is history, just going round and round in circles, everything the result of fate and blind chance.

Then there is another view, and in the light of our text it is a little more directly interesting for us – that is, the modern scientific view which tells us quite definitely that there is to be an end of history. They talk about the second law of thermodynamics. Now what the second law of thermodynamics really says is this – that the world is like a clock which has been wound up but which is gradually unwinding itself and running down, and that there will be a time when it will have run down altogether and life on this planet will cease. There are a great many scientists today who believe this on purely scientific grounds. There will be an end of time, and a point will be reached when life will no longer be supportable. And that will be the end of history.

Yet another view I want to mention is the common view of many professional historians, and I think you will agree that this is interesting and significant. It was, for instance, the view of the late H. A. L. Fisher, the author of a monumental 'History of Europe'. It was put perfectly by a member of this school in these words: 'History itself, according to these professional narrators, is a meaningless, lawless, shapeless sequence of events.' That, I suggest, is the common view of the professional historians today. Here are men whose business in life is to study history. They look at the facts, they arrange and collate them, they do research upon them, and then they try to see if they can discover any sense or rhyme or reason, any purpose, or any philosophy, which they can lay before us with respect to them. And this is their conclusion – history is a meaningless, lawless and shapeless sequence of events.

Those, then, are the commoner views with regard to history which are held at the present time. We cannot now deal with them one by one. I just want to hold them over against what we find stated so clearly in the Bible, what we find here in these words of the Apostle Peter.

Is it not surprising and amazing that anyone can still believe in the theory of inevitable progress and development? Do not the facts which you and I have witnessed during this present century utterly disprove it? Can it be said that the world is advancing and that man is becoming better and better? As we look at life today, and at our world, can we really claim that we are superior to those who have gone before? Surely, it is time we began to examine again the theory that has held sway for such a long time, and which in many ways has produced the complacency which has been the source of so many of our recent troubles. And there is another thing about this theory which makes it quite unthinkable – it is an utter violation of any true idea of human personality, and especially of the personalities of men living at the present time or at any given point in history. This view of mankind roughly, is, that you and I do not matter as such. We are nothing but parts of this process which is going to lead to ultimate perfection. We are just cogs in the wheel that has to go round until perfection is eventually produced. According to this view, man will ultimately live a wonderful life and will really enjoy being in existence. But what of us? Well, they say, unfortunately it is just our part to lead to that – we, as such, do not count. It depreciates personality and the value of the human individual, and all the time it is interested only in that ultimate state of perfection that is going to arrive.

As for the view of cycles, there is, as I have granted, a great deal to be said for it. But surely, at the same time, we must agree that there is something in history beyond this turning round in circles. Civilisations have come and gone; that is perfectly true; but is it not true at the same time that the whole world is clearly moving forward as a whole? In the past you had civilisations in China, but they did not affect the rest of the world. You had the same thing in Egypt. But today the world is one in a sense in which it has never been in the past. What happens today happens to the whole world. It is not surprising that a war today becomes a world war. Travel, science, all these things have brought us together. The machine has done that. And anything that happens in the world today affects the whole world, so that in addition to the revolving of these individual cycles and wheels, there is, I suggest, a movement of the whole which strangely confirms the biblical view and conception of history.

As for the view of the professional historian, all we need to say about that is, that it is just typical of the ultimate scepticism and hopelessness of the man who takes a materialistic view of life, and who does not accept the biblical teaching with respect to God and man and the universe. I would say this for the professional historian that, apart from this Book, there is everything to be said for his view. Take the Gospel of Jesus Christ right out, and I think we have to admit that these gentlemen are very scientific and clear-headed, and have kept themselves from being carried away by beautiful idealistic theories with respect to life.

However, let us take all these theories and put them over against the biblical view. What does that enunciate? It is altogether different from everything else. *History, says the Bible, first and foremost is definitely under the control of God.* It is not blind, unintelligible or unintelligent. It is not the out-working of blind force and unseen powers that have no rhyme nor reason. We must not say of it that it is meaningless, lawless and utterly shapeless, because we can point to certain historical events which very definitely and clearly show a purpose. You have only to read the history of the children of Israel to see that. You have only to look at the Person of Jesus of Nazareth to see that. You have but to take the history of the Christian church in order to see that there is another plane, another order of events. That is the first great pronouncement of the Bible – it assures us that the whole historical process is in the hands of God. As we have pointed out before, it tells us that God started the process, that God invented time, introduced time, brought time into the scheme of things, and that God erupts into time and has His hand on the clock of time. That is the first statement.

And let me point out incidentally, in passing, that the Bible does not argue with us about this question of history; it makes its statement and we are left in the position that we either accept the biblical teaching and revelation, or else, finally, we are left with the scepticism of the modern historian. The world and its theories and its philosophers stand utterly baffled and bewildered today. But over against all that is this great revelation which claims to be super-natural and essentially miraculous. It does not say that it is scientific in our sense of the term scientific; it says, this is God's revelation, and if you only look at history in the light of it you will see how it is being worked out.

First and foremost therefore, the Bible states that God controls history; then its second statement is, that *the key to the understanding of history is the fact of sin*. But what does that mean? Let me put it briefly like this. According to the Bible, after God had created man, and had made him a perfect being and placed him in a perfect world, man rebelled and sinned against God. So another element came into life which was discordant, and opposed to the mind and will and purpose of God. A new factor, evil, came into life and into the world of man. According to the Bible, all the contradictions, all the troubles, all the problems have arisen from that, and that alone. Now you remember the Bible tells us that when man sinned and disobeyed God, not only did he affect his own story but he affected the story of the whole creation. God, we are told, cursed the ground because of the sin of man. There would never have been any thorns and briars but for sin; man would never have had to earn his bread by the sweat of his brow but for sin. You remember how the Apostle puts all that in the eighth chapter of the Epistle to the Romans: 'the creature was made subject to vanity, not willingly, but by reason of him who hath subjected the same in hope'; 'the whole creation groaneth and travaileth in pain together until now'.

In other words, not only is human history different from what it might have been, the very world in which we live is different. You and I have no conception of what this world was when God created it; we cannot visualise the grandeur; we cannot conceive of Paradise. The perfection was something we cannot even grasp. Sin has changed creation, the world is no longer what it was, the animals are not what they were, nothing is the same. That is not to say there is no beauty and wonder and glory in creation, but it does say that, in comparison with what it was meant to be, it is almost ugly. Sin has affected man and his history and the whole of the creation in which he finds himself, and that, of course, is to be seen right through the long story of man's history here upon the face of the earth. That is why you have these apparent cycles. Man has retained certain powers though he sinned against God, and he has shown this in various plans and designs which he has purposed and carried out.

You remember the great story at the very beginning which tells us how men in their cleverness and their ingenuity said, 'Let us build a tower'. And they began to build it, but they had not gone very far when God smashed it and frustrated their purpose and confused their language, and thereby showed that He was Lord over all. That kind of thing has been happening ever since; men have constantly been trying to get on without God, and God allows them to go so far, but then suddenly He intervenes and all is destroyed. That is why history is contradictory; that is why you seem to be having these recurring cycles; that is why so many people have become cynical and confused, or to use a common word, frustrated. During the past hundred years we have been trying to rebuild the tower of Babel. We were very confident that we could make ourselves good by our own efforts. God allowed us to try, and then suddenly the world we had built was smashed by a world war. All that is just God showing us that, because of sin, there can be no uninterrupted progress. It is God bringing down the pride of man. Thus it comes to pass that you have a kind of renaissance, and then you go back to a dark era. That is why so many are ready to believe the professional historians at the present time. The explanation of that, according to the Bible, is sin. So if we do not start by accepting the biblical doctrine of sin, we cannot expect to understand history, we cannot expect to understand this modern world in which we live. That is why there are troubles and contradictions and frustration – it is man at enmity against God; and while that persists this kind of thing will persist.

But let me move on to the next statement. The Bible shows in connection with salvation that there is not only a plan, but there is a developing and progressive plan; there is a distinct purpose in the mind of God. Now that is the next point we see very clearly – that *in the Bible there is a history of salvation*. And that is the whole glory of our Gospel. Because of sin everything went wrong, and if God had left it at that, the story of the world would have been just one perpetual torrent of sin and evil. But, thank God, there is something else; it is the theme of the Bible – the history of salvation. The Bible is not the history of the world, it is the history of salvation, of God's action in the world. God gives a promise, He calls a man named Abram. He turns him into a nation. He does various things with that nation; He gives a testimony concerning Himself to all other nations through that nation. On and on it goes, it is all leading to something; and then, in the fulness of time, Christ came, the centre of history. Then He did certain things which led up to His death on the cross, but it is all according to the 'determinate counsel and foreknowledge of God'. God's plan is here, it is working out, it is going on, it is evolving. God is bringing it to pass. The history of salvation clearly shows and indicates the purpose.

But let me come on to the last point – it is that *there is to be an ultimate and final consummation*. That is what Peter reminds us of in this verse. The plan of God which has thus been started, and which is continuing today, will go on until the final consummation. What is happening in this world at the present time is that God is calling out His people. He is dealing with individuals, rescuing them, delivering them out of the world, and He is putting them into a new kingdom. He is adding them to this realm of super-history, and it is all leading up to the end; and the end is the return of Jesus Christ into this world. It is clear in this Book from beginning to end – the return of Christ to judgment! What is that going to involve? It will involve, according to the record, the judgment of the whole world. Sin, evil and all who belong to that realm will be destroyed. Not only that – and this is the particular detail which Peter adds – the earth, the world, creation as you and I know it today, will also be destroyed. He tells us that, as the ancient world was destroyed by the Flood, so God will destroy our present world by fire. There are many in the modern world who really think that it is more than ludicrous for anybody to believe in anything like that today. My only reply to that view is this, that it is always included as part of the biblical teaching concerning salvation. If I believe in this message concerning salvation, the atonement and all these other matters, what right have I to reject this teaching concerning the ultimate, final consummation? It is here everywhere, and if I believe that this Apostle was definitely inspired when he wrote, I must accept it, and I do accept it. 'The day of the Lord will come as a thief in the night; in the which the heavens shall pass away with a great noise, and the elements shall melt with fervent heat, the earth also and the works that are therein shall be burned up.'

There have been two main views as to what that means. Ultimately they really differ very little one from the other. Some hold the view that the earth and the cosmos, the whole creation as we know it, will be literally and completely destroyed and that God will create a new earth. But according to the other view, what will happen is that the earth, as we know it now, will be entirely destroyed, but the ultimate elements that constitute it will remain, and out of them God will fashion a new world. An example of this was the way in which, at the time of the flood, the world was then destroyed, in a sense, and yet God remade it, refashioned it. There are many who believe that what we find in the first two verses of the Book of Genesis will, in a sense, happen again. What happened then was that the Spirit brooded over the chaos. The world, they say, had been made 'in the beginning', but as the result of evil it had entered into a state of chaos. God brooded over that chaos and brought into being a new world.

I say it does not ultimately matter which of the two views we believe; but what does matter is that, as Peter puts it, 'we, according to his promise, look for new heavens and a new earth'. What is absolutely certain is that when evil and sin have been destroyed and removed, the world, the earth as we know it now, will likewise have been destroyed. Then there will be produced a new heaven and a new earth. This is the very thing, says Paul, to which the whole creation is looking everywhere, and for which it is longing – creation 'waiting for the manifestation of the sons of God'. Those who are Christian will be present in that new world in glorified bodies, reigning with Christ, enjoying that eternal state with Him. The animals will be different, creation will be different; everything that is ugly and painful and foul will have been removed. There will be no more disease, there will be no more death; crying and sorrow and suffering will all be removed. There will be a glorified earth and a glorified heaven, and glorified men and women will live on such an earth and under such a heaven.

That is the biblical view of the ultimate end of history, and according to Peter, Christian people are those who look forward to it. 'Nevertheless we, according to his promise, look for new heavens and a new earth, wherein dwelleth righteousness.' How do I feel about history today? What do I feel about things as they are at this present time? How do I keep myself going? what is it that enables me to live? Am I living in the hope that something wonderful will happen, and that all our troubles will be banished and all will be well in a year's time, or two years', or perhaps ten years' time? Am I still clinging to something that is going to happen in this life and in this world for my happiness? If I am, then according to the New Testament, I am worldly minded, I am carnally minded. That is not the biblical view at all. The Bible tells us that the Christian man is one who really lives in the light of this blessed Book, who believes that this world, because of sin, must ultimately be destroyed. Have you noticed how in the predictions of the return of our Lord to this world there is always that element of apparent hopelessness, of things getting worse and worse – 'When the Son of man shall come, shall He find faith on the earth?' That is the teaching of the New Testament. It does not promise us some amazing millennium as the result of man's effort. No! the prediction is 'wars and rumours of wars,' and 'troubles'. If we are Christian, we must be expecting that kind of thing. We must not be depressed by it. The hope of the Christian is the new heaven and the new earth, the glory which is awaiting us with God in Christ. 'Well,' asks someone, 'are you not depressing with regard to the immediate?' I am realistic in the immediate. Surely it is the fool who tries to persuade himself that all is well, and that all is going to get better, without any basis of hope. Listen to your professional historians; they say that hope is not justifiable, and they are right. There is but one hope, there is but one comfort. Whatever we may have endured in this life, whatever the world may do to us, if we are children of God, we are heirs of God, we are joint-heirs with Christ. And, as certainly as we are alive today, there is a new heaven and a new earth coming, and if you and I belong to Christ we are going to live in that world. That is the doctrine that was preached to the first Christians. That was the doctrine that enabled them to die gladly amongst the lions in the arena. That is the doctrine which made them say that rather than deny their Lord they would willingly die. That is the faith which has sustained God's people throughout the ages. It is the only optimism today, it is the only comfort. Oh, let us diligently search into these things. Let us read our Bible again from this standpoint. Let us wait for that blessed hope, let us get into that state in which, with the Apostle of old, we may even long for and look for the glory that is yet to be revealed, which is God's promise to His own children in Jesus Christ our Lord.

20

The Blessed Hope

'Seeing then that all these things shall be dissolved, what
manner of persons ought ye to be in all holy conversation
and godliness, looking for and hasting unto the coming of
the day of God, wherein the heavens being on fire shall be
dissolved, and the elements shall melt with fervent heat?
Nevertheless we, according to his promise, look for new
heavens and a new earth, wherein dwelleth righteousness. Wherefore, beloved, seeing that ye look for such
things, be diligent that ye may be found of him in peace,
without spot, and blameless.'

Chapter 3:11–14

In these verses the Apostle continues the theme he has already been
dealing with in the previous three verses. We have already described
it as the 'Christian view of history', and in the last chapter we
considered what we may describe as the 'negative' side of that
Christian view of history. We were at pains to show that the Bible
clearly teaches everywhere, not only a definite end to history, but
that the end will be an end of judgment, introduced and ushered in by
the return of our Lord and Saviour Jesus Christ as King. He will
judge all men and women who have ever lived, and there will be a
final judgment of men and of angels. That will be followed, not only
by the condemnation and destruction of the ungodly, but further-
more by what we described as the destruction of the world as we
know it. The heavens and the earth, we are told, shall pass away, and
the elements shall melt with fervent heat, the earth also and the
works therein shall be burned up.

Now that is what I called the 'negative' side. Fortunately,
however, the picture does not end there. Peter goes on to give us a
positive picture of that to which the Christian can look forward.
There is nothing for the ungodly to look forward to except final,

ultimate destruction. Apart from Christ there is no hope whatsoever; and what we are told everywhere in this Book is that those who do not believe on the Lord Jesus Christ have nothing to look forward to except a state of punishment and of destruction unrelieved and without end. It is a terrible and terrifying thought, and yet it is the plain, clear teaching of the Bible everywhere. But thank God there is another side, there is a hope held out for the people of God. 'Nevertheless we,' says the Apostle – here is the Christian hope already – 'Nevertheless' – here is something different – we, according to his promise, look for new heavens and a new earth, wherein dwelleth righteousness.'

Now this is undoubtedly the most glorious promise which is to be found in the entire Bible.This is, of course, the thing to which everything we read in the Bible is ultimately meant to lead. This is the grand object and purpose of salvation; and there is nothing, perhaps, that is quite so sad and regrettable in the history of the Christian church, especially in the last fifty years or so, as the way in which this ultimate glory of the Christian message has been almost completely forgotten and ignored. The fact of the everlasting, or eternal state is recited in the Creeds, but how infrequently do men pay attention to it. We have been so concerned about the state of affairs here on earth that we have forgotten the glory which is to come. Men have talked so much about 'bringing in the kingdom of God on earth' that they have forgotten this glorious vision of eternity which is held out before us in so many places in Holy Scripture.

That is what the Apostle refers to here, and it is something to which frequent reference is made in many places in the Bible. Take for instance, the Apostle Paul's reference to it in the first Corinthian Epistle where he says, 'Eye hath not seen, nor ear heard, neither have entered into the heart of man, the things which God hath prepared for them that love him . . .' Then in the same Epistle a little later on he says, 'Know ye not that the saints will judge the world?' and again he goes on to say, 'Know ye not that we shall judge angels?' He was dealing with a very simple problem in connection with the church at Corinth. There were disputes and differences of opinion. This, said Paul, in effect, is ridiculous. Don't you realise that you, as God's people, as saints, are, in an age to come, going to judge the world and to judge angels? Well, surely, if you are going to do that, why don't you do this lesser thing?

Then you remember also the words of our Lord Himself where he says in Matthew 19:28, 'Verily I say unto you, that ye which have followed me, in the regeneration when the Son of man shall sit in the throne of his glory, ye also shall sit upon twelve thrones, judging the twelve tribes of Israel.' Now this is the interesting word, – regeneration'. 'Know ye not that ye which have followed me, in the regeneration . . .' – when everything shall be made anew – that is what it means. In other words, when the present heaven and earth shall have passed away and there shall be a new heaven and a new earth, then, in that regeneration, you shall sit upon twelve thrones judging the twelve tribes of Israel. And you remember how the Apostle Peter, in the sermon which is reported in the third chapter of the Book of the Acts of the Apostles, beginning at verse 19, puts it: 'Repent ye therefore, and be converted, that your sins may be blotted out, when the times of refreshing shall come from the presence of the Lord, and he shall send Jesus Christ, which before was preached unto you: whom the heaven must receive until the times of restitution of all things, which God hath spoken by the mouth of all His holy prophets since the world began.' There is the same idea – the time which is coming when all things shall be restored. 'The restitution of all things' into the state of glory which God had intended for them.

Again the Apostle Paul, in the eighth chapter of the Epistle to the Romans, says very definitely, that 'the Spirit itself beareth witness with our spirit, that we are the children of God: and if children, then heirs; heirs of God, and joint-heirs with Christ'. An heir must be an heir to something, and Paul makes it plain and clear that we are heirs of this great new world which is coming, this new earth, this new heaven, for he goes on to say, 'I reckon that the sufferings of this present time are not worthy to be compared with the glory which shall be revealed in us'. And then, you remember, 'For the earnest expectation of the creature waiteth for the manifestation of the sons of God; for the creature was made subject to vanity, not willingly, but by reason of him who hath subjected the same in hope. Because the creature itself also shall be delivered from the bondage of corruption into the glorious liberty of the children of God. For we know that the whole creation groaneth and travaileth in pain together until now. And not only they, but ourselves also, which have the firstfruits of the Spirit, even we ourselves groan within ourselves, waiting for the adoption, to wit, the redemption of our body.' Now that is, perhaps, one of the most magnificent statements of this doctrine that has ever been made.

But then, in addition to all this, we get it stated in a very plain and explicit manner, especially in the Book of the Revelation, the last Book of the Bible, with that glorious account of it in the twenty-first chapter. There, in a sense, in that one chapter, the whole doctrine and the whole truth is laid open before us, and we see that in a particularly clear manner if we compare and contrast that chapter and, in a sense, the whole Book of Revelation, with the early chapters of the Book of Genesis. That is, perhaps, the best way of grasping this doctrine. In the Book of Genesis we find the creation of the world; then in this last Book, and especially in the twenty-first chapter, we find this new creation, this 'regeneration' of which our Lord spoke, this 'restitution of all things' of which Peter speaks. And there you see the great contrast. God made the world; then sin came in and with it chaos, but God is going to remake the world. We have been reminded that it does not say that it will be a different world; but what it does say is that the world as we know it is going to be purged and purified from sin until there is nothing left which is the result of sin. And all will be perfect.

But let us look at it like this by way of contrast. In the Book of Genesis we have an account of the creation; in the Book of Revelation we have the new creation. In Genesis we are told how the moon and the sun and stars, the luminaries, the lights in the heavens were brought into being; in the Book of Revelation we are told that there will be no need for such luminaries because the glory of God will be the light of this City. In Genesis we have an account of how Paradise was lost; in Revelation we see Paradise regained. In Genesis we see the power of the Devil, the serpent, the fallen angel who came in and brought about the fall of man, and all the misery and wretchedness and iniquity that has ever followed in the long history of mankind; in Revelation we see the Devil conquered and mastered and ultimately destroyed and thrown into the lake of destruction, and rendered powerless. In Genesis you see man, because of his sin, fleeing from God, hiding himself from the face of God in the garden, shrinking from God, trying to get away from Him – he has been trying to do that ever since, – but in Revelation, as the result of the Gospel and its blessings and its goodness and mercy, you find God dwelling with man, and man dwelling with God and in the light of

God, the estrangement and the fear of God removed, and there, in perfect communion, they dwell together. In Genesis you see man disobeying God, eating of the forbidden tree, being thrown out of the Garden, and then being prevented by the flaming sword and the cherubim from getting to the Tree of Life and from eating its fruit; in the Book of Revelation (chapter twenty-two) man is allowed freely to take and eat of the Tree of Life – the very thing originally forbidden him, now given to him as the greatest boon and blessing.

The great promise that is held out before us, is the thing that Peter has in mind. 'Nevertheless we, according to his promise' – the promise which runs right through the Bible – 'look for new heavens and a new earth . . .' After the judgment and the destruction of the ungodly, after the world as we know it is burned with fervent heat, there will be this new heaven and new earth. What it means is that the fire will have burned out from the cosmos every taint of sin, thorns and briars, diseases, everything that causes pestilences, everything that leads to earthquakes and calamities. All will be removed, the earth will be purged of every such thing – that is the meaning of the fire. It will burn out everything evil, and the result is that there will be 'new heavens and a new earth, wherein dwelleth righteousness', of surpassing beauty and wonder and glory.

Now here we are in the realm of something that is truly wonderful and amazing. Our imaginations are too feeble to grasp it, and yet I have tried to remind you of what we are told in the Scriptures. We are not told much more than that: 'Eye hath not seen, nor ear heard, neither have entered into the heart of man, the things which God hath prepared for them that love him. But God hath revealed them unto us by his Spirit . . .'; and He has revealed them unto us in this Book. That is the teaching; that is the thing, according to Peter, on which Christian people should concentrate their gaze. We talk about the beauties of the world and creation as it is at the present time – and there are surpassing beauties in nature – and yet, according to this Book, when we, the children of God, shall see this new creation, this glorified earth, the beauties that we speak of at the present time will pale into insignificance. There will be such glory that the very mind of man at present cannot grasp and understand it. The wolf shall dwell with the lamb; the lion shall eat straw like the ox; there shall be no quarrelling, no sorrow, no sighing; all that will be removed. Read again that twenty-first chapter of the Book of Revelation and meditate upon it – that is the thing, says Peter, with which we are concerned.

Now that being the vision, that being the glorious prospect that is held out for Christian people, what should be our reaction to it? Peter tells us here in this verse. He says three things. I am merely going to note them. The first thing is that Christian people should be *looking for that*; secondly, they should be *preparing for it*, and thirdly, they should *hasten its coming*. Those are the three things which he tells us here. Let us just glance at them very briefly.

The first effect is that we should be ever *looking for it*. Did you notice how Peter keeps on repeating this word 'look' in verses thirteen and fourteen? That is the first thing the Christian does – he looks for these things. Now that word does not need any explanation. Perhaps the simplest way of putting it is this. It is the same word as the one which is used of the man sitting at the Beautiful gate of the Temple in the third chapter of the Acts of the Apostles. You remember the story. We are told that Peter and John were going up to the Temple at the hour of prayer, and there was a man who had been laid outside the Temple gate by his friends, a man who had been a cripple from his birth. He was put there to receive alms from people, and there he sat. Then Peter and John came along and the man, mechanically probably, held out his hand to receive something. But Peter, addressing him, said, 'Look on us,' and we are told that he looked at them 'expecting to receive something of them', and that is the very word used here – 'expecting, looking, waiting for, anticipating'.

What does this mean? I think we must work it out like this. The Christian's expectation and hope are not based upon this world. I sometimes think that this is perhaps the particular message that is needed by this age. In ages past there have been different principles and doctrines which have needed emphasis. I suggest that perhaps this is the doctrine above all others that needs to be emphasised today. The Christian's hope and expectation are not based upon this world. The very centre of the Christian position is to believe that this world is doomed, and that there is no question about it. That is, of course, why the Gospel flies right in the face of all the pathetic optimism of the last hundred years which led so many sadly astray, and which has in turn led to this present cynical generation of men and women. Our hopes were so built up with respect to the things that were going to happen here in this world, and in time; and we have seen the exact opposite. But all along the Gospel has been here, warning us and showing us that our hope in this world was utterly false.

Now we must be perfectly clear as to how this teaching should be put and how it works out. I heard a man the other day put what he thought was the Christian message in this form. He said the message to the world at the present time is, 'Repent or perish'. He told us about atomic power – that to him was the most important thing – and he said his message was that, unless the nations of the world decide to apply Christian principles, and outlaw atomic power altogether, well, then this atomic power is going to destroy the world. Therefore the message is 'Repent or perish'. That sounds very plausible, and yet I am anxious to show that it is not the Christian message. The Christian message is this: the world will not repent, the world is doomed. We have passed through two world wars. Would you not have thought that if anything could have sobered a race of people, that would have done so? But it has not. Instead there has been a hardening of the heart, and reports which have been written by missionaries of experiences in concentration camps during the war show that, far from leading men to Christ, it has hardened them.

Now that is the very thing the Bible tells us – that rebellion against God will continue, and that as things become worse rebellion will increase and become intensified. No, the world cannot be frightened into a belief in God, the Bible is eloquent on that theme. They will hate Him all the more. The world is doomed. The message is not repent or perish; the message is that the world is going to perish. That does not mean to say that the world is going to perish soon, it does not mean that I commit myself of necessity to the belief that atomic bombs and power are going to usher in the end. The world may decide to outlaw atomic power, but that is not going to save the world. It may prolong the course of history – we do not know, and we are not to be concerned about the times and the seasons – but what we do know is that the world is doomed to an utter, final destruction. The message of the Gospel is not a message addressed to the world in general, it is a message to men and women to save themselves out of that world which is doomed. It is a message which says, 'If you do not want to be involved in that condemnation, repent and believe on the Lord Jesus Christ – come out of it.' So that the message to the world cannot possibly be to nations at large or to the world as a whole; it is a message which pronounces doom, judgment, and destruction.

Let me hasten to say that this doctrine does not for a moment mean that the Christian should be unconcerned about the state of this world. It does not mean that at all, but it does mean that he should never 'lose his head' over what we may call social reforms. Now that has been the tragedy of the last hundred years. It seems to me that the men who are more responsible than any others for the state of the world, and especially for the state of the church, today, were the so-called preacher-politicians of the last century who displayed such enthusiasm and zeal and energy in trying to reform the world and society, and who gave the impression that education was more important than salvation. They were men who talked about this world and what could be done here and now, and who turned the attention of men and women from the world that is to come. The tragedy is not so much that they believed in reform, but that they became over-zealous, and pinned their faith to reform. It is the business of Christian people, believing that this is God's world, to control sin and the evil effects of sin; and that is why, according to the Scriptures, governments, authorities and powers have ever been brought into being. It is God who ordained the State, it is God who ordained magistrates and kings. But what is their function? Their function is, in a sense, entirely negative – it is to prevent the world from becoming a worse place. The function of Government and human activity is to restrain evil and its effects, although it can never produce a perfect condition.

So, then, the Christian is not only to believe in human government and enactments, he is to take a part in it. But the moment he begins to pin his faith to it and to believe that it can save the world, then he is contradicting the Gospel, he is denying the Christian faith. We must not pin our faith to this world, our hope must not be set upon it. The Christian is a man to whom the main thing, and the great thing, is that glory, that world that is to come. 'Look for'! 'We look for new heavens and a new earth.' The question that should be facing everyone of us is, Are we looking for these things? Peter says it is quite inevitable. You cannot believe this doctrine, you cannot accept the prophecies from beginning to end, you cannot accept this message, without looking for these things, waiting for them, expecting them. I fear that we, as we contemplate this glorious truth, must feel condemned and upbraided as we realise how much of our time and thought and expectation we give to this world and its affairs, and how little we think of that other world. And yet if we but realised it, that is the real world — 'the things which are seen are temporal, but the things which are not seen are eternal'. If we believe this Christian Gospel, those are the things which are before us. Very well, let us look at them; if we believe them, let us expect them. There should never be a day in our history or in our story, but that we stop and pause and meditate about these things and contemplate them. We talk so much about present suffering–oh, I am not here to make light of that, but that as Christians we must not stop there. We must think positively of that which is coming, think of the new heavens and new earth, think of this glorified creation. That is the thing to which we are going if we are in Christ. Very well, let us look for it, and spend our time in contemplating and meditating upon it.

But let me move on to the second point. The Christian not only looks for these things, *he prepares for them*. Peter puts this again very plainly, 'Seeing then that all these things shall be dissolved, what manner of persons ought ye to be in all holy conversation and godliness?' And again in verse fourteen, 'Wherefore, beloved, seeing that ye look for such things, be diligent that ye may be found of him in peace, without spot, and blameless.' Now this is the basis of the New Testament appeal everywhere, for Christian conduct and Christian behaviour. And again let me say that this is the way in which the New Testament always puts it. The New Testament never appeals for morality and ethics and conduct and behaviour in and of itself. Never! The New Testament never asks men to live a good life merely for the sake of living a good life. Its appeal on these lines is always in terms of this 'blessed hope'. So that there is nothing, in a sense, which is quite so contradictory as the position of the Christian who objects to the ethical demand of the New Testament. Peter says this is logic – there is no need to argue about it, it is inevitable, it is so absolutely reasonable. If you say that the thing you are looking for, and waiting for and expecting, is a world in which there is righteousness and no sin, how can you continue to do that which belongs to the realm of sin? It is a self-contradiction. That is his argument, and he puts it to their common sense and to their logic. That is why it seems to me that those who approach holiness, as being but the carrying out of a list of rules and regulations are denying the very New Testament teaching itself. That is not the way; the world tries to do that; that is not the Christian appeal at all. The Christian appeal is this – you claim that you are children of God, you say that you believe this Gospel; very well, if you really believe that, it is time you began to prepare for it. Listen to John saying the same thing – we do not know 'what we shall be: but we know that, when he shall appear, we shall be like him; for we shall see him as he is. And every man that hath this hope in him purifieth himself' – of course, it is inevitable. If I say that that is what I desire, well, let me give practical proof and demonstration.

Ah yes, but there is something else. I must live this godly, moral, holy Christian life because otherwise, when the day does come, I shall find myself ashamed. 'Wherefore, beloved, seeing that ye look for such things, be diligent that ye may be found of him in peace, without spot, and blameless.' What does the Apostle mean? He means this. The day is coming when our Lord will return, and 'every eye shall see him'. You and I shall see Him. That is why we sing that hymn of Murray McCheyne's –

> 'Then, Lord, shall I fully know,
> Not till then, how much I owe'.

We shall see Him, the blessed Son of God, who, though He was equal with the Father and co-eternal, there enjoying the everlasting bliss of eternity, came out of it and humbled Himself, emptied Himself, divested Himself of the insignia of His glory and became man on the face of this earth, endured all He endured even to the death on the cross in order that you and I might be forgiven, that you and I might be delivered from sin, that you and I might be made heirs of this glory that is awaiting us. We shall see Him! Then we shall see what it meant to Him and what it cost Him. And if you want to face that, says Peter, in peace, well, give diligence that you may appear before Him without spot and blameless. When you then see Him, and see the meaning of His life, and what it cost Him to redeem and bring you to that glory, then you will remember the time on earth when you played with sin, and how, though you said you were a Christian, you really enjoyed the world and gave yourself to it and spent your time in looking at it and its affairs, and you will feel you are a cad. You will feel you are worse than a cad; you will feel so ashamed, you will not be able to look at Him who has done so much and suffered so much. Ah, says Peter, if you want to avoid that, be diligent now and prepare yourself for the day, for His coming and for your entry into that glory.

Lastly, we must not only look for this and prepare ourselves for it, we are *to hasten its coming*. 'Looking for and hasting unto the coming of the day of God,' he says in verse twelve. This again is a great mystery. If these things are determined, how can we hasten them? Peter says exactly the same thing, you remember, in the sermon recorded in the third chapter of the Acts. It surely means that we must not think of these things in terms of dates, we must not think of them in terms of time; it is a question of moral conditions. The end will come when the moral conditions are such as God deems to be necessary. Well, we can hasten that by preparing ourselves, by preaching the Gospel, by telling others about Him. The end will come when the fulness of the Gentiles and the fulness of the Jews will have come in, when all will have been gathered in, when all of the redeemed will have been drawn out of the world. Let us hasten that by preparing ourselves, let us hasten it by spreading the Gospel, by preaching, or by supporting missionary work, and the work of the church in this land; in fact by everything we can do to hasten the coming.

Now that, according to Peter, is the Christian reaction to this glorious Gospel; that is the blessed hope of this wonderful doctrine. What a vista, what a vision! I wonder whether we have seen it? I think perhaps the simplest way to test that is to ask ourselves these questions: What is our reaction to the present position? Are we utterly depressed by it, are we even surprised at it, are we disappointed? Do we feel it is all wrong? Are we still pinning our faith to what man can do? If so, we haven't the Christian hope. The Christian is the man who expects nothing from this world. He is not surprised at the state of the world today because it is all foretold and it is the only thing you can expect from it. He does not pin his hope to it, because he knows it is doomed. He therefore spends his time looking at this other vision – something of which no one can ever rob him. The world, evil and Satan can never spoil us of our inheritance. If you are Christ's, you are a 'joint-heir with Christ'. He has entered into the inheritance, and as certainly as He has entered in, all who belong to Him shall likewise enter in and be with Him. Look for it, expect it, prepare for it, hasten its coming.

21
The Consolation of the Scriptures

'And account that the longsuffering of our Lord is
salvation; even as our beloved brother Paul also according to the wisdom given unto him hath written unto you;
as also in all his epistles, speaking in them of these things;
in which are some things hard to be understood, which
they that are unlearned and unstable wrest, as they do
also the other scriptures, unto their own destruction. Ye
therefore, beloved, seeing ye know these things before,
beware lest ye also, being led away with the error of the
wicked, fall from your own steadfastness.'

Chapter 3:15–17

In these verses the Apostle, having completed his doctrinal exposition, ends his letter with an appeal, and, in a sense, his final appeal.
The great need of these Christian people, he tells us, in the light of all
that he has been saying – and, therefore, our great need also – is the
need of steadfastness, the need of stability, the need of endurance.
You notice how that idea keeps on recurring in these verses. That is
why we have to account the longsuffering of our Lord to be
salvation; that is why he refers to certain people who are unstable;
that is why he ends up by saying, 'Seeing, beloved, ye know these
things before, beware lest ye also, being led away with the error of
the wicked, fall from your own steadfastness.' That, he says, is the
thing which is needed above everything else – this quality of
endurance, patient endurance, stability, strength, continuance.

Now this, of course, is in a sense the great theme of the whole of
the New Testament. We could spend much time in just giving a list of
quotations from the New Testament to show how, above everything
and every other appeal, the great appeal which runs right through is
this appeal for continuance, for endurance, for steadfastness, for
strength. Our Lord Himself constantly makes this point, but never

more clearly, perhaps, than in those words in which He says: 'Men ought always to pray and not to faint.' Fainting is the greatest danger of all – this collapsing, giving in, going out, backing out. He constantly warns His disciples against that danger. That is why He tells them so much about the trials they will have to endure in the world – 'In the world ye shall have tribulation.' He prepares them for it all because He knows that the greatest temptation that is going to assail them is the temptation of flagging under discouragement and persecution. So he prepares them for what was coming; and He constantly exhorts them to prayer, to diligence and to this holding on.

You find it in exactly the same way in the various Epistles written by the Apostle Paul, as Peter reminds us in this very section. You remember how Paul tells the Galatians that 'in due season we shall reap if we faint not'. It is an appeal to them to continue, to hold on, to keep going forward. And then, of course, I need scarcely point out that it is above everything else the whole message of the Epistle to the Hebrews. You are going to receive certain blessings, says this letter, if you hold fast the confidence which you had at the beginning. This is the refrain that runs right through the Epistle. That is the whole point of the glorious argument in the eleventh chapter. What is the point of referring to that list of Old Testament saints? Well, those men were living in a hard, contradictory world; but they went on in spite of everything. Like Moses, they all had their eye on 'the recompense of the reward'. They were 'seeking for a city which hath foundations'. The whole appeal of the Epistle to the Hebrews is for steadfastness, for confidence, for continuance, for patience in well-doing. You get it in exactly the same way in the first Epistle of John, and surely it was one great reason why the Book of Revelation was written. It is a book which gives a preview of what is going to happen in order that we may be prepared for it. It is one of the great outstanding themes of the New Testament as a whole. There is nothing which gives a more false representation of the teaching of the New Testament than the idea that it is just a book which merely tells us to believe on the Lord Jesus Christ and that then everything will be perfectly all right, that there will never be troubles or problems any more, and that we shall be able to rest at ease and be wafted in that passive state to heaven. Not at all! It is a 'fight of faith', and 'through many tribulations ye must enter into the kingdom of God'. All along it is an appeal for this very thing that we find here, for endurance, and for steadfastness.

Now why should that be necessary? I suggest that there are three main reasons. The first is the delay in the Lord's coming. I say the delay, perhaps I ought to say the apparent delay. I mean by that, that these people, these early Christians, having listened to the preaching of the Apostle, had somehow got hold of the idea that our Lord was coming back immediately. And because He did not come at once they began to question and to query. That has been the great theme of this Epistle – why does He not come? And we have already seen Peter's answer – God's calendar is a moral one, and to Him 'a thousand years are as one day and one day as a thousand years'.

A second factor which tended to produce this falling away, and this failure, was the work and the teaching of the false teachers. We need not refer to them again; it is the whole theme of the second chapter, as we have already seen. But Peter refers to it once more in this seventeenth verse – 'being led away with the error of the wicked'. The wicked are the false prophets, and they are still with us. It is not an easy thing to be a Christian today. There are so many ideas and thoughts and suggestions and insinuations which would discourage us, and would indeed positively encourage us to slackness and indolence, to a falling away, to a failure to stand. We are set in a very difficult position. Never, therefore, is this exhortation to steadfastness more needed.

Then, perhaps, the third factor, and the one which Peter wishes to emphasise particularly in this section, is what I might call our natural instability, our natural waywardness, the natural tendency to indolence. Is it not a very remarkable manifestation of sin that the natural man who, when concerned with material things is characterised by energy and enterprise, should, when it becomes a question of standing loyal to Christian principles, be affected by instability and indolence. I sometimes feel that there is nothing at the present time which should make those of us who are Christian feel so much shame as the way in which we can so easily be put off from our Christian views. When we observe the contrast between the world and ourselves, is it not rather sad and pathetic? It takes a good deal to stand between the man of the world and his plans and the thing in which he believes. He will endure almost anything to obtain that thing which he likes and in which he believes. But far too often we give the impression that it takes very little indeed to stand between some of us and our loyalty to the Gospel – this Gospel which tells us that we are sons of God, that we are going on to a glory which transcends our highest imagination, that we are heirs of God and joint-heirs with Christ. We say we believe that, and yet how easily can we be deflected from it. Now those are the reasons that led the Apostle to make this appeal; and these factors are still prominent amongst us and still powerful in their influence.

The question is, then, how do we resist these temptations and tendencies? How can we be steadfast, how can we continue as men worthy of the name? To use the language of Paul, how can we 'quit ourselves like men and be strong'? The apostle answers those questions here. How does he do so? Well, let me point out, first of all, what he does not say to us. What is his appeal? In the first place, it is not an appeal to our courage as such, it is not an appeal to grit. I put it thus negatively because at the present time there is a great danger of our applying what was being addressed to us in a material sense, to the spiritual conflict also. We are living in a time of difficulty, and these appeals are made to us. You remember the appeals that were made during World War II; they were appeals to our grit, to our manliness, to our strength. Now that is not the appeal which the Apostle makes here. It is very important that we should realise that. The Christian, as I want to show you, does not go on and hold on simply in terms of manliness and human grit. Neither does Peter make an appeal to them to view the situation philosophically. Again, we hear a great deal about that. There are people who can go on, not because they have any particular manliness or courage, but because they have decided that they might as well be philosophical about the situation. 'What is the use of grumbling?' they ask; 'there is the situation; we have to go through with it.' But while from the natural standpoint that is quite sound, it does not radically help us to confront the situation. Many a time has man said, 'I will just take a philosophical attitude. Things are as they are, events are unfortunate, but it is no use crying over spilt milk. No doubt events will improve.' He does not lose his temper, he just accepts the situation in that way – the result of being philosophical. That is not the appeal here; that is not the way the Christian does it.

Nor is it an appeal to some mechanical resignation. Peter does not just say to them, 'Well, put up with it; it isn't very good, but, well, there it is, shoulder it, get on with it, and put up with it; do the best you can, you may as well resign yourself to it.' That again is not the Christian way. Neither does he appeal to them to live on their past experiences. He does not say, 'Now things are not as you expected. The Lord has not returned. What are you to do? Why don't you think of the wonderful experiences you have had. Look at the thrilling moments you had in life, go back to the mountain-top experiences. Find something there to cheer you up. And in the light of past experiences go on today and go on into the future; live on your experience and on everything which has been helpful.' Again I say that that can be very valuable in a natural sense, and on a purely human plane; but that is not the method of the Gospel.

Now these negatives are important for this reason, that far too often we must all plead guilty to the fact that, in our Christian life, we overcome our difficulties and our problems by some such psychological method instead of doing so by the spiritual method. But surely, says someone, you are not opposed to psychology? I am opposed to psychology if it comes between us and that which is true. Psychological suggestion and treatment can be of temporary help to those who are not Christian; but for a Christian man to comfort himself, and establish and strengthen himself by psychology alone, can be a denial of the truth of the Gospel. Far too often you find that the Christian church herself has been a promoter of psychology instead of presenting the Christian message with its comfort and cheer. 'Ah,' people say, 'that is nice. I feel better for being in that atmosphere.' That may be so, but I would remind you that there are many things which can produce that effect. It may be brought about by drugs or by taking alcohol. You forget your troubles; they cheer you up for the moment. But that is not the Gospel method.

How does the Gospel do it? Well, the Gospel method of establishing us is to impart knowledge to us, to give us learning; it presents us with truth. 'Account that the longsuffering of our Lord is salvation; even as our beloved brother Paul also according to the wisdom given unto him hath written unto you, in all his epistles, dealing with these things.' That is the method. So as you and I confront the contradiction and the problems of this hour, the thing we are exhorted to do is to read the New Testament, to come back to this revelation and this truth. Now why should we do so? How does that help? That is the question. Why should I, as a Christian, confronting the modern world, say, 'Now I am not going to listen to any of the things that are being said by mere man. I am not going to try to help myself by trying man's psychology. I am going to the New Testament, I am going to see the truth as it is there unfolded and expounded, I am going to believe that.' Why should I do this?

Peter answers that question in this passage, and here are his reasons. In the first place I should read the Scriptures and accept this teaching because I believe it is *the revelation which has been given by God*. I base my whole life upon this teaching because I believe the Scriptures are divinely inspired. Now this is how Peter puts it: 'Even as our beloved Paul also according to the wisdom given unto him hath written unto you.' I am saying this to you, says Peter, not as Peter but as the Apostle of Jesus Christ to whom this wisdom has been given, and I ask you also to read the Epistles of my beloved brother Paul to whom also this wisdom has been given. Now that is fundamental. After all, Peter was a fisherman stating a philosophy of history. This man who wrote these words is in effect telling us that he, in and of himself, has no understanding or knowledge. He is saying that which has been given to him by God, it is the wisdom received, the revelation given from above. It is not I, I am simply announcing these things to you. I am not a scientist. I do not say the world is going to be destroyed because of my scientific understanding. It has been revealed to me, it has been given to me. The Scriptures are divinely inspired, they are not human views and philosophies; they are the revelation of God and His purpose with respect to man.

Not only that, you notice that Peter here places the writings of the Apostle Paul, and therefore his own writings, on an equality with the Old Testament Scriptures. 'As also in all his epistles speaking in them of these things; in which are some things hard to be understood, which they that are unlearned and unstable wrest, as they do also the other scriptures, unto their own destruction.' That is a tremendous claim. These people, says the Apostle, are misunderstanding some of the things which Paul says in his letter, but they do exactly the same thing with the other Scriptures also, and when he talks about the other Scriptures he is referring to the whole of the Old Testament Scriptures. So that here he puts his appeal, and that of Paul, on an equality with the Old Testament Scriptures which every Jew regarded as uniquely inspired of God and given by Him.

There, then, is our first reason for accepting this teaching, this knowledge. This Book is the revelation of God's mind. And I say once more that I am driven in the last analysis to one of two positions; I either believe and accept this as a revelation from God, or else I trust to human ideas and human notions. And it is past my comprehension how anyone can possibly do that in view of the history of this present century and the way in which all the forecasts and views and ideas of man have been falsified. Here we have the view of God.

The second reason for reading the Scriptures is that *they give us full information concerning all these matters about which we are so exercised.* 'Account that the longsuffering of our Lord is salvation; even as our beloved brother Paul also according to the wisdom given unto him hath written unto you; as also in all his epistles, speaking in them of these things; in which are some things hard to be understood, which they that are unlearned and unstable wrest, as they do also the other scriptures, unto their own destruction. Ye, therefore, beloved, seeing ye know these things before, beware lest ye also, being led away with the error of the wicked, fall from your own steadfastness.' The Scriptures, thank God, deal with this very situation, and that to me is what makes the New Testament an increasingly thrilling Book. I know of no Book that is so contemporary as the New Testament. As I look at the modern situation, here is the only place I find anything satisfactory. I read other books, they all try to diagnose our time and the problems of our time, but again we remember what Dr Joad said in his review of a certain contemporary book, 'An excellent diagnosis, but no solution whatsoever.' Here is the only place I know of in which these things are really dealt with. Here is the only Book I know of that prepares me for a difficult world. Here is the only Book I know of that prepares me for the world as it is at this moment.

Having listened to and read the idealistic, humanistic philosophies of the last century, no one would expect two World Wars in a quarter of a century. With our education and culture no one would expect the godlessness and the immorality that we are witnessing at the present time. But here is a Book that tells me to be prepared for these things. 'In the last days perilous times shall come.' It tells of moral muddle, it tells us to be prepared for many signs and wonders and voices which are so deceiving that, 'the very elect' would be fooled by them. It prepares us for these things. It tells us that the delay in the coming of the Lord is nothing but salvation – 'Account that the longsuffering of the Lord is salvation.' We have already dealt with it and understood how it enables us to see that God has a purpose in it all. God is so loving that He is still giving the world an opportunity to repent – that is the meaning of the apparent delay. It warns us against the false teachers that are round and about us. But above everything else, and, thank God for this, it gives us a glimpse of the glory that can never pass away, which can never be affected by atomic bombs or by any devilry the mind of man may invent. It gives us an insight into those things which will then be fulfilled. That is how it prepares us. In every respect the Gospel gives us a perfect provision and full preparation.

But now finally let me deal with the last point which the Apostle makes here. It is quite right thus to view life and its attendant circumstances in the light of the Scriptures, but, says Peter, you must be very careful that you approach the Scriptures in the right way. Now this is something of unusual interest. Peter tells us it is not enough just to read the Scriptures; we must read them in the right way lest we may be guilty of wresting the Scriptures to our own destruction. If ever there was a time when this particular warning was needed it is surely the present. Peter tells us that there were certain people who were misunderstanding certain things which were being preached by the Apostle Paul. You will find that made very clear in several of the epistles. For instance, in the Epistle to the Romans Paul says that some people were slanderously reporting him. Certain people had been saying that the Apostle's teaching on justification really amounted to this, that because we are justified by faith, because we are saved by grace, we may do evil that good may come. Sin as much as you like, they said, all is well; the more you sin the more you will realise the sin, and the more you will need forgiveness by God, and the more grace you will receive. Let us do evil that good may come. That is how they were wresting his teaching to their own destruction.

Moreover, he tells us in the first letter to the Corinthians that there were some people who were trying to show that the resurrection had already happened. These people were wresting his teaching on the resurrection to their own destruction. Then in the second chapter of the Second Epistle to the Thessalonians, he again tells us that some people had been saying that he, Paul, in his letters had said the day of the Lord had already come. Do not believe it, says Paul; it is false representation, it is the very opposite of what I said. And he goes on to correct them. Now they had been doing exactly the same thing with this particular doctrine which we are now considering. So Peter is very emphatic that we must be extremely careful when we read the Scriptures that we approach them in the right manner.

What then is the right way of reading the Scriptures? Let me give you the headings as they are suggested by the Apostle's teaching. The first thing is the Scriptures must always be read *carefully and studiously*. We must never read them hurriedly, we must never rush our reading of the Scriptures and we must never jump to conclusions. There is nothing more fatal than just to open your Bible and look at a verse, or to extract a verse here and there out of its context – the Scriptures must be read through carefully and studiously. Shall I be misunderstood if I say that the most dangerous Book in the world is the Bible, because it is the Word of God, because it is the greatest Book, because it is a Divine Book, because if we misread it we can, as Peter says, wrest it to our own destruction. Therefore, I say, let us approach the Scriptures carefully and studiously.

The second point is, we *must read it as a whole*. We must not just read a portion here and there, or a particular section that may happen to appeal to us. At a time like this, especially, nothing is so important as to read the whole Bible. The danger is that people should say, 'Well, I am feeling tired and depressed and things are rather difficult. The Psalms are very comforting; they seem to understand me.' So they turn to the Psalms, or to a certain favourite passage in the New Testament. But I say, read the whole Bible, go through the history, read the law, read the Prophets, see its ultimate outcome – read the whole Bible and not just favourite parts.

Then, thirdly, we must read the Bible *with fairness and with an open mind*. In other words we must not read the Bible just to conform our own ideas and support our own theories. We cannot enter into this now, but this is what Peter has in mind, and this is what Paul has in mind when he corrects this tendency – the danger of coming to the Scriptures with your own ideas and theories. Read the whole of the New Testament; do not read it with a theory in your mind. I need not tell you of the many ways in which that is being done today. Think of the many theories that are current; look at the strange doctrines that are current, look at the cults that are round and about us, look at the notions that some people harbour about our own nation and country. And the trouble is that they tend to see these things everywhere in the Bible. That is what I mean by going to the Bible with a theory instead of with an open mind, and then, instead of reading the Bible and allowing it to speak to you, you are just looking for a confirmation of your own theories and ideas. That is one way of wresting the Scriptures to your own destruction. In other words we must come with an open mind, and if we do not understand we must say so, and we must be content not to have a perfect theory. We must say there are certain points in the Scriptures which we cannot fathom.

Further, we must turn to the Scriptures with *a spirit of humility and with a readiness to learn*. Now there is a glorious example of that in our text. Looked at in a purely personal way it is wonderful. Peter says, 'Account that the longsuffering of our Lord is salvation; even as our beloved brother Paul also according to the wisdom given unto him hath written unto you.' That is the spirit! What does it mean? You remember how we are told in the second chapter of the Epistle to the Galatians that Paul had to withstand Peter to the face. Peter at Antioch had gone astray; he had misunderstood the doctrine of justification, and he had told the Gentiles that they must in certain senses become Jews. And Paul had had to reprimand Peter. There he is, a great man in the Christian church, in a sense the leader, and yet this man Paul questions him and corrects him and puts him right. Now many of us in that situation would never have forgiven Paul for that, and we most certainly would not have recommended the people to read his Epistles. But this is how Peter put it, 'Even as our beloved brother Paul also, according to the wisdom given unto him, hath written unto you.' Here is a man who is humble, here is a man who has recognised that he was wrong and that Paul was right; he was prepared to listen and to learn – that is the spirit! We must go to the Book in that spirit of humility and with a readiness to listen and to learn. Though my pet theory may prove to be wrong it does not matter; I must go in that childlike manner; even as Peter listened to his beloved brother Paul.

In other words, finally, we must approach the Book *in a prayerful manner*. We must realise the greatness of its message, we must realise the feebleness of our own minds, we must realise our tendency to be governed by carnal, worldly, merely human thoughts. So I should never open this Book without praying, without humbling myself and asking God to give me understanding, and by the Holy Spirit to open my mind, to open my intellect, to open my heart. I must go to it with reverence, with a spirit of supplication that I may receive unction and knowledge from the Holy One. Why? Because this Word of God can be a dangerous word to me, for I might wrest it to my own destruction.

That then is the Apostle's method of facing the tendency to fall and to falter and to wander away. That is the way to be steadfast, that is the way to be loyal and to be true, and to continue without faltering. Not just a little psychological encouragement, not just turning over the pages and feeling you are being entertained by reading the Scriptures and studying the doctrine, but doing so in this humble and reverent manner. If you do that, says Peter, all the taunts of the scoffers and all the heresies of the false teachers will leave you quite unaffected. The world may persecute and even threaten to kill you, but seeing these things, having a view of the glory that awaits you, you will be able to smile at it all and stand firm and continue steadfast in your most holy faith. Amen.

22

Growing in Grace (I)

'But grow in grace, and in the knowledge of our Lord and
Saviour Jesus Christ. To him be glory both now and for
ever. Amen.'

Chapter 3:18

'Grow in the grace and in the knowledge of our Lord and Saviour
Jesus Christ.'

These are the Apostle's final words to these Christian people to
whom he has been writing. He has developed his doctrine, he has
worked it out in detail with them. He has given a full explanation of
their position and their outlook. He has warned them against the
dangers which are likely to confront them. And especially in the verse
immediately preceding this last verse, as we saw last time, he has
been urging upon them the importance of really grasping the truth.
That is why he impressed upon them the importance of a careful and
reverent study of the Scriptures. The reason for that was that there
was a danger of their being led away with the error of the wicked,
and that if they were so led away they would fall from their own
steadfastness.

The Apostle then comes to this final word which he introduces
with this word 'but'. In contra-distinction to all that he has said –
avoiding this error of the wicked, the false teachers; avoiding the
tendency to fall away and to slip and to get into trouble – as a
contrast to all that, they are to 'grow in grace', or rather 'grow in the
grace and in the knowledge of our Lord and Saviour Jesus Christ.'
The way in which Peter puts this is full of interest. He suggests
obviously, and at once, that the only way to avoid falling in the
Christian life is to advance. The only way to avoid slipping back is to
go forward. There is no such thing as being static in the Christian life,
for the good reasons which we shall soon be discovering; and there,

then, is the kind of principle or key to the understanding of his entire teaching on this point.

Now this is a well-known and familiar verse. It is in many ways an epitome of the New Testament appeal to Christian people. The New Testament is full of exhortations to us to perfect ourselves in godliness; it has this constant call to holiness and sanctification. And all that teaching is, in a sense, perfectly summed up in these words, 'Grow in the grace and in the knowledge of our Lord and Saviour Jesus Christ'. That is the sum total of Christian duty; it expresses, I say, perfectly and concretely, everything which you and I are called upon to do in this Christian life. This therefore, is something which really should demand our very careful and close attention, and I am happy to attract your attention to it at this particular season of the year which is known as the period of Lent. It is not that we believe in the mechanical observance of times and seasons, but that any occasion which calls upon men and women to examine themselves and their lives is something which is essentially good. Our one quarrel, finally, with the whole Catholic view of the Christian life, is not that it believes in the period of Lent, but that it does not believe in observing Lent always throughout the year. Our one quarrel is that these times are isolated instead of being observed perpetually. Now I say that here surely is the theme of Lent, here is the essential Christian and New Testament doctrine with regard to the living of the Christian life.

It is a very large subject, and it seems to me that the best way of dividing it is this. First of all, we must try to discover together what the Apostle means by 'growing in grace and in the knowledge of our Lord and Saviour Jesus Christ'. Then having done that, the next obvious step is to consider how one is to grow in grace and in the knowledge of the Lord Jesus Christ. Then thirdly, how does one determine whether one is growing? It is not enough to consider this question theoretically and from the outside, the ultimate object is to discover whether we are growing. How does one do so? What are the tests? What are the possible methods? What are the fundamental dangers and pitfalls in connection with this whole matter of self-examination and inspection of ourselves in our Christian faith?

The point at which we must start, then, is to discover exactly what is meant by this whole idea of growing in the grace and in the knowledge of our Lord and Saviour Jesus Christ. Now this way of putting the New Testament doctrine of sanctification and holiness is something which leads us at once to some of the very vitals of our faith. That is, of course, what Peter was anxious to do. He was anxious to leave these people with a final word which would always remind them of what they had to do, and one cannot imagine a more perfect synopsis of the whole Christian duty than what we have here. It is all here in embryo, and as we analyse this verse I think we shall see that it does hold us face to face with the basic elements of our faith.

Now what is suggested first of all by this word 'grow'? What are the thoughts that are immediately insinuated into the mind by this conception of growth? There, I think, we are reminded of something that is basic. The very word 'grow', the very idea of growth, suggests to us immediately that *being a Christian means receiving a new life*. There can be no growth unless there has been a birth, and birth means bringing, or coming to life. So that when the Gospel exhorts us to grow in grace and in the knowledge of our Lord and Saviour Jesus Christ, it pre-supposes a life, a birth, a beginning, the possession of something which is very definite.

Here, of course, is the very first, and most fundamental step. All these appeals for holiness in the New Testament are only addressed to Christian people. There is, I would say, a fundamental respect in which it is true to say, that the Gospel is not interested in the conduct and the behaviour of those who are not Christian, except in a purely negative sense. I mean by that, that the Gospel never comes to a man who is not a Christian to tell him to live a better life. That is in a sense a denial of the Gospel. The Gospel never calls upon an unregenerate man to improve himself and make himself better. That is morality, not Christianity. There is always this vital presupposition in the New Testament appeal for holiness; it only speaks to those who have received a new life. It only addresses those who are born again. So that the very word 'grow' introduces immediately and automatically the whole Christian doctrine of regeneration and of the rebirth. Now that, of course, is the very point which Peter has in mind; because his whole emphasis, as we have seen, has been that these people to whom he is writing must realise that they are altogether different from those who are not Christian. They have received a Divine nature, they have become 'partakers of the Divine nature, having escaped the corruption that is in the world through lust.' He told them this at the beginning, and he now ends on precisely the same note.

So the first question that we ask ourselves as we confront this exhortation to grow in the grace and in the knowledge is, are we alive? have we life? have we been born again? The Christian, in other words, has a different seed of life in him, or I can go further, and say the Christian is essentially different from the man who is not a Christian. He is different in kind. Now this is really basic. The Christian is not only better than the man who is not a Christian; he is different. He is one who has been born from above, born of the Spirit – these are the New Testament terms – he is always conscious of having received a new life. He is one who conforms to the definition given by the Apostle Paul, 'If any man be in Christ, he is a new creature; old things are passed away; behold, all things are become new.'

This obviously is the starting point. In any self-examination, in any desire to grow and develop, we must be conscious of this life; we must be aware of the fact that God in His infinite grace has imparted to us His own nature; we must, in other words, be conscious of this vital difference. The Christian is not just a man like every other man. Let me put it this way. I would say that far too often we tend to think of the Christian as someone whose conduct of life is the same as everybody else's, but that he has added on certain things to his life. Now that, I say, is an utter travesty of the New Testament teaching; and my argument is that this word 'grow' makes that utterly impossible. Its contention is that the Christian is not a man who adds something to his life; but that his life is essentially different, he has a different order of life. There is a new being, a new existence, a new quality incarnate in his life. Christ comes into the Christian, and I say that without this idea of life, growth is something which is utterly impossible. So the very exhortation to growth leads us immediately and directly to the cardinal New Testament doctrine of the re-birth and of regeneration.

Then having said that, we can go on to the second deduction. *This life, like all other forms of life, should lead to growth.* That is something, of course, which is always characteristic of life. The very fact of life in and of itself contains the whole idea of growth. Think of the smallest seed. Within it inherently is the possibility of growth and development. Think of the smallest animal and you see the same thing. Think of the smallest plant or flower – wherever there is life there is always this inherent possibility of growth. Now that is exactly and precisely the case with respect to the Christian life. So that we can say there is no better test that we can apply to ourselves, to discover whether we are truly in the Christian life, than this very test of growth. Is what I regard as Christianity something that is capable of growth, or is it not? If it is not capable of growth it is not Christian. It may be a number of other things that are very good, but it is not Christian. Let me put it like this. There is all the difference in the world between the vital process of growth and the mechanical enlargement of anything without life. You can add to something which is lifeless, but you cannot make something which lacks life grow. Take, for instance, a mound of earth; you can add more earth, but you do not say that that pile of earth has grown. Growth is something essential and vital.

Here, again, we have a test which is very thorough and sensitive and delicate. This has been the cause of stumbling to many in the Christian life, as the record of the church so very plainly shows. I say that the fact that there is the possibility of growth in our Christian experience is one of the most delicate and sensitive tests as to whether we have life or not. Let me give an illustration. I think we can see the difference very clearly in the life of a man like Martin Luther, or if you like, in the life of a man like John Wesley. You can see it in fact in the life and experience of anyone who has written an account of his spiritual pilgrimage and who has contrasted a pre-conversion and a post-conversion period. Take a man like Luther. There he was, a very religious man. He was a monk, and there I see him fasting and praying in his cell. There is a man who is trying, as he thinks, to grow in the Christian life. What does he do? Well, he fasts, he prays, he gives alms, he does good works; and yet, having done all that, he knew perfectly well that he had not grown at all, he had no more life at the end than at the beginning. That man has been adding things to his life but he has not been growing. He has been adding merit to merit, but he knows at the end of it all that there is no life. Then, you remember, he becomes converted, he receives this new life, and from then on he is conscious of a growing process, of a development, of real growth.

You see exactly the same thing in the case of a man like John Wesley – an excellent, moral young man, a member of a good

Christian home. His one interest in life was religion, his one desire to be better. He forms his Holy Club at Oxford, he goes preaching in prisons and thereby suffers sarcasm and scorn; he gives up the Fellowship in his College and crosses the Atlantic to preach to the pagans in Georgia. And yet he knows that he does not have any true life. He does not feel he has grown or developed or advanced. There is a man who has been adding on plus after plus, but there is no development or growth. Then he receives life, and from the moment he receives life he is conscious of growth, of true organic development.

Now there, I think, we see this very vital principle. Life contains within it, inherently, the whole possibility of growth, and should lead to growth; but apart from that life there can be no growth. I can, I say, add morality after morality, but that is not to grow. So I suggest the second test which we apply to ourselves is this: Am I aware of growth in my Christian life? Can I say that I am growing in the grace and in the knowledge of our Lord Jesus Christ? We shall later be dealing with a number of tests – I am now putting it in general. As I look back across the year, as I look back ten, twenty or thirty years, or however long I have been in the Christian life, am I aware of some organic development and increase? Is there real growth in my Christian life? There is nothing more vital and important than this sharp, careful distinction between the process of trying to add to the life and a growth in the life. It is all inherently suggested by this very word 'grow'.

Then just a passing word about *the process of growth*. In a sense I have already dealt with one section of this. The process of growth is something which is vital and not mechanical. It is very difficult to define it; there is something very elusive in this very idea of growth. When we come to look at the methods or the ways in which one should grow, and when we look at the tests of growth we shall again be reverting to the same point, but there is something mysterious about growth. It is something that, in a sense, you cannot observe directly – you are aware it is taking place but you cannot see it happening. You remember our Lord likened it to a man who sowed seed in his ground and how while he slept the seed sprang up – the mystery of growth. That is something which is true always of growth and of this life process. But we can say that it is always a vital process; it is never a mechanical process. It therefore is to be judged in terms of an organic whole rather than in separate parts.

I must emphasise the importance of this distinction. If you take up so-called Manuals of the Devout Life you will find that many of them are written by Roman Catholics because they have always been specialists in this matter. I think you will see in them that the principle of the difference between the mechanical and the vital process is really most important, because the whole Catholic conception of growth tends to be mechanical. It separates and isolates particular things and its whole way of measuring holiness tends to be in terms of, are you adding this, or are you not adding that, have you added this to your life? You count your beads, as it were; you put up your list on the wall and tick off each deed until the list is completed. Now that is mechanical, it is not a vital process. It seems to me that the mistake at this point is to confuse the things that promote growth with the growth itself; and as I think we shall see, all you and I can do ultimately is to obey certain conditions that tend to promote growth. We cannot produce growth directly and we must always bear in mind that growth is a vital and not a mechanical process.

The other point I should like to make is that *the process of growth is of necessity a process which is progressive and gradual* – growth is never sudden. Here, of course, I am saying something which is highly controversial, because I think you will find there are schools of thought with regard to this matter. There are those who in preaching holiness and sanctification would have us believe that a man can suddenly be sanctified. They very often compare the process of sanctification with the fact of our justification in one act of reception, saying that you can receive your holiness and your sanctification in the same way. That has been, as you know, the characteristic teaching of a very well known school of holiness. They say you can be made holy at once in an act, you can arrive there, you can be placed in that position. Now I am suggesting that that does violence to this very essential process of growth. The whole New Testament picture, surely, is one of growth and development. It talks about men being 'babes in Christ' – a babe cannot suddenly jump from a babe to manhood. It happens gradually, you know not how; you just know that that person is no longer a babe, he is no longer a boy, he has become a youth and then he has become a man. You cannot mark off these stages. It takes place gradually – you see the babe, you see the boy, and then you see the youth and then the man. It has happened gradually and imperceptibly. He has gone from step to step and stage to stage. And holiness is not something that can be received once and for all in one act. We 'grow in grace', we grow in holiness, we grow in knowledge. It is something which is gradual, it is something that is progressive, it is something that goes on throughout our entire Christian life in this world until eventually we attain unto 'the measure of the stature of the fulness of Christ' in that glorified life that awaits us beyond.

Now this, again, I feel, is a very important distinction, because failure to recognise this has accounted for much unhappiness in the life of many a Christian person. There are many Christians who spend most of their lives in going round from Convention to Convention, hoping that eventually they are going to receive what they call 'IT', seeking to get it, hoping that something tremendous will take place and that they will receive holiness and sanctification as they have already received their justification. Now the New Testament, I suggest, does not teach that; indeed, the New Testament makes it very plain and clear that there is no such thing as justification without sanctification. Christ is made unto us 'wisdom and righteousness and sanctification and redemption'. If you have Christ at all you have the whole Christ. If you are 'in Christ' you are 'in Christ'. It is impossible for a man to have justification without the seed of holiness and sanctification being in him at the same time, and that seed is to grow and develop. Indeed, there would be no point whatsoever in all these New Testament appeals to us to grow and develop and to put off the old man and put on the new man, if it were something that was to be done in one act. No, no; growth of necessity is a gradual and a progressive matter.

Well, those are certain thoughts suggested to us by these short words 'grow' and 'growth'. But let me say just a word with regard to *the respects in which we can grow*. Peter does so very plainly. First of all I am to grow in the grace of our Lord and Saviour Jesus Christ. What does that mean? I sometimes think that this is one of the most difficult phrases in the New Testament – grow in grace, grow in the grace of our Lord Jesus. What does it mean? I think in the first place we must say it does not mean that I grow in graciousness – it includes that, but it does not mean that. Neither does it mean, in and of itself, that I should grow in my possession of the graces of the Christian life. It does include that, but it isn't that. What then, does it mean? It must mean this – that as Christians we have been brought into the realm of grace. We are all of us either under the law or under grace – we are either under the wrath of God or we are under the grace of God. Now what Peter is saying is something like this – you, as Christians, are now in the realm of grace. In that realm, grow in the life into which you have been brought by the death of Christ and His resurrection, and as a result of His grace develop and expand and increase and go forward.

And surely also it must include this, that to be a Christian means that I am the special object of God's favour and kindness. As a Christian I can receive and experience that favour of God in varying degrees and in varying amounts. The more I live the Christian life, the more obedient I am, the more will I experience the favour of God. That is growing in the grace of the Lord Jesus Christ. There He is, waiting to show me His favour and to shower His favour upon me. Well now, says Peter, so live that you will experience that more and more, and will enjoy your Christian life increasingly – that is growing in the grace of the Lord Jesus Christ. In the realm of grace I am increasing, I am growing, and my experimental knowledge and experience of His favour is something which I am increasingly conscious of. That is what is meant by growing in grace. So that again we can put that as a question. Am I increasingly conscious of the favour and of the kindness of God? Can I, as I contrast myself with what I was at this time last year, say that the favour and the kindness and the mercy and the goodness of God to me are something of which I am more greatly conscious than I have ever been before? If so, I am growing in grace.

But I am also to grow in 'the knowledge of the Lord Jesus Christ.' What does it mean? That is Peter's way of saying that I am to grow in my understanding of the truth. As Peter has been elaborating this I need only give a summary. It means that I should increase and grow in my knowledge concerning Him, in my knowledge of what He has done and of what He has brought to this world. I can summarise it in this way. As a Christian I am not to stop merely at a knowledge of forgiveness and a knowledge of salvation; I am to grow in my understanding and in my knowledge of the whole scheme and plan and purpose of salvation. I am to learn everything that Peter has been telling us in this Epistle. I am to see the whole plan of the ages and the plan of the world and of the cosmos. I am to understand increasingly the nature of the spiritual conflict which is going on in this world round and about me. I must not stop at a sense of personal forgiveness of sin, I am to see myself in the whole economy of God. I am to be aware of this mighty spiritual struggle that is taking place in the heavenly places. I am to see God gradually working out His plan even in the realm of history and I am increasingly to understand the final consummation of it. That is partly what is meant by growing 'in the knowledge of the Lord Jesus Christ.' There is knowledge concerning Him, and the implications of that knowledge. So that I must busy myself with Christian doctrine. I must learn to understand the doctrine of God and His Being, the doctrine of the Trinity, the doctrine of man, the doctrine of sin, the doctrine of salvation, the doctrine of the ultimate and the last things. I must go into all these so that I may grasp the knowledge concerning the Lord Jesus Christ more and more.

But I think that, in addition, it means this: not only the knowledge concerning Him, but a knowledge of Him. I must grow in my knowledge of the Lord Jesus Christ, by which is meant my communion with Him; my sense of a personal relationship to Him must increase. You remember how Paul puts that very perfectly and tells us that this was his one ambition – 'that I might know him'. That's it! There is a mystical knowledge of Christ possible to us. The Christian is not left with a mere knowledge concerning Christ, there is a knowledge of Christ. You remember how Peter puts it in his first Epistle; 'Whom having not seen ye love.' You can only love a person whom you know. You mustn't stop at knowing things about Christ; there must be a sense of personal knowledge. I want to grow in that, says Peter, and you *must* grow in that. So we grow in the grace and in the knowledge of the Lord Jesus Christ in that dual sense.

Then a final word. *Why is it thus important for us to grow in both these main respects?* The answer is, of course, that it is the only way to stand firm and solid, and it is the only way to meet the contradictions of this life and of this world. The more I know the favour of Christ the more I shall be able to smile in the face of adversity. If I really know Him and receive His favour then I will be able to say with Paul, 'I am persuaded that neither death, nor life, nor angels, nor principalities, nor powers, nor things present, nor things to come, nor height, nor depth, nor any other creature, shall be able to separate us from the love of God which is in Christ Jesus our Lord' (Romans 8:38 and 39). It enables me to say that. But not only that, the whole picture of the difference between the child and the grown-up person shows us another reason why we should go on. The child does not understand, and that is why the child is always liable to disappointment. The child varies according to its surroundings. The child lacks this capacity to see things truly, and because the child lacks understanding, the child, I say, is either very much alive or very depressed. Now there are many Christians like that, and it just means that we are babes in Christ.

Another inducement to growth is that a child always lacks a sense of discrimination, and anyone who lacks a sense of discrimination is always a ready prey to false doctrines. That is why Paul says, 'That we henceforth be no longer children, tossed to and fro, and carried about with every wind of doctrine' (Ephesians 4:14). It is the immature Christian who always rushes to the latest cult or movement. So we must grow in order that we may develop a sense of discrimination.

And in the same way, the child is always very dependent upon its feelings and impulses, and judges according to them. It is exactly the same in this Christian life. That is why Peter ends with this great exhortation. You are in a difficult world, he says. How are you going to stand and face it? Here is the answer: 'Grow in grace', appreciate His favour more and more. And grow in knowledge. Get an understanding of these things, see the whole sweep of truth, get rid of the childish foolishness and become an adult man, and as you do so, says Peter, you will never fall, you will never be carried away by the error of the wicked, but you will quit yourselves like men, you will be strong, you will be worthy of the God who by his grace gives you this new gift of life and has made you an heir of eternity. Therefore 'grow in grace and in the knowledge of our Lord Jesus Christ'. Amen.

23
Growing in Grace (II)

'But grow in grace, and in the knowledge of our Lord and
Saviour Jesus Christ. To him be glory both now and for
ever. Amen.'

Chapter 3:18

We are considering here this final exhortation of the Apostle in
which he sums up, and puts in this positive form, what in reality has
been the whole of his exhortation to them right through the Epistle.
He has outlined his doctrine. That must come first. Having put that
plainly and clearly to them, he now ends with this exhortation to
them that they should put into practice all that he has been
indicating. It is the subject, then, of 'growing in grace and in the
knowledge of our Lord and Saviour Jesus Christ.' We have already
tried to consider in general what that means, and we found that there
were a number of principles which were of vital importance. We saw
that this exhortation implies life; that there can be no growth
without life. That is vital. The Christian is not a man who adds a
number of good deed to his life, he is a man who has received the gift
of a new life which then grows and develops. We considered also the
various other principles with respect to the nature of that growth, its
gradual character and its increasing character.

We now go on to another consideration, namely, how are we to
grow in grace? If that is what is meant by growing in grace, the
question arises, how are we to do it?

As we come to consider this question, perhaps the best starting
point will be to indicate that it is a fact beyond dispute and beyond
doubt, that this whole matter of growing in grace, and especially a
detailed consideration as to how it is to be done, is something of
which we have heard very little during the past fifty years or so. Now
I would contrast this period with what has formerly been the case in

the long history of the Christian church. There was a time when nothing was commoner than frequent sermons and exhortations on this subject, and indeed there was a multiplicity of books on what was called the Devout Life, or on the Holy Life, and this whole question of growing in grace. But I think you will agree with me that for the last fifty years or so that has not been so. We have heard comparatively little about it. It has not been in the forefront of the teaching of the church as it used to be. That it used to be in the forefront, I say, is something which is entirely beyond dispute. If you look at the history of the Roman Catholic Church, for instance, you will find that it has always had a very prominent place in their teaching. I take it that they have more literature on the question of the Devout Life than any other section of the Christian church. Their whole doctrine with respect to those whom they call 'saints' is proof of that in and of itself.

But this was not confined to the Roman Catholic Church. In many ways the outstanding fact about the Puritan literature, the great literature of the seventeenth century, was its insistence upon this principle of growth in grace and of the development of the spiritual life. I find constantly, as any others confronted by this subject must find, that if I am to obtain a real analysis of the nature of the Christian life and the laws governing it, I have to go back constantly to the works of the great Puritans like John Owen and Thomas Goodwin and Richard Sibbes and others. It is a fact, not without interest, that probably the greatest work ever written on the Holy Spirit and His work, is that monumental work of the great John Owen, who at one time preached here in London in the seventeenth century. And the Puritans were always concerned about this – it was the thing that was always in the forefront of their lives. How could they grow in grace; how could they make certain of their inheritance of the kingdom of God and be sure that eventually they would arrive there?

Now the same thing is true very largely of the 18th century. There is no doubt at all that it was works of this kind that prepared the way for, and led to that great evangelical awakening, and to books like William Law's *Serious Call*, or the book of that great man, Philip Doddridge, on *The Rise and Progress of Religion in the Soul*. Those two books have had a tremendous influence upon religious life. William Law had a profound influence upon George Whitefield and

John Wesley, and Philip Doddridge's book was the means of converting men like Wilberforce. Then Wilberforce's own book, *A Practical View of Christian Religion*, had in turn a great influence upon Lord Shaftesbury.

I mention these things in order to substantiate my contention that these things were not only prominent but were in the forefront of Christian life and Christian teaching in former times. You go back to those centuries and you find that men were concerned about this above everything else – the culture of the life of the spirit, growth in grace, development within the kingdom of God, how to be more like God and how to know God better. That was the great thing. But we must confess that for the last fifty years or so we have been hearing little or nothing about these questions; and it is very difficult to find a book written on that subject during that period. When one desires literature on this aspect of the Christian life one still has to go back to these older works.

Now it is a matter of interest to discover as to how there has been this difference. To me there is only one adequate explanation, and that is, a new view of the Gospel. As I am never tired of pointing out, this came in during the middle of the last century. The emphasis was turned from the personal to the social, and increasingly men have come to think of the Gospel of Jesus Christ in general terms, something that is concerned about the general uplift of the race. In the same way the church is regarded as an institution that has to make vague and general pronouncements on peace and war, on politics and industry, and so on. That has been the great characteristic of the last sixty to seventy years; the whole interest has been social and general, instead of being personal and direct and intense, and the result naturally is that we have heard very little about the culture and the development and the nurture of the Christian life. In other words, this is nothing but a manifestation, and a very significant one, of the whole decline in the level of spirituality in the church of God. As the interest has been widened, so there has been less intense cultivation of personal devotion and of the personal spiritual life. We have been so concerned about trying to make the world a better place through the Gospel that we have ceased to become better men and women ourselves, and we are witnessing this tragic lowering of the level of life in every respect at this present hour. Forgetting that society consists of nothing after all but a collection of individuals, and trying to improve the mass at the expense of the individual, we have found that both the mass and the individual have gradually been sinking to a lower and ever lower level in a moral sense. That has been the explanation in general.

The explanation, I think, in particular, in evangelical circles, has been the false teaching with respect to holiness, namely, that holiness is something at which you can arrive suddenly and as the result of one action. If I believe that in one action I can receive something that makes me holy, and all I have to do is to maintain that level, well, obviously, I shall not be very interested in manuals that tell me about growth and development in grace. And that is what has been happening. People have believed that you become justified in one act and sanctified in another; and then you just go on maintaining that position. Thus this characteristic New Testament teaching about the culture and the nurture of the Christian life has naturally dropped into the background.

That, I think, is the explanation of the state of affairs in the church with which we are confronted. But surely, if we take the New Testament seriously, we must return to this subject, for this exhortation to grow in grace is to be found everywhere. There is nothing that is more characteristic of the New Testament than this particular appeal, and I say we must return to it, not only for our own peace and happiness, but especially if we want to carry any influence and weight in the world that is around and about us at the present time. There are those who are tempted to say, 'Why do you thus spend your time talking about a personal development of the Christian life; isn't it being rather selfish?' This is the argument that is often produced; they say, 'Fancy, at a time like this, with the country in so much trouble, with the world in so much trouble, instead of talking about what can be done about the industrial position, instead of indicating how you think more goodwill can be produced, how the food problem can be solved, and so on; fancy, at a time like this, directing our attention to ourselves and our own souls! Isn't that to be utterly selfish? Isn't that the trouble with you Christians, that you seem to be oblivious of the world and its state and spend your time examining yourselves? Isn't it morbid and utterly selfish?'

Now there is nothing that shows such a complete misunderstanding of the New Testament doctrine as criticism of that kind. It will be a very simple thing for me to prove to you that the men who have actually influenced the course of the history of this country and of the world at large most of all, have been the men who have given exceptional care to this very question of personal growth in grace and in the knowledge of our Lord and Saviour Jesus Christ. Let me give just an instance or two.

I take it that no one will be anxious to dispute the contention that in many ways the true greatness of this our own country was laid down and established in the seventeenth century. A true understanding of the history of this country and its greatness must lead us back inevitably to Oliver Cromwell. There was the man who made this country count in the councils of the nations. It was then that this country began to stand out in position and prominence, and the man most responsible was none other than that Great Protector. Now if ever a man spent a great deal of time on this question of growing in grace and the culture and the nurture of his own soul, it was Oliver Cromwell. It was because of that, in a sense, that he became the man he was. He felt that the first thing that mattered was his relationship to God, and you cannot explain Cromwell except in terms of his direct application of himself to this personal obligation to grow in grace.

I have already mentioned William Wilberforce, who was responsible for the emancipation of the slaves. Do you know his story? He was converted, as I have said, by reading *The Rise and Progress of Religion in the Soul*. Read the story of William Wilberforce and the so-called Clapham Sect that worked with him, including such men as Zachary Macaulay, and the Thorntons and the Venns. These holy men knew that the greatest thing in life was their own relationship to God. These were the men who pioneered great reforms, and the first thing in the life of these men was this very matter of growing in grace. It was so, too, with the great Lord Shaftesbury and his helpers in passing the Factory Acts. Indeed, the same was true of Gladstone. I am mentioning but a few. You can trace the origin of the greatest institutions, and the most beneficent movements in this country, and you will find every time that you come back to a man or to a group of men whose first concern in life was personal growth in grace. Indeed, the whole case can be put like this: when men cease to put this in the first position, not only do their own lives cease to grow, but the whole life of the country deteriorates. The great call, we are told, at the present time, is the call for leadership, which means disinterested men with a noble view of life. Why are there but few such men? I suggest the answer is because we have forgotten this doctrine. Men have been out for themselves. They say: 'Why should I trouble myself, why should I be interested in politics or the general state of society?' It is nothing but pure selfishness, and that is due to a lack of spirituality. In other words, the direct road to a national recovery is the recovery of this personal sense of vocation, this personal desire to know God and to live a life that is well pleasing in His sight. So we advocate this, and turn to it again, not only for personal reasons but in a sense still more so for its general effect, and even for the sake of its national importance.

Very well, having said that, we come back still to the practical question – how is one to grow in grace? what is the method? Here we divide up our subject into two main sections. There are, roughly speaking, what we may call the Catholic idea and the Protestant idea. Now the Catholic idea is not confined to Roman Catholics. You will find it in any other type of belief that calls itself Catholic – it is as true of the Anglo-Catholic or of the Scottish-Catholic as it is of the Roman Catholic. The whole Catholic view of the devout Christian life conforms to a certain pattern, the essence of which can be put in this way. It regards holiness as a special vocation. It says that if you want to be holy, if you want to grow in grace, you have to take that up as the exclusive business of your life. Hence you see monasticism and the various religious orders. The Roman Catholic is one who divides up Christians into two groups – the religious and the laity. The religious are the people who grow in grace and develop. The laity, on the other hand, cannot do that because they are too busy, and too preoccupied with other things. So you have your two groups of Christian. What is there for the laity? Well, the laity can receive merit from the others, the others who have taken up the spiritual life as a vocation and who become 'saints'. These 'saints' are not only holy in themselves, they are so holy that the laity, the ordinary Christians, can borrow from their works of supererogation and thereby they can develop. Now that is in essence the Catholic view of this question of growing in grace. You have to come out of the world, you cannot remain in any profession or in business. It is something which is for special people, and it becomes the exclusive business of your life. You have to be celibate, so marriage is incompatible with it. You have to cut off certain things in a drastic manner and then you have

[234]

to follow the mystic way. You have to go through the various stages such as 'the dark night of the soul', and the state of purgation, and finally you enter into a state of union with God. We need not bother about details; it is the principle that is of interest to us.

What are we to say with regard to this whole Catholic conception of holiness? Well, it seems to me that our ultimate and final criticism of it is, that it is based upon an utterly false view of growth, and that is why I dwelt upon the principle of growth earlier. My criticism of the Catholic conception of this matter is that it virtually teaches us that we live to grow instead of teaching us that growth is nothing but the essential result of living. Growth, according to the Catholic conception, is the thing for which you live and they spend the whole of their time in living to grow. Or, if I may put it in another form, I would say that the trouble with that attitude is that it approaches the question of growth directly instead of approaching it indirectly. It is the hot-house plant conception of growth and development, rather than the natural one. It tends, therefore, inevitably to lead to that false division of Christians into two groups that I have mentioned.

Now let us hold over and against that, what I have described as the Protestant view. The Protestant view starts with a general principle. It says there are certain laws which govern growth in every realm and in every department of life and of living. It starts by saying that we cannot make ourselves grow. We cannot produce growth, and there is a sense in which you should not even try to produce growth. What have we to do, then? Well, says the Protestant view, you must approach it indirectly rather than directly. You remember our Lord's statement that we cannot add one cubit to our stature. He was referring there to physical growth or to the extension of life. But there is a sense in which it is equally true that we cannot add a single cubit to our spiritual growth, either. What can we do, then? Well, according to the Protestant view, this is what we can do. I cannot make myself grow but I can observe certain conditions which promote growth, and which are essential to it. And that is what I have to do. Now perhaps I can put this best in the form of a phrase that I encountered while reading a book recently in quite a different connection. It had nothing to do with spiritual matters at all, but it was a phrase which struck me as being very applicable. 'Health,' it said, 'is not something which can be produced by medicine and surgery.' Now I think that this is a very striking and profound remark. Health is not something which can be produced, or made, by medicine and surgery. I think that is the most perfect criticism I have ever known of the whole Catholic conception of this question of growing in grace. You cut yourself off from the world because it is impossible to become holy if you live in the world or in business. You must be celibate, marriage is incompatible – I say that is surgery. And in the same way, in its positive aspect there is an artificiality about it, there is a false attempt to produce growth – it is trying to produce health by drugs. That is the attempt to grow in grace by means of medicine and surgery – the direct effort, the belief that by doing things you can make yourself grow.

Now over and against that we must put the Protestant, the New Testament conception. That is, that all we have to do is to realise that there are certain conditions that lead to growth, that encourage growth, and that promote growth. Your business and mine is to fulfil those conditions, and if we fulfil them the growth will look after itself. Thus we are delivered from morbidity and introspection, from an unhealthy view of the Christian life, from monasticism and that incorrect, ascetic view of life. And we see that in the midst of life and our ordinary vocations we can be growing in grace, and we can become a holy people, as the New Testament Christians themselves did.

If that is the principle, what then are the details? What are these conditions that are essential to growth, to life and to development in every realm? Let me just note them for you. First and foremost we put food and drink and air. That is true in the natural realm, and I say it is equally true in the spiritual realm. As growth physically is impossible without food and drink and air, so in the same way spiritual growth is equally impossible without corresponding food and drink and air, in a spiritual sense. Think of a babe growing, think of a little animal growing, think of a plant growing. You will find it is absolutely true, there must be food, there must be drink, there must be air. What does all this mean in a spiritual sense? Well, it sounds very elementary, yet how often do we forget these things, and how prone we are to neglect them! There are certain things I must partake of if I am to grow in grace. What are these things?

First and foremost there is this Book. Here is the food of the soul – 'As new born babes,' says Peter in his first Epistle, 'desire the sincere milk of the Word that ye may grow thereby.' Peter has been saying it all along. If I do not feed on this Book, well then I simply cannot grow. There is no need to argue about this matter. You will find invariably that the people who do not grow in grace are the people who are neglecting to read their Bible. On the other hand the people who have grown have been regular daily students of this Book. It is the food of the soul provided by God Himself. What else? Prayer! In prayer one not only comes into communication with God, one receives the life of God. In waiting upon God, one receives of Him. Each one of these things, obviously is worthy of a sermon in itself – I am only giving them as general headings here.

Next to that the 'means of grace' – attendance on the preaching of the Word, partaking of the Lord's Supper – these likewise are the food of the soul. Go back again to the great periods in the history of the church and you will find invariably that at such times men took every advantage, every opportunity, of attending upon the means of grace. John Wesley, for instance, used to say that he always observed that the people who failed to attend his preaching service at five o'clock in the morning were always those who failed to grow in grace. It was one of his cardinal signs and tests – the means of grace. What else? Well, meditation, thinking about the soul, pausing in this busy, loud and raucous world to remind ourselves that we are 'here today and gone tomorrow', that there is within us that which is immortal and eternal, that God has given us something that was meant for Himself. Meditating upon this, meditating upon ourselves and our growth in grace, our relationship to God, thinking about death and the judgment and eternity – how vital this is! Then, the reading of books which will help us to grow in grace, books about people, biographies, the history of revivals. I do not know what your experience is, but I find these things are essential, and invariably as I read about saintly men of God, as I read about the periods of revival, as I read books that help me to understand these things, I feel my soul is being fed. This is the food of the soul.

What is the next great principle? It is that I must avoid everything that is harmful to the life and the growth of my soul. If you do not protect an infant from infectious fevers he is not likely to grow. In terms of the garden, if you do not weed your gardens the weeds will take up the sustenance and your plants will cease to grow. It is exactly the same in the Christian life. If I want to grow, I must avoid everything that is harmful to my spiritual life. I will not insult you by staying to emphasise this principle. You will find it everywhere in Scripture. If we are friends of the world we cannot be friends of God. If I want to grow in grace, I clearly must avoid things that are opposed to that life, and the mind and the way of the world are definitely opposed to it. Reading the newspaper, I find, does not help me to grow in grace very much, with its insinuations and suggestions, with its advertisements of that which is low, with the prominence which it gives to that which is opposed to the life of Christ. Likewise so much of the literature which we have in the world, and so much of its amusements and pleasures, are inimical to our growth. It is for Christians to work out these things for themselves. We all know what hinders our communion with God. The principle is this: knowing that, being aware of that, which stands between me and this life, I must cut it out. I have no time for it, I must keep myself in an atmosphere that is not a hindrance to the life of my soul.

The next great principle is exercise. It is not enough to have the right food. It is not enough to avoid that which is harmful. If there is to be growth the life must be exercised. Take the babe, take the growing animal – if you confine them and prevent them from moving and developing there will be no growth. What does this mean to the Christian? It means positive Christian living. It means putting into practice what I claim to believe; it means active Christian work; it means taking an interest in the propagation of the Gospel. It is as we exercise ourselves in that way that we shall find ourselves growing in grace. If our interest in these matters remains on the intellectual level, and if we do nothing about it, we shall find, I think, that we shall cease to grow.

What is the next principle? It is rather an odd one, and yet a very vital one. Food and drink and avoiding that which is inimical, exercise, and next – rest! How often this is forgotten – rest! Take that infant – if he is not given the right amount of rest, even though you are giving him the right food, and though you are avoiding that which is inimical, he will not thrive. Rest is of tremendous importance; the right amount of sleep and rest to the plant is vital; you must not be fussing about it constantly, it must be left alone. You remember how our Lord put it in the parable of the farmer that sowed his seed and then rested and rose night and day. How vital this is in the realm of the soul and spirit. If you haven't a quiet mind you will not grow. You may be reading your Bible very diligently, but if your mind is not at rest and at peace you won't grow. There are some poor people who spend their time trying to grow in grace by continually praying to God, but who do not succeed. There are people also who suffer from what we may call spiritual mumps and measles – they develop that pained expression on their faces, they are always full of questions; they do not understand why God does this, they cannot fathom why God does that. Now how can we obtain this rest? The great principle is, to realise that we are justified by faith, and live by faith. We must realise that we do not make ourselves Christians. We must know something about this rest of faith, and when we cannot understand, we must say 'I don't know, but I believe God works, and all things work together for good to them that love Him.' We must learn to rest and recline in the arms of God, and believe where we cannot prove; and without cultivating that aspect of rest and a quiet mind, there will be no true growth.

But let me just mention the last principle – it is the principle of discipline. In other words, having recognised all those other things, I must be regular in my carrying out of them. I must not read my Bible and pray spasmodically, I must do it constantly. I must avoid that which is evil all the time, reckoning there is no such thing as a spiritual holiday. I must be regular and constant. And in addition I must inspect myself and my life, and overhaul myself constantly. In other words, I must indulge in self-examination. Now in order to show what I mean by self-examination let me read, as I close, a list drawn up by the saintly John Fletcher of Madeley in the eighteenth century in order that he might show the simple people over whom he was vicar how they might examine themselves. These, he says, are the questions you can ask yourselves, in order:

1. Did I awake spiritual, and was I watchful in keeping my mind from wandering this morning when I was rising?
2. Have I this day got nearer to God in times of prayer, or have I given way to a lazy, idle spirit?
3. Has my faith been weakened by unwatchfulness, or quickened by diligence this day?
4. Have I this day walked by faith and eyed God in all things?
5. Have I denied myself in all unkind words and thoughts? Have I delighted in seeing others preferred before me?

6. Have I made the most of my precious time, as far as I had light, strength and opportunity?
7. Have I kept the issues of my heart in the means of grace, so as to profit by them?
8. What have I done this day for the souls and bodies of God's dear saints?
9. Have I laid out anything to please myself when I might have saved the money for the cause of God?
10. Have I governed well my tongue this day, remembering that in a multitude of words there wanteth not sin?
11. In how many instances have I denied myself this day?
12. Do my life and conversation adorn the Gospel of Jesus Christ?

That, according to Fletcher, is the way to examine ourselves. We take these questions seriously, we realise we have a soul, a spiritual life, and we are anxious that it should grow, and having observed those conditions of growth we make certain that we observe them all by just asking ourselves questions similar to these day by day.

That is the Protestant method of growing in grace. Realising that God has given us the gift of life, realising that certain conditions are essential to the preservation and the increase in life, we must practise them, and as we do so we shall find that we are 'growing in grace and in the knowledge of our Lord and Saviour Jesus Christ'.

God in His grace grant us this wisdom and enable us thereby to grow. Amen.

24
Growing in Grace (III)

'But grow in grace, and in the knowledge of our Lord and
Saviour Jesus Christ. To him be glory both now and for
ever. Amen.'

Chapter 3:18

We consider once more this great and vital subject of 'growing in
grace and in the knowledge of our Lord and Saviour Jesus Christ'.
We have already looked at it from two standpoints. We have
considered what it means and the definition which is given of this
process in the New Testament – the nature of the life and the
character of the growth. Then, also, we have considered together how
to grow – what exactly we have to do in order that we may grow.
Again we were of necessity compelled to consider something of the
character of the Christian life, and we saw the main New Testament
teaching was to the effect that our chief business is to observe certain
conditions. We cannot make ourselves grow. Growth is something
that cannot be produced by us; but we can observe certain conditions
and obey certain laws; and if we do so then growth will result. We
saw the absolute necessity of food, drink and air in a spiritual sense;
we saw also the necessity of exercise and activity, and the equal
necessity of rest. Then we saw that if we observed these conditions in
general and if we checked them by a periodical self-examination and
self-inspection, we would have the right to anticipate growth. We
also gave a few illustrations to show that, when these conditions are
observed, growth is the inevitable result.

Well, now, the next question before us is, *how do we know that we
are growing; how does one measure growth in the Christian life?*
This is surely an essential part of this injunction. We are commanded
to grow, but there are some people who obviously think that they
have already grown, that they have already arrived. If their view is

correct, there is no object in appealing to them to grow any further. Any doctrine of perfectionism in any shape or form is in and of itself a contradiction to this exhortation to grow. Those who believe that they can suddenly arrive at the standard, do not believe in growing; they believe in maintaining themselves at that maximum standard. That is not growth. So I argue that as an essential part of this exhortation, we must face the questions: How do we determine whether we are growing? and how do we measure any growth that may have taken place in us? Now here again I would point out how vitally important this subject is from a very practical standpoint. We are not to be concerned only about our own life; we are not to regard ourselves as hot-house plants; we are not to spend the whole of our time in just contemplating ourselves and feeling our spiritual pulses and taking our spiritual temperatures. That is morbidity and valetudinarianism in a spiritual sense. That is not what we are concerned about. We are concerned about the whole subject because, as I have already emphasised, the greatest need in the world today is efficient Christian people.

The tragedy is that we talk about the church in general; and while we have been talking so much about the church for so many years, the church has had less and less influence because there are an insufficient number of Christian people. The church has always had her maximum influence upon this world when there has been the greatest number of individual Christians. All our resolutions, and every recommendation we may send to Parliament or to the Prime Minister, will be utterly ignored unless they feel there is a great body of the community behind these resolutions. So that, from every standpoint, the call to us is to grow in grace individually in order that we may function more efficiently, and in order that large numbers may be benefited as a result. Now that is why the New Testament constantly exhorts us everywhere to grow in grace, and to make sure that we are growing in grace. It is, as I have been pointing out, the great command which is found everywhere in the New Testament. It was the exhortation which these writers and apostles always addressed to the young, infant church – the New Testament church.

We live in a time of confusion and of uncertainty, a time of bustling activity; never perhaps was it more incumbent upon us to measure and test ourselves in terms of the New Testament teaching than it is today. There are many indications, surely all must agree, of a certain tendency to manifest what one is compelled to call the childish state in connection with the life of the church. I think you will see this as I put before you some of the indications of what we may call childhood in grace, or the 'babe' condition in grace.

Now there is one preliminary point to which we ought to refer before we come to the detailed discussion, and that is, that there are many who feel that of necessity, this exhortation leads directly to morbidity and introspection. They say, Are you not rather calling upon us to contemplation of ourselves? Was not that the whole trouble with monasticism and with that entire view of the Christian life which believes in segregating itself away from the world? Are you not exhorting us to that, to spending the rest of our lives in just looking at ourselves, and examining ourselves? Shall we not become rather useless persons, utterly morbid and introspective? While I admit very readily and frankly that there is that danger, and that there are many people who, as a result of this exhortation to grow in grace, have become morbid and introspective, I say that it is because of their abuse of what is here commanded. The fact that some people do this in a false way is surely no reason why it should not be done at all. The opposite to the false is the true, and there is a way of self-examination which avoids the danger of morbidity and introspection.

I would suggest that there are two things which, if we observe them, will always safeguard us against this danger. The first is, that we must always keep our eye on the glory of God and not on ourselves. In other words, I must be concerned to grow in grace, not that I may grow, but to the glory of God. In other words, the object of growth is not only that I may be better than someone I know to be worse, or better than I used to be; it is that thereby I may glorify God, that God may use me more, that I may be a more efficient instrument in the hand of God. In other words, the motive must be right. It must never be in personal terms. Perhaps I can put it like this. It must not be my ambition to become holy as such; I am to be holy because God is holy; I am to be holy because, if I am holy, I shall thereby display the glory of God in a manner which will be well-pleasing to Him. I must not look at the end in and of itself. It is the same as in the realm of our physical being when people are over-concerned about health. The healthy man, in a sense, is the man who forgets about health. If a man is the whole time considering and contemplating his health, it is a sign in and of itself that he is not healthy. Now that is exactly true in the spiritual realm. I must not put it up as my aim and object; indeed it must not be considered at all in terms of myself, but rather in terms of the honour and glory of God. And as long as I keep that in the forefront, I shall be delivered from any tendency to, or danger of, morbidity.

The second great principle is that I must never start upon this process of self-examination without reminding myself at the beginning, in the middle, and at the end, of the cardinal doctrine of justification by faith only. I mean this. If I start upon the process of self-examination without reminding myself that I am justified by faith only, there can be but one result of my self-examination, and that is, that I shall feel I am not a Christian at all. I shall feel utterly hopeless and shall be thrown into a state of morbidity. Now this, of course, is the danger that confronts us when we read certain well-known and famous manuals of devotion. Take the famous *Imitation of Christ*, by Thomas à Kempis, in many ways a very valuable book, and yet in many ways an extremely dangerous book, because it tends ultimately to teach justification by works. It tends ultimately to give the impression that we make ourselves Christian by what we do. And, I say, if we start with that idea, this self-examination can but drive us to despair. There is only one safe way of examining ourselves, and it is to start by reminding ourselves that we are saved solely by the grace of God in Jesus Christ, and that if we move heaven and earth, or ascend into the heavens or go down into the depths, we can never make ourselves righteous before God. Nothing can save you and me but the fact that Christ died on the cross for us – there is our salvation!

Very well, I start with that. I then examine myself and I find things that condemn me. I find failure and unworthiness, and so on; but if I have started with the doctrine of justification by faith, all the things that I discover, and all the blemishes, will drive me back more to Christ. But if I have not started with Him, and with His death upon the cross to make atonement, I shall discover that it will but drive me to despair and to morbidity and introspection and a sense of hopelessness. Therefore I say that, as we examine ourselves in the period of Lent, or when we examine ourselves at any time, let us make certain that the result of our examination will always bring us back to the cross. If you come there you will never be morbid, and you will avoid that which unfortunately characterises the monastic, and what we earlier described as the Catholic, view of the holy, sanctified life.

Well, that was a preliminary warning before we move on to the details of how one is to know that one is growing in grace and in the knowledge of the Lord. This, of course, is a vast and a vitally important subject, and I can attempt to do nothing more than just to give you headings. I have come to the decision that it is better to give a general review of the whole position rather than to divide it up into too many sermons. How does one know that one is growing in grace? Now there is a false way and a true way. One false way is to compare ourselves with other people whom we know to be worse than ourselves. To say that is to sound almost childish, yet I think we shall have to admit that it is one of our most constant dangers. We none of us like to end the year with an adverse balance, and a very simple way of avoiding that is to compare ourselves with somebody worse than we are. And it is a very simple thing indeed to do that in this modern world. It is a very simple thing to see all the sin round and about us, and to read the morning newspaper and say, 'Well, I am not like that, and therefore I am all right.' The standard is so low that of necessity you are satisfied. That is an utterly false method.

The second great error, I suggest, in this matter of self-examination is to measure our growth in grace in terms of activity – what we do. Here again is a great danger, the danger of assuming that much activity is of necessity a sign of growth. Let me dismiss this point by putting it like this. You see an illustration in the natural realm which surely ought to put us right on that once and for ever. The child is generally much more active than the adult person; so that if we estimate our growth merely in terms of activity we are setting up a characteristic of childhood and the childish state as the measure of growth.

Well, turning from that, what is the true method? There is only one answer. The way to measure growth is to come to the standard measure, and that is this Book – the Word of God – the Bible. The only way to discover where we stand is to read what the New Testament has to say about the Christian man. That again sounds obvious, and yet I suggest to you that it is an easy thing to read the

New Testament without examining ourselves at all. One can read this Book so mechanically that one is never tested by it at all, and yet here is the only test. There are amazing pictures of the Christian man in the New Testament; there are delineations of the Christian life and of the kind of people we must become. There are the biblical characters – you look at those Old Testament saints, and the Apostles; you look at the first Christians and the kind of life they lived, the things they said, the ambitions they had. Now the way to test ourselves is to look at these people, then to look at ourselves in the light of these pictures and these great principles that are here enunciated. Then you can, if you like, go on to read the lives of the saintly people who have lived since the end of the New Testament. There again is something that is most valuable, though it can be dangerous, dangerous in the sense that we may try to imitate and recapture their experiences instead of just contemplating their faithfulness to the New Testament pictures. So we can look at it in that way, but above all, and beyond all, we must look at our Lord Himself. Think of the frequent exhortations to do that, as for example, 'Let this mind be in you that was also in Christ Jesus.' That is the test – our likeness to Him and our conformity to the kind of life He Himself lived.

Very well, that is the method – we come to the Book and there we find the yard-stick, the measure, by which we can measure ourselves. How do we do it in actual practice; how do we divide that up? I think there are two main divisions. The New Testament has negative tests, and it has positive tests, as to whether one is growing. Or I can put it like this: a very good way of measuring myself is to read again in the New Testament of what a babe in Christ is like – that is the negative test. If I am growing I am no longer a babe. The positive test is to look at the New Testament picture of the adult Christian. I can do both things. Now what I want to do very briefly is to give you some of the characteristics as we find them in the New Testament of these two types of Christians.

Let us look first at some of the things that characterise the babe in Christ; the one who does not grow, the one who has not grown. It is such a vast subject, again, that it almost baffles classification. I have tried to classify the traits and the characteristics in this way. Let us look at some of the general characteristics of the babe in Christ by observing the characteristics of immature life in the natural realm.

There is, in this sense, an application of natural law in the spiritual world. What is true of the natural babe is true, in principle, of the spiritual babe. What are the characteristics? Well, the Apostle has already been telling us in this very chapter that one of the characteristics of the child is that it is unstable. You remember how Peter has told us that Paul's epistles deal with these matters, 'in which are some things hard to be understood, which they that are unlearned and unstable wrest, as they do also the other scriptures, unto their own destruction; ye therefore, beloved, seeing ye know these things before, beware lest ye also, being led away with the error of the wicked, fall from your own steadfastness'. Instability: the child is unstable, changeable, easily depressed, easily frightened and easily discouraged. There is hardly any necessity to comment upon these things. But transfer all that to the spiritual realm. The Christian person who is always becoming panicky is obviously a babe in Christ. We are set in this world, and there are things happening round and about us – are we easily discouraged, are we easily depressed? Do these things that happen immediately make us question the whole of our faith and the love of God to us? Are we unstable and changeable? If so, we are but babes in Christ. Nothing is so characteristic of that stage of life and development as just that.

The second thing that characterises the babe is that he is lacking in understanding and discrimination. You will remember how the Apostle Paul puts this in his great passage in the fourth chapter of the Epistle to the Ephesians: 'That ye be no more children, tossed to and fro, and carried about with every wind of doctrine.' You see what he means. There were people in the early church who were babes in Christ. They had received the Gospel and believed it, and had become members of the Christian church. But there were false teachers, people going about teaching heresies, and these babes in Christ thought they were rather wonderful and interesting. Then somebody came and said the exact opposite and they went after him. The babe is always the first victim of the latest cult – any sort of refinement, any doctrine, any new theory, and immediately they jump to it and accept it. 'That ye be no more children, tossed to and fro, and carried about [like a cork on the surface of the wave] by every wind of doctrine' that chances to come along. That is always a sign of a babe in Christ – the kind of person who rushes into any new religious movement and thought. He is a babe carried about by every wind of doctrine. Now this is not my idea, it is the New Testament teaching.

What next? Well, the next characteristic of the babe in Christ is what I can put in a word that I dislike very much, but which is expressive, the word 'exhibitionism'. The child is always at some time guilty of this spirit of exhibitionism. It means this – too much interest in self, too ready to talk about self, too ready to call attention to self. This is very elementary psychology, but it is something of which the child is always guilty, and the business of parents is to check such tendencies in children. The child always likes to be the centre of the circle. It is one of the results of sin and the fall – exhibitionism – self manifesting itself. As we get older we are a little more subtle in the way we do it. The child in his innocence is not conscious of what he is doing; he is not aware of this folly. The child does it openly, but the adult talks about his good deeds, talks about his activities, or tells his experiences, of marvellous and wonderful things that have happened. The application is perfectly obvious. There is a type of Christian, unfortunately (God knows we have all suffered from this, and maybe are still suffering – God have mercy upon us if we are) the kind of person who, the moment he begins to talk, talks about what he has done and seen, and gives you a list of his good deeds – exhibitionism! What a subtle thing it is, and perhaps it is one of the last temptations to leave us, even tempting us to say that we are humble! We can be proud of our humility, indeed I think we always are if we try to give the impression of humility. If our humility is not unconscious it is exhibitionism. So long as we are in the stage of always letting people know what we are doing, and giving an account of ourselves in any shape or form, it is exhibitionism.

Then the next general characteristic of the child is a love of that which is entertaining and spectacular and exciting. I do not think you will dispute this; the child always likes these things. You present a lesson to a child in a very different way from that in which you would present or express it to an adult. Well, transfer all that to the spiritual realm and you will find it equally true. A babe in Christ is always interested in experiences, and if he hears of anybody who is going to stand up to give an account of his experience he will rush to hear it. In the same way, of course, meetings and thrills! The child likes entertainment, he likes large numbers of meetings, the more meetings the better, the more thrills and excitement the better. All that is characteristic of the child mind and the child state. You remember the exhortation in the New Testament – 'Study to be quiet'. We read, too, about people with 'itching ears', always wanting to be hearing something, people who do not like meditation. They do not like contemplation, they are not very fond of reading and study. The exciting, the spectacular, the entertaining, above all appeal to them. These are some of the general characteristics of the child.

But let me give you a few of the particular characteristics. What an extraordinary description we are given in the third chapter of the first Epistle to the Corinthians of the characteristics of the child. The child in Christ is always more interested in the teacher than in the truth taught. The Corinthian Christians divided up into factions; some believed in Paul, some in Apollos, some in Cephas, and some were followers of Christ; and there they were, always talking about the preachers. One said, 'I am of Paul,' another said, 'I am of Apollos.' Now so long as you are like that, says Paul in effect, you are babes in Christ, and I have fed you with milk, for you cannot stand anything else so long as you are like that. It is to me one of the saddest things in the New Testament to read what some of those members of the church at Corinth had been saying about a man like the Apostle Paul. There is no better illustration of babyhood and childhood in Christ than the two letters to the Corinthians. They really are worthy of careful consideration from that standpoint. Paul tells us more concerning the babe in Christ there than anywhere else. There were members of the Church at Corinth who had the inestimable privilege of listening to the Apostle Paul preaching. (If I were offered an opportunity of going back into any great scene in history I am not sure but that the thing I would ask for above everything else would be an opportunity of sitting and listening to the Apostle Paul preaching.) Yet you know there were people who had heard him and sneered at him and said that 'his presence is weak' – he is not much of a man to look at – and they were discussing the mighty Apostle, this servant of God. 'His presence is weak and his speech contemptible' – he writes powerful letters, but he is not much of a man to look at or to listen to. They were babes in Christ. Those people were Christian but they were interested in the appearance of the preacher rather than in the truth. Would you imagine that anybody listening to the truth of

God coming from the lips of that holy man would even remember what he looked like!

Yes, and they were interested also in the way in which he said it. 'His presence is weak and his speech is contemptible.' Apollos was much more eloquent than Paul; he was a great orator, Paul was not. I think his preaching was very different from what we would anticipate or expect. 'His appearance is weak, his speech is contemptible', but it is only babes who are interested in things like that. But the babes are very interested in the personality of the preacher, in his appearance and method and manner of speech. Well, those are the things that create the party spirit, they are the things that divide churches into sections. May I put it in this way – if you are more interested in your denomination than you are in the truth of God, well, you are a babe even though you are old. Denominationalism is a sign of spiritual babyhood – doing things because it is my group, my denomination, my organisation, rather than because it is the truth of God committed to us which drives and constrains us to do them.

What else? The child, as we have been reminded, is interested more in experience than in relationship. Let me put it like this: the child is more interested in activities and results than in relationship. You remember how our Lord rebuked His disciples. They had been casting out devils, they had been preaching very successfully and they were filled with elation. But He said to them, 'In this rejoice not, that the devils are made subject to you, but rejoice rather that your names are written in heaven.' The child is interested in activities and results, in what he is doing and what happens; but Christ says, Rejoice rather in the relationship – that your names are written in heaven.

Let me sum it all up like this. The child is always more interested in gifts than in graces. Read the thirteenth chapter of the first Epistle to the Corinthians on this matter; and the twelfth chapter is equally important. The trouble in Corinth was due to the fact that they were interested only in the gifts, such as tongues and miracles and healings, but Paul says, 'Yet show I you a more excellent way' – 'faith; hope and charity; these three, but the greatest of these is charity.' The child is interested in the flashy, spectacular gifts; the one who is grown up is interested more in the graces of the Christian life.

That brings me to the positive side. It is the exact opposite to all I have been saying, we must not be like that. We must develop out of that. What else? I can put it under three headings. Personally I can be certain I am growing in grace if I have an increasing sense of my own sinfulness and my own unworthiness; if I see more and more the blackness of my own heart. If I am satisfied with myself I am not growing; if I am not satisfied, it is a sign of growth. Let me put it in this way — if I am more concerned about being delivered from sin than from particular sins it is a sign that I am growing. The child is interested in particular sins, the man who is growing is aware of a sinful nature from which he longs to be delivered.

What about the Christian's attitude to the world? Well, the sign of growth in grace is an increasing understanding of the nature of the spiritual conflict that is going on in this world. In other words, the man who is growing is the man who is less and less surprised at what is happening, and at the state of the world. The man who is growing in grace desires the world less, and is less tempted by it.

But above all, I would say that the sign of growth in grace is when a man is grieved by the state of the world. This is how Paul puts it in the second Corinthian letter: 'We groan, being burdened.' This world to the Christian is a sinful world; he groans because of it; he is driven to prayer because of it; he is driven to praying for revival; he is concerned about society and its terrible condition.

But, lastly, the best of all tests of growth is a man's attitude to God. Do I love God more than I did? Do I desire God's glory more than I used to do? Oh! let me put it in one phrase — Do I desire *Him* more and more, and not just what He can do for me? The child wants gifts and is always rushing for the gift, and, alas, so many of us still come to God like that, interested in His gifts, interested in what we can get from Him, regarding Him as just an agency to bless us. There is no better test of growth than that a man desires God because He is God, desires to know God, is not so much concerned to be getting things from God as to be in His Presence and to feel the radiance and to know himself in the blessed filial relationship. 'Forgetting those things that are behind, I press forward,' says the Apostle. That was his great ambition — 'that I may know Him.' Ah! that is the ultimate test. Delivery from the realm of experiment and experience and gifts, and all these things which are perfectly legitimate and quite all right as long as we do not live for them, and being increasingly drawn to the centre and desiring Him and Him alone. May God give us grace

to examine ourselves in the light of this teaching, and may we be able
to say with humility and yet with confidence that we have advanced
somewhat, that we have grown somewhat, and that our main object
and desire is to know Him, and to be more like Him for His glory.
Amen.

25
The Glory of God

'But grow in grace, and in the knowledge of our Lord and
Saviour Jesus Christ. To him be glory both now and for
ever. Amen.'

Chapter 3:18

'To Him be glory both now and for ever', or, as another translation
puts it, 'To Him be glory both now and to the day of eternity'. We
thus look at this Epistle for the last time in this particular series of
meditations. These are the closing words. We observe that the
Apostle ends his letter as he began it. He began by saying, 'Simon
Peter, a servant and an apostle of Jesus Christ, to them that have
obtained like precious faith with us through the righteousness of
God and our Saviour Jesus Christ: grace and peace be multiplied
unto you through the knowledge of God and of Jesus our Lord.'
Thus, I say, the Apostle ends as he began; and that is something that
is truly characteristic not only of him but of all the other New
Testament writers. We have seen in working our way through this
particular letter that Peter, as a wise pastor, has been very rightly and
naturally concerned about the problems of the people to whom he
was writing. It is right that we should discuss our own personal and
peculiar problems; but the church ultimately is not an institution
which is concerned merely or primarily with a discussion of the
problems of men and women. The main function and business of the
church is to proclaim the Lord Jesus Christ. So Peter, as it were,
hurries to end his letter on this note, 'grow in grace'. After all, he says
in effect, that is the big thing, that is the important thing. But even to
put it like that is to think too much in terms of the people to whom he
was writing, so on he goes to say, 'to whom be glory both now and
for ever, Amen'.

Now there we have a perfect illustration and example of what I would call the healthy-mindedness of the New Testament. You see, the New Testament is not a textbook on psychology. It does not start with us, and just consider us, and then end with us, leaving us perhaps a little bit happier for the time being, and feeling very nice and comfortable. That is not the great purpose of this Book. It is the good news concerning Jesus Christ. It is the Gospel, it is a declaration from God and it is concerned with something that God has done. You and I come into the picture because it was designed for our benefit; but it starts, not with us, but with Him. Anything that may be true of us, or that we may derive, is secondary to this major theme. Now surely in the world as it is today we should thank God for this. The world is very much immersed in doubts and problems. The books are concerned about this, even the very novels have apparently entered into that vortex. They have all become so subjective, so self-centred, so introspective. Modern man with all his boasting has become a problem to himself, and he spends most of his time in looking at himself. That is why he is so miserable and unhappy; that is why, in an intellectual sense, he is so inferior to his forefathers. He has turned in upon himself, and there is an unhealthy morbidity about him. But, here, we find ourselves in an entirely different realm, what we may call the realm of grand objectivity where we are asked to cease looking in upon ourselves and to look out upon Him. Peter exhorts us to grow in grace, and we have been at pains to point out that if we adopt the New Testament method of doing this, as distinct from the methods which we have described as Catholic, and others which are psychological, we shall be saved from that danger – the danger of introspection. This follows because the most essential principle in growing in grace is to look at Christ and not to look at ourselves. As we look at Him we shall become like Him; as we meditate upon Him we shall desire Him more; and as we seek to please Him we shall incidentally be growing. It does not turn us in upon ourselves, it always draws us out to Him.

Now the last words of this Epistle put all that very plainly and clearly to us. You cannot read these letters of Peter, you cannot read any of the New Testament letters whatsoever, without seeing that Jesus Christ is the centre of all, and He is the constant theme. It is a Book about Him, everything looks to Him – forward to Him, back to Him; it is all an exposition of Him. We are reminded, then, that the Christian life is essentially a life of relationship to Him. Christianity is Christ. It is not a number of views or a collection of ideas; it is not a number of terms and categories which, if we apply them and use them and meditate upon them, will do certain things to us. It is all about Him, and I say that this letter we have been considering together in these studies makes that quite unmistakable. Peter cannot keep away from it. He has to deal with various problems, but all along he brings them back to Christ. He started by saying he wanted them to grow in the knowledge of Christ; he ends with the same thing. He tells them how he was on the holy mount with Him, how he beheld His glory – all along it is Christ. Peter was a man whose whole life and outlook were entirely governed and controlled by Jesus Christ. Christ had changed everything for him, and ever since he first met Him, and first understood Him, He was the key to the whole of existence, to every problem and to every situation. And thus when he ends his letter it is inevitable that he should end with the words we are considering together now. He so loves Christ, and he is so concerned about Christ, that his great ambition in life is that all glory should be given to the Lord Jesus Christ.

What does it mean? It means that Peter felt that everything he had, and everything that everyone else had, should all be devoted to the Lord Jesus Christ. That is what he meant by saying, 'to Him be glory both now and for ever'. It is his way of expressing his desire that Christ may receive all the honour and be magnified, that Christ may be glorified by the whole world and the whole of creation. We see exactly the same thing as we read the second chapter of Philippians. It is 'that at the name of Jesus every knee should bow, of things in heaven, and things in earth, and things under the earth; and that every tongue should confess that Jesus Christ is Lord, to the glory of God the Father'. That was the thing that really filled the minds and the hearts of these people, and that was their burning desire and their greatest ambition. And it is to that that the Apostle exhorts these people thus at the end of his letter.

What he says in effect is this – Are you so living that the glory of your lives is going to Jesus Christ? Are you concerned about His glory; are you desiring to promote His glory? Now if we illustrate this by means of something else, perhaps it will be still more clear. We know what this means in terms of country; we know what it is to stand for our country and desire her name to be great. We all know something of the response to an appeal like that; and in response to an appeal like that, men are prepared to die. We know what it is to stand for, and to be anxious for, the honour and glory of great men or of a great cause, or of something in which we are particularly interested and which appeals to us strongly. Now what Peter is saying is that Jesus Christ should be like that to the Christian. He should be the centre of his meditation, the law of his life, the One he loves with his whole being. His main ambition in life should be to bring everybody to acknowledge Him and to praise Him, to submit themselves to Him and to do everything they can to promote His honour and glory, and to make Him stand out supreme in the whole world of men. That is exactly what he means, and that is his last and final appeal to the people to whom he is writing.

Now, I suggest that that is a call that comes to us who claim the name of Christ at the present time. The Person of Christ must stand out, and we must be very careful to make it clear that we are not concerned with a collection of ideas, but that our whole position is a personal relationship to this Person. Our proclamation is that He is not only worthy to be praised, but that He deserves all the glory that man can give to Him.

Someone may ask, Why should this be done? What are your reasons for saying, 'To Him be glory both now and unto the day of eternity'? Incidentally, let us notice that last striking phrase before I answer the question. There is something rather odd and almost paradoxical about it – 'day of eternity'. 'Now and for ever,' says this Authorised Version. Well, Peter no doubt is keeping in his mind here what he had been saying earlier in the self-same chapter, 'Beloved, be not ignorant of this one thing, that one day is with the Lord as a thousand years, and a thousand years as one day.' So he talks about 'the day of eternity'. Here you are now, he says, in time. But, as he has been explaining to them, the end of time is coming. The end will be ushered in by the return of our Lord, and the kingdom of glory will be set up in a new earth under a new heaven. That is what he means by 'the day of eternity'. Let Christ be glorified amongst you now, continually, and until 'the day of eternity' – that glorious day of which he has been speaking.

Well, now, why should He thus be glorified; why do we Christian people say that He is worthy of all this honour and glory? Let me suggest some answers to the question. The first answer to the question is that *He is to receive all glory and honour because He is*

God. Jesus Christ is *God.* Putting it negatively, if Jesus Christ is not God, then this statement of the Apostle Peter is nothing but blasphemy. God alone is worthy to be glorified and honoured by the whole world. It is God alone, because He is God, who deserves all the glory. To Him all the glory is to be ascribed. Peter says here, 'to whom' – the Lord Jesus Christ – 'be glory both now and for ever, Amen'. What is the implication? Unmistakably, that Jesus Christ is God; and that is our central Christian affirmation; that the Person, Jesus of Nazareth, who was born as a Babe in Bethlehem, who lived for thirty years an ordinary life, following the occupation of a carpenter, and who set out to preach at the age of thirty and who 'went about doing good', working miracles and teaching the people for those three years – we say that that Person is none other than the second Person in the Blessed Trinity – God. On what grounds do we say this? On what do we base our affirmation that this Jesus, to whom we thus ascribe all glory, is really God the Son? One almost apologises for asking that question, but in view of certain recent publications it seems to me to be necessary still that we make certain affirmations clearly and unmistakably.

On what grounds do we say that Jesus of Nazareth is the Son of God, the unique Son of God, and that He is God Himself, the Second Person in the Trinity? The first answer is the *Virgin Birth*. Here is a doctrine clearly stated in the New Testament. There are people today, even in prominent positions in the church, who say that that is something which is scientifically impossible. But the Christian church has never claimed that this is something which science can understand. The Gospel of Jesus Christ is, avowedly and confessedly, supernatural. One does not expect the natural man to understand. Indeed, Paul says that the natural man cannot understand. We do not start by saying that the generation of Jesus Christ is the same as that of every other person who lived on earth. We say, No! He is essentially different. We affirm that He was born of a virgin, that He was 'conceived by the Holy Ghost', that it is a supernatural action – the Virgin Birth. He is different in His birth. He starts differently. He has come into the world; He has not been generated in the ordinary fashion and manner. We claim, therefore, that He is God, were it merely because of the very way He came into this life and world.

And then we look at His claims for Himself and His teaching. We observe how He contrasted Himself with all who had gone before Him, how indeed He puts Himself above and in a position superior to all the ancient teachers. He says of Himself, 'Before Abraham was, I am', 'I and the Father are one'. He claims for Himself a totalitarian allegiance from men; He called upon men to leave their work and their vocation and to follow Him. He sets Himself in that position in words and in actions. He claims a uniqueness, He claims to be One with God. He claims to have an intimacy and an intimate relationship with God which no other man ever had.

We likewise point to the miracles. Again I am reminded that certain people tell us today that we really must cease talking about the miracles, and that with our modern scientific knowledge a belief in miracles is utterly impossible. To that there is but one simple reply. A miracle by definition is something that science cannot understand because it is supernatural. A miracle does not mean that a law of nature is broken; it means that a law of nature is superseded. And there is no scientific knowledge or understanding or advancement which has in any way, or to the slightest conceivable extent invalidated the claims of the New Testament concerning miracles. The New Testament presents us with its miracles as something out of the ordinary, and to say that it is unscientific to believe in miracles is just to make a thoroughly unscientific statement. Science is something which is concerned with the realm of things which can be touched and measured and verified by experimentation. A miracle, by definition, is something above and beyond that. To attempt therefore to put science and the miraculous in contradictory positions is, it seems to me, to fail to understand both the meaning of science and the meaning of miracles.

Let me put it from the New Testament standpoint. If you take the miracles out of the four Gospels what have you left? If the miracles are not true, what can I believe? If I cannot accept the records of these men about Christ's actions, can I accept what they say about the words and the teaching? If I take all the miracles out and say they are false or exaggerations, can I believe anything at all? I have nothing, as we found in dealing with the question of authority in the first chapter of this letter. The position in which we find ourselves as Christian people is that we either accept the testimony of the four Gospels, of the men who were with Christ and who saw Him, and who were witnesses of His life and death and resurrection, or else we believe, and accept, and base the whole of our life and outlook upon the suppositions and the statements of modern men – it is one or the other. We have no authority apart from this Book, and either it is right or it is wrong. I can understand the man who says it is altogether wrong and who rejects it; but the man I cannot understand is the man who claims that modern thought is the ultimate authority and then applies that to this Book, and takes out of it what he does not like and accepts that which pleases him. That seems to me to be a complete denial of the New Testament. The New Testament tells us to ascribe glory to Christ because He is God. And it tells us that He revealed the fact that He is God by the miracles He worked – 'Though ye believe not me, believe the works,' He said. The miracles of Christ attest His deity and proclaim that He is indeed God.

What else? The *Resurrection*. Again we are told that no modern man with scientific knowledge can believe and accept the fact of a literal physical resurrection. But if there had not been a literal, physical resurrection, would there have been a Christian church at all? Look at those disciples after the death of Christ! Are they the sort of men, or were they in a condition to start a movement that would soon 'turn the world upside down'? No, there is only one explanation – it is the Resurrection that led to the church. It was the Resurrection that gave the assurance to them that He was the Son of God. The Resurrection! It is in the light of these very things that are so denied – the Virgin Birth, the Miracles, and the Resurrection – that we state and affirm that He is *God*, and that because He is God we ascribe all glory and honour unto Him.

And then add to that the sending of the Holy Spirit on the Day of Pentecost. That is the ultimate proof of His deity. Having done all, He proves He has authority by sending upon them 'the Promise of the Father'. That is the reason for ascribing all glory unto Him – He is God. This amazing Person is none other than the second Person of the Blessed Trinity.

In the next place, we ascribe all honour and glory to Him also *because of what He has done*. There is the eternal Son of God, He leaves the Eternal bosom and the courts of heaven. You remember the language of Paul in the second chapter of the Epistle to the Philippians – He humbled Himself, though He was so glorious. He counted it not robbery to be equal with God, and yet He divested

Himself of all the signs of His eternal glory and was born a Babe in Bethlehem. Look at that Babe, look at that Boy at the age of twelve in the Temple, look at that young man during those silent eighteen years, sharing the ordinary life of men. Remember that He is the Only Begotten Son of God, the Second Person in the Blessed Trinity. There He is in all His loneliness. He humbled Himself, He took upon Himself the form of a servant, just like an ordinary person. He mixed with His own people and worked with His hands, though He was the Son of God. And then look at Him and watch Him in His public ministry. Listen to His teaching, observe again His works. Look at Him as he has to suffer at the hands of His enemies – the scribes and the Pharisees and the Doctors of the Law – the insults they heap upon Him, the misunderstandings from which He suffered! And then look at Him on that marvellous Palm Sunday when suddenly the people, rising above and beyond themselves, seem to have seen, though without understanding, who He is. Follow that great procession and His triumphal entry into the City of Jerusalem. But you must go on to Gethsemane and the agony and the shame of it all, and then – the cross. He humbled Himself even unto death, yea, 'even the death of the Cross'. Think of the crown of thorns, think of the nails, think of the thirst, think of the sweat and the agony, the cry of dereliction, and then the death, and the burial in the grave. Now, says Peter here, He is to have all glory and honour because of what He has done. And this is exactly the argument of the great Apostle Paul in his letter to the Philippians – it is because of all this that 'God hath highly exalted Him and given Him a name that is above every name, that at the name of Jesus every knee should bow, of things in heaven, and things in earth, and things under the earth'. So that if anyone asks today, Why should I ascribe glory to Him, that is the second answer. Not only because He is who He is, but because of what He has done. This blessed, glorious Person has come down to earth and has endured all that; and it is for that reason that we praise Him and magnify His Name, and give Him such honour and glory.

But you do not stop at that – to Him be all glory and honour and praise *because of His present position*. For the Gospel does not stop at the burial and the grave. It goes on to speak of His Resurrection, and it goes on to say that after that Resurrection He ascended up on high. It tells us that He is seated there at the right hand of God's authority and power, that He shares the throne with God, and that at this moment this very self-same Person is there in glory reigning with God. Now these are things which are so transcendent, and so marvellous in their very nature, that our minds seem to be baffled and bewildered, and we cannot contemplate them; but these are the statements of the New Testament. You start in the heavens, you see Him coming down, you follow His earthly course, then you see Him back again in heaven. And every one of these things is a reason for ascribing honour and glory unto Him.

The Apostle has been working out this particular point in detail in the body of the Epistle. He has been asking these people to endure, he has been giving them comfort in their sufferings. His ultimate consolation for them is this, that Christ is on the throne, that the Son of God is in glory, that whether we know it or not, whether we believe it or not, the fact is that this Person who suffered under Pontius Pilate and who died and was buried in a grave is now seated at God's right hand at this moment. He is King of kings and Lord of lords; all authority has been given to Him, all power is in His hands. He has already opened the book of life and history, He is already the King on His throne, and we are to ascribe all glory unto Him for that reason also.

What else? Well, the next reason is that we are to ascribe glory to Him *because of what He is going to do*. Here, again, you see once more that Peter in this last word is but gathering up into a sentence everything he has been saying in his Epistle. Here we are upon the face of this earth, in a world which has emerged out of two World Wars, in a world where there is talk of wars and rumours of wars, in a world of sin and contradiction and shame: and the call to us is to give glory to Christ. Why? He does not seem to be glorified, men deny His Deity, they deny His miracles, they deny His resurrection. They would make Him just a man, a teacher. The majority are not thinking about Him at all, and are not concerned. The world is against Him, why then should I ascribe all glory to Him? The further answer is that that blessed Person, who is there seated at the right hand of God at this moment, is going to come back into this world. He will come on the clouds, He will come into the world, not riding upon an ass, but seated upon the clouds of heaven in glory transcendent, and all who see Him will acknowledge and know Him. 'The day of eternity' is coming. The kingdom of glory is going to be ushered in. The Christ who was crucified, the Christ who is forgotten, the Christ whom men deny, is nevertheless coming in glory, and He will set up His kingdom and He will reign for ever. Why am I to ascribe glory and honour to Him? Because I believe that; because I, with the eye of faith, see all that happening; because I now know it is true; because I anticipate the glory that is yet to be revealed.

But let me give the last reason for ascribing all glory to Him. I am to glorify Him because He is God, because of what He has done, because of His position in glory now, because of the glory that is yet to be revealed concerning Him. But if you want a still more personal reason, the reason is – that it is as a result of all I have been saying, of all that He has done, that it is at all possible for us this day to know God. My ultimate reason, therefore, for glorifying Him is *because of what He has done for me*. Without Him where are we? We are the children of wrath, we are born in sin and shapen in iniquity. We have broken the laws of God, and God looks upon us with displeasure. In the eye of the law we have no hope. We are wretched in life and doomed and damned beyond death. But Christ has come and has done what we have described; and the result is that God forgives us, we are reconciled to God, we are made children of God and all things are become new.

Why should I glorify Christ? Well, because of the new life He has given me, because of the hope He has given me, because he makes life different, because He changes everything. He has made life endurable and bearable; He has delivered me out of that wretched, unhappy life of trying to live for pleasure, trying to forget my problems, with no hope in life or anything beyond death but darkness and blackness itself. He has died for my sins and has reconciled me to God. It is He who has brought me into the kingdom of God. It is He who gives me the assurance that whatever man may do I shall be with Him in His glorious kingdom, and shall spend eternity in His glorious, blessed presence. To Him be glory both now and to the day of eternity! Many things may happen between now and the day of eternity. It does not matter, they cannot affect Him, they cannot change Him, they cannot deflect Him from His purpose. And finally nothing can separate us from His love. To Him, God the Son; to Him who made Himself of no reputation, who went even to the death of the cross; to Him who rose triumphant over the grave; to Him who is seated at the right hand of God; to Him who will yet come and bring in His glorious kingdom; to Him and to Him alone, be glory both now and until He comes, and 'to the day of eternity'.